THE TEACHINGS OF KIRPAL SINGH

ABOUT KIRPAL SINGH

Kirpal Singh (1894-1974) of Delhi, India began, at a young age, an intense search for a true spiritual Master. For years he investigated the claims of yogis and saints representing many schools of thought. His search culminated in initiation by the great saint of Beas, Baba Sawan Singh. For twenty-four years he diligently studied under his Master's guidance, and was chosen to succeed him in the spiritual line. Thereafter, he served as a spiritual Master for twenty-six years and initiated more than 120,000 disciples throughout the world. He is the author of over twenty books on various aspects of spirituality. In addition, he served as president of the World Fellowship of Religions, and was the organizer of the World Conference on the Unity of Man. In 1974 he appointed Darshan Singh as his spiritual successor.

Sant Kirpal Singh Ji
(1894-1974)

THE TEACHINGS OF KIRPAL SINGH
Volume I

THE HOLY PATH

*Compiled and selected from
the writings of Kirpal Singh*
by Ruth Seader

SAWAN KIRPAL PUBLICATIONS

Library of Congress Catalog: 81-51513
ISBN 0-918224-13-6

First published by Sant Bani Press in three volumes:
Volume I, The Holy Path, 1974
Volume II, Self-Introspection & Meditation, 1975
Volume III, The New Life, 1976
Published in one volume in 1981 by
Sawan Kirpal Publications,
Bowling Green, Virginia 22427, and
2 Canal Road, Vijay Nagar, Delhi-110009, India
  Second Printing, 1985

Printed in the United States of America

Baba Sawan Singh Ji
(1858-1948)

Sant Darshan Singh Ji
(1921-   )

Preface

WHEN OUR beloved Master Sant Kirpal Singh Ji graced our shores with His benign presence in 1972, five manuscripts containing a categorized compilation of Master's writings were given to Him in Philadelphia for His approval with the request that possibly some additions could be added to them from the tour. In Sant Bani Ashram some two weeks later, it seemed to me that Master should not read the books now, but wait for the revisions and additions. I went to the Master to see if the books could be returned. Master was sitting on His bed in the beautiful house that the dear ones had lovingly built for Him at the ashram. The five books were on His night table. I found out that the Master had already read the books; I was quite surprised. With His busy schedule in New York, Boston, and at Sant Bani, when did He find the time? He told me that the three books should be printed. I said, "Master, there are five books." Master looked at me with a surprised yet playful expression and said questioningly, "Five books, let me see." With that He took each of the five books, one by one, and started counting slowly—"one . . . two . . . three . . . four . . . five . . . ." Master looked at each book very long and hard, with His full and concentrated attention. I realized that Master was charging each book, the words of which were already charged as they came from previously printed discourses. He counted them once, and then recounted them, slowly and carefully. He shook His head and said, "Yes, there are five books," adding "These books will help many people."

Later, on three separate occasions, Master again said three books and I said, "No Master, there are five books." After two years there came the realization that the five manuscripts would best be released and printed in three volumes: Book I: *The Holy Path;* Book II: *Diary/ Meditation;* Book III: *New Life in The World/New Life In God.* The lesson: when the Master takes five books in His holy hands and says, three books, you know it for certain as you gaze on the five books that there are really three books there. The Master is always right.

RUTH SEADER

Table of Contents

THE HOLY PATH

The Holy Path

Man's Plight: Attachment to the World

SO ALL TRUE MASTERS say that realizing God is a simple matter—What is there to realizing the Lord? Just uproot the attention from here and plant it there. It is simply a matter of withdrawing and gathering together the scattered attention.[1] The whole thing depends upon your attention, or *surat* as it is called, which is the outward expression of your soul. Wherever you keep it engaged or attached, those very thoughts will always be reverberating within you. We have to make the best use of things of course, but we are not to become attached to them. If we can only attach our soul to something higher within us, we would be alright. But if our attention is diverted through the outgoing faculties, so much so that it becomes identified with the outer things, what is the result? You cannot withdraw your attention from them. It is a question of the attention or surat, whether you keep it engaged to the outside things or invert and attach it to your Overself. So for that, you must see where you are driven away through the outgoing faculties of seeing, hearing, smelling, taste and touch. These are the five outgoing faculties working through the five physical outlets. Unless these are withdrawn from outside, you will not be able to have some awareness of your own self or

3

be able to contact the Higher Self or God within you, which is Light and Sound Principle.[2]

Whatever you do, whether for one day, two days, ten days, a month or two, naturally becomes a habit. Habit is strengthened into nature. If you want to go to one place, and you are attached somewhere else, your mind will go one way while your feet will go the other way. You know what is needed? God is within you, but unless you withdraw from outside, how can you contact Him? If you are attached to outside things, you cannot withdraw from outside. If you leave this building, you are the same. When you leave this body, you are not changed. You are what you are now. After leaving the body, you cannot become a learned man.[3] If you are attached here while living in the world, your attention will still be in the world even after leaving the body. Where will you go? Where you are attached. Where should we attach ourself? The soul is a conscious entity, it should be attached to the Overself, which is all Consciousness, even in life. Then while remaining in the world, you won't be attached to the world. You will be in the world and yet out of it. When you leave the body, you will go to the feet of the Lord.[4]

As long as we remain with the body, the body is glorified, but we are prisoners within it, and remain so until we are released by the Controlling Power. And how can this Power be experienced? It cannot be known by the senses, for while the senses, mind, and intellect are not still, there is no experience. So God, cannot be known by senses, mind, intellect, or even pranas. He can be experienced by the soul alone, when practically through self-analysis the soul comes to know itself. By separating matter from consciousness, we can learn what it is that controls all our faculties. You can say that we come to know the attention, for without the attention even the senses do not work. You will have noticed, for instance, that if your attention is fully focused on something, you will not hear if anyone calls you.[5]

So we must have control over all our outgoing faculties. We should be able to use them when we require, not to be dragged outside. It is for this reason that the diaries are intended. You must know where you are attached. You are given some contact within by the grace of God. You see the Light of God within you, hear the Sound Principle. When you turn your whole attention to the Sound Current, it will, like a touchstone, drag you up. Even those who are given a contact with the Lord within will lose it if they do not keep their self restraint. Only if you have some control over yourself, can you direct your attention wherever you like.[6]

So we are here to make the best use of all outward things, but not to be attached to them. We should make them a stepping stone to reach the Higher Self. If you are addicted to or become identified with any enjoyments outside, so much so that you cannot even withdraw from them, then how can you invert and have that contact within you with God, which is given at the time of initiation? So these outer faculties should be under our control. Whenever we like, we should make the best use of them, but they should not drag us out.[7]

When you see for yourself that you are the indweller of the physical house and not the dwelling house itself, which you tenaciously believed hitherto, your angle of vision is altogether changed, and you begin to see everything in a different vision. You can understand this more clearly from a single example. It is the reflection of your own soul current, when attached to anything, that gives you a feeling of pleasure or enjoyment. You are sitting in an opera house enjoying the show, along with others sitting around you. The play is on, and everybody is immersed in the so-called pleasure. All of a sudden, a messenger comes to the hall and breaks the news to you that your son has accidently fallen from the housetop and is lying unconscious because of a severe shock.

In spite of this harrowing news, the play is going on as it was, but your attention is distracted, and you are overtaken by sorrow and remorse on account of the great attachment to your dear son, who has been hurt, with the result that the same nice show which so much engrossed your attention is now insipid and void of all pleasure.

It shows that the pleasure was not inherent in the show but was just the reflection of your own single-minded attention that you had bestowed upon it. This very principle works everywhere and at all times. The Master knows it and sees it working as vividly as we see each other. Now He comes to our rescue and tells us to bind our attention with something which is of a permanent nature and enjoy everlasting happiness or bliss. All that we see with the aid of our physical eyes is in a perpetual flux and is constantly changing in form and color.[8] That which we believe is giving us satisfaction is not true; it is merely that our attention is there and the enjoyment comes from that, so happiness is not in the thing but in ourselves. How can pure consciousness (the soul), get any happiness out of matter?[9]

At the Mercy of the Mind and Senses

THE LORD is not separate from us and we are not separate from Him. But because of extroversion at the plane of senses, we have lost our identity. What is required is that we should disengage our attention from worldly pursuits and 'tap inside' as Emerson calls it. This is the act of receding back. This does not mean that we should supress our senses. But they should be channelized in such a way so as to assist the spirit on the physical plane as well as on the inner.[10]

Mind in its present state is burdened with a huge *karmic* load of past lives. It is enthralled by the outgoing faculties of senses and is thus driven helplessly into the mire of sense-gratification. The alphabet of spiritual progress commences with the control of mind. It is said that unless mind is stilled, we cannot have experience of Self-realization. The human body is just like a chariot wherein soul is the rider, mind is the driver, intellect is the reins, and senses are the powerful steeds running amuck in the mire of sensuous gratification. It is for this reason that for having a retrace of the facts, the senses are to be disciplined, intellect stilled and mind controlled so that the inner experience of the soul can be had. Mind is accustomed to roam about externally through ages. Unless it is offered something more joyous within, it cannot be controlled. The four main attributes of mind have to be divinized before any perceptible right understanding of the subject can be arrived at. Just as at the present we are so greatly impressed by the facts of externality of life that we have little or no knowledge of higher spiritual truths full of Divine beatitude, which is gross ignorance; similarly unless we have firm conviction of this life of the Beyond, there is no hope of our mind taking the right turn. It is only in the presence of the Living Master, who has full command and control of His mind, that we find radiant reflections of inner stillness and equipoise of the mind. A Saint has exclaimed aptly:

> *If you are firmly resolved to proceed to the Beloved Lord, you should put one foot on the mind and the other will enable you to reach the alley of the Friend.*[11]

Self is the friend of self and self is the foe of self. The mind, acting as a slave to the senses, running after the sense-objects, debases itself. As a reckless sower of the *karmic* seeds, it has, per force, to reap and garner an abundant harvest, in life after life, in an endless series. The poor soul in the light and life of which the mind works is hopelessly and helplessly relegated to the background and the mind assumes the supreme command of the citadel of the body. What a pity! The princess of the royal blood is swayed by the wiles of a trickster who himself is being pleasurably duped by the siren songs of the senses and, is unwittingly dancing to their tunes on the stage of mundane life. No wonder that it poses a menace to the security and integrity of the soul, running a handicap race with formidable and at times insurmountable hurdles in the way. We have, therefore, to subdue this inveterate foe before we can smoothly tread the spiritual path. To subdue the mind by force is impractical. It has to be won over steadily by persuasion and by giving it some fore-taste of the real happiness which a Master Saint alone can do.[12]

Human mind is so fashioned by Providence that it does not like to be captivated. It is ever restless unless it reaches its true abode. It is an agent of the Negative Power tied to each soul and will not allow the latter to proceed to the True Home of the Father. The Masters instruct us for taming it for the higher purpose of spiritual progress. As a matter of fact mind is helpless against the onslaught of senses which are in their turn driven into the jungle of gratification. A careful analysis will show that the lower categories of creation who are endowed with one sense prevailing as uppermost are done to death or live their whole life under captivity. For instance, moth is over-whelmingly fond of light on account of its sense of sight, which takes its precious life. A moth will never hesitate to burn itself on the burning candle. Flower-fly is fond of smell and outer fragrance. It rushes on to the blossoming flowers and prefers to die in it than leave it. Fish is the fastest creature and enjoys its life in running waters. It has weakness of taste or lure of tongue. The fish-catchers put some eatable on the rod and the fish is caught helplessly in the noose and serves as an eatable. Deer is one of the most nimble-footed animals which can rarely be overtaken by a horse, but it has a weakness for hearing. The hunters go to the wood and beat the drum in such an enchanting manner that unaware the deer is irresistably driven near, and places its head on the drum and loses its freedom for lifetime. Elephant is one of the mightiest creatures but it has the weakness of lust which provides for a not very difficult way of capturing it by digging deep pits in the jungle and covering them with grass and bushes. An artificial she-elephant like a decoy is placed over it. The lustful animal rushes towards it and is thrown into the deep well, where it is kept for several days hungry and thirsty. When it is taken out it is so weak and feeble that it is put under the iron goad for the entire life. From all this, it is pretty clear that the souls which are considered as bound in lower forms of creation are so much over-powered by one sense, where lies the safety of human souls who are endlessly enticed by all the five powerful senses of sight, smell, sound, taste, and touch. By sheer habit, it has become mired, roaming the world over like a wild elephant in a forest. Feeding fat on the lusts of the flesh, from moment to moment, it has grown out of all proportions. The spiritual disciplines are irksome and galling to it for they impose serious restraints on its free movement. This is why the mind does not relish any discipline, and plays all kinds of tricks to evade them, posing at times, as an honest broker pleading on behalf of our friends and relations and whispering sermons on our duties and obligations towards the world in varied aspects of life. Unless one is very vigilant and is equipped with a quick discernment, one fails to see through its pranks and falls an easy prey to them.

It is the outstretched gracious hand of the Master which helps us to wade through jungles of sensuous wilderness. Ethical discipline, if cultivated under the protective guidance of the Master is helpful for spiritual progress. Ethics and spirituality go hand in hand. The former is the soil and the latter the seed which thrives and blooms in favorable circumstances.[13]

The human form, because of the soul within it, is the highest in all creation, and is accepted as the form next to God. It is next to God, a part of God, having the same nature, is itself a conscious entity, and yet with all this, it is full of misery. Having tied itself to the mind, the passions and attachments of the senses are dragging it from one place to another. The pleasures of the world control the senses, the senses control the mind and the mind controls the intellect. This process is called *kam* (passionate desires and other appetites). Kam also means work, and if we put this desire or drive into reverse and become engaged in the opposite type of work, then we will achieve the true peace of being. A true Master always prays, "Oh Lord, keep my intellect in Your control."

At present the whole system is wrong, for the horse should have been pulling the cart, but instead the cart is in front. The soul should be giving strength to the mind as and how it wishes, but the mind, intellect and senses are stealing the strength, with the soul a helpless slave to them. It is all wrong. That is why Masters have advised to "Know thyself," for it is the only way to cut the evil from the root. Have you been able to control your senses and make them do whatever you wish, stopping their action whenever you desire to? Have you reached that stage? A certain piece of machinery has an electric motor which is connected to the powerhouse. There are many sections comprising this machine, and one can switch off any section in a second. Similarly, we should be in control of our being, and be able to switch off our whole machinery if we wish to.[14]

God is within you, He is not to come from outside. It is your I-hood or ego that stands in the way. This ego comes up when you are conscious of the body, whether physical, astral or causal. When you rise above the physical body, the physical I-hood is eliminated. When you rise above the astral body, you lose the astral I-hood. When you rise above the causal body, then you will completely understand who you are. Your will is the will of the Lord. The Lord's will is within you.[15]

When we come to this world the greatest knowledge we can have is that only in the physical form can we realize the Truth or God. How can we know God? He cannot be known through the senses, mind, intellect or through the pranas (vital airs). If God is to be realized, only the soul can do it. When can the soul get this experience of realization? When it has freed itself from the mind and the senses.[16]

As long as we do not have an inner experience of the soul, we remain in utter darkness. Bookish knowledge becomes a headache as it draws the mind out into the world through the senses and makes us feel identified with the senses by constant association with the world. On the contrary, self-knowledge satisfies the innate craving and hunger of the soul for peace and happiness. All that we need learn is the Book of Man, for the greatest study of man is man.[17]

We frequently see the lifeless physical forms being taken to the cremation ground, and have perhaps on occasion lit the flame with our own hands, but it has never occurred to us that we will also die one day. This can also be attributed to the fact that being the reflection of the Truth, we consider we are eternal and all happiness. God is all bliss. We also want all happiness, and for this reason we are constantly searching for it. How long does our earthly joy last? For as long as our attention, which is happiness, is attached to the source of it. It may be a good thing or a bad thing, but by putting our attention there we get some joy out of it, because essentially we are all bliss ourselves.

Why are we not fully aware of this innate nature? Because we have forgotten who we are. The start of all this forgetfulness was the birth into the physical form. This body is the origin of illusion. We are not the body— we are the indweller. The body is attractive because we (the soul) are enlivening it. We are surrounded by the senses, and with aid of the intellect we attempt to think of a solution—but if only we would awaken within ourselves... The whole world is asleep, through attachment and forgetfulness; all is illusion. Being identified with the body, the soul loses itself in attachment more and more, creating a new world for itself—a world of delusion, derived by seeing things in different appearance than they actually are. We think that the body and all its surroundings are part of the Truth—and this is a delusion. Can we not observe that the body and its conditions are never consistent? How can one who has become an image of the body and is indulging in outer practices, expect to rise above the body? There is only one solution, and that is to search out one who has himself escaped from the illusion; it is an impossibility for us to free ourselves.[18]

The Way Out: Guru, the Greatest Gift of God

IN GURU NANAK'S *Jap Ji Sahib,* he tells us:
There is One Reality, the Unmanifest Manifested;
Ever-Existent, He is Naam, the Creator, pervading all;
Without fear, without enmity, the Timeless,
The Unborn, Self-existent, complete within itself.
Through the favor of His true servant, the Guru,
He may be realized.

The truest riches and the greatest gift of God is the Godman, the person who, having realized himself, is established in his Godhead. He is in a sense a polarized

God or pole from which God manifests Himself amongst His people. Limitless and infinite as God is, He is beyond comprehension by finite powers of perception. He can, however, be apprehended in the Master somewhat as a vast sea can be apprehended at the beach with bathing ghats, where sea waters gently flow in so bathers can have a safe dip.

As like attracts like, man must of necessity have man as his teacher, for no one else can teach him. The way to God, therefore, lies through man. Some Godman alone can tell us of the "Way out" from the world and a "Way in" into the Kingdom of God, now a lost province to mankind in general. The fall of man was brought about by man and the regeneration of man too is to be brought about by man. But there is a world of difference between man and man—the latter being God-in-man.[20]

When people see the Guru living like an ordinary human being, eating, drinking, etc., they become careless in thought and respect. You should always remember that a Master's life is two-in-one. He is the son of man, accepting all as brothers, having no ill thought for anyone, living like a true human being, sharing happiness and misery with others. He also suffers in the sadness of others, and sometimes sheds tears of sympathy too. But, as his true Self, he leads the souls within and up. Those unfortunate people who consider him merely a man, remain at the level of man and lose the golden opportunity.[21]

The greatest prayer a person can therefore offer to God is that He may, in His unbounded mercy, establish

his contact with His prophets who may lead him Godward. The Godman or the Prophet shows him the
Way—the Grand Trunk Road that leads to God. It is
nothing but the Sound Current or Sound Principle differently called by different sages: the Word or the Holy
Spirit by the Christians, Kalma, Bang-e-Asmani or Nida-
e-Arshi by the Mohammedans, Udgit, Akash Bani, Naad
or Sruti by the Hindus, and Shabd or Naam by the
Sikhs.[22] Zoroaster calls it Sraosha and the Theosophists
"The Voice of the Silence." Christ speaks of it as "The
Voice of the Son of God." God overflows in the Guru
and unites man with the Word to reach back to His true
Home.

This Sound Current is the means to salvation. It is the
Master Key that unlocks the Kingdom of Heaven. It bestows life eternal on man and restores him once again to
the Garden of Eden from which he was driven away by
disobedience to God. What greater boon can a man seek
from God but restoration to the Kingdom lost by him.
It marks the end of his long exile through countless cen-
turies as He hails back the lost sheep to His fold. The
Master is the kind Shepherd who, out of compassion,
does all this for erring humanity. Such high souls hold a
commission from the Most High.[23] No longer is he an exile in the world but an inheritor of the Kingdom of God,
established once more in his native Godhead.

This is the true fulfillment of the covenant between
God and man, and the true resurrection or rising from
the dead as vouchsafed by the Son of God to man. This
is the fulfillment of God's Law and the purpose of hu-

man birth. Herein lies the greatness of Master-souls. They effect a reunion between man and God. The long-drawn period of separation comes to an end, and the lost child is restored once again to the Father. It marks the Grand Homecoming through endless trials and tribulations. The Saving Grace of God is stirred by the Godman and the purpose of life is fulfilled. Henceforth, the Son and the Father are not only reconciled but become one.[24]

It is a question of grafting—grafting a branch of one tree into another tree. What happens? The fruit of the second tree while retaining the shape and color of its own, acquires the taste and flavor of the other. This is exactly what happens when the Guru-power or life-impulse of the Guru works upon the disciple. While remaining as before, the disciple is now no longer his previous self, for he has been bought with a ransom. To be one with God (*Fana-fil-allah*) one has first to be one with the Godman (*Fana-fil-sheikh*). This is the easiest way to reach God.[25]

We have as yet no experience of God, and have therefore no conception of Him nor of His powers. Our knowledge of Him, however little it may be, is a secondary one, derived from the study of books or heard from persons as ignorant of Him as we are. In such a state we can contemplate nothing. But there may be a person who may have direct knowledge of God and be inwardly in tune with the infinite. There is a peculiar charm in His company. His weighty words of wisdom at once sink deep into the mind. His utterances, charged with His power, have a magnetic influence. One feels a kind of serenity and an inward calm in his holy presence. He does not reason of God. He simply talks of Him with authority, because he has a first-hand knowledge of Him and consciously lives in Him every moment of his life. Such a person may be termed a Prophet, a Messiah, or a God-man. The Gospel tells us that God speaks through His Prophets or the chosen ones. It is but a natural thing. Man alone can be a teacher of man and for God's science we must have some Godman to teach us that. Sant Satguru is the pole from where God's light is reflected. From him alone we can know of the path leading to God; and he can be a sure guide who can be depended upon, in weal or woe, both here and hereafter. From what has been said above, it naturally follows that God-man or Sant Satguru is the right person to be approached in the first place and to whom all our prayers should be addressed. Faith is the keynote of success in all our endeavors. We must, then, have firm and full faith in the competency of the Master. With love and humility we must make an approach to Him if we want to make a beginning in the spiritual science. We must pray to him sincerely from the depth of our heart. We should think it fortunate indeed if in his grace he accepts us for imparting knowledge of self and knowledge of God—which in fact is the seed-knowledge from which all knowledge springs.[26]

We should go to the Satguru and plead to him to take us out of here—"He has the love, and we are prisoners—He also has come as a prisoner, just for our sakes—He put on this bag of filth, this human form, just to release

us. O Satguru, if you do not help us, then who can?"
He who has left the house and is standing on the roof can
catch hold of another's hand and drag him up. The powerful Guru drags the soul out. By giving a boost, the complete Master gives an experience of rising above the body
consciousness. We need this help, otherwise how would
we rise above by ourselves? We get an inner contact and
a taste of the Maha Ras—Greater Nectar which withdraws one completely from the outer attractions. So with
Naam, the mind can be controlled. And to receive connection with Naam, one must go to the Satguru.[27]

How does one determine a Great Master? Swami Ji
Maharaj in *Sar Bachan* has answered this question very
beautifully. He exhorts that as and when you hear about
a Saint or Master, just go to him and in deep humility
and reverence sit near him. Just look into his eyes and
forehead like a child with deep receptivity. You will feel
an upward pull of the soul and divine radiation from his
eyes and forehead. Besides, if you have any questions in
your heart, these will be answered automatically by his
discourse without your effort. Over and above all the
testing criterion for the Perfect Master is to have the conscious contact of holy *Naam* within, the lowest links of
which in the form of Divine Light and holy Sound Current must be had on initiation. Again he should be competent to afford guidance for his initiates in the astral
plane and must protect the soul at the time of their physical death.[28] . . . When you go to a God-realized man,
with full sincerity and humility question him as much as
you like, and when you are satisfied, take his path and

work for it. You should also remember that no true Master will impose his will on anyone, but he will develop one's better understanding until the subject has some appeal.[29]

Man hesitates and fears to approach a Master Saint because his living is tarnished, maybe less in one and more in another. Never fear to go to a Master Saint because you are a sinner. He is meant more for sinners than for others. He has a remedy for every wound. Approach him and through him will be found a way to become rid of sin. If one is far away, he can be contacted through correspondence. He has means and methods to meet every case. He is competent.[30]

Godmen come into the world not to make any new laws, nor to destroy the laws as they exist, but only to uphold the universal divine law, unchangeable as it is. Their message is one of hope, fulfillment, and redemption for those in search of the divine in man and, as such, they constitute a great cementing force transcending all denominational creeds and faiths and presenting a workable way out of theoretical polemics of the so-called religious strongholds. They soar high into the ethereal atmosphere of the spirit and like a skylark establish an abiding link between the mundane life on earth and the free and untarnished spiritual haven. All religions are theirs and yet none binds them, for they place before humanity what is essentially sublime in essence at the core of each.[31] They do not come to establish a new religion and they preach from no particular script; from their celestial abode they come with a law peculiar unto themselves, and this is why the worldly people often fail to understand them. As for the strict trials and tests of fitness, it is gratifying to know that these have been done away with during this Kali Yuga (Iron Age); but whenever necessary they do put searching questions to the aspirants.[32]

The Master always speaks with an authority born of conviction for he has a first-hand knowledge of everything, which comes from his direct communion with the Universal Cause or Original Source.[33] . . . Every word uttered by a Saint is pregnant with unalterable truth which lies far beyond the human ken.

> *They are the mouthpiece of God and whatever*
> *they utter comes to them from above,*
> *Though it may appear to be coming from*
> *mortal throats.*

Whoever has a sincere yearning for the Lord will most definitely get Him. Many will say, "I want God," but they should analyze their desire and see why they are wanting God. It will be discovered that they really want the health of their children, wealth, name and fame, the removal of their unhappiness, or peace in the hereafter, and many other things. Everyone seeks solicited favors; no one really wants God and God alone. All cry out for worldly satisfaction, and God goes on granting their wishes. The Father Kirpal (Merciful) has ordered thus: Whatever a child wants, he shall be given. And he who truly desires the Lord and the Lord alone—most definitely he will get his heart's desire. Such single-pointed devotion is the ideal condition for realizing the Lord.

> *I do not want Swarg* (heaven) *or Vankunt*
> (higher heaven) ;
> *I only want to repose in the lotus feet of my*
> *Guru.*

How can one reach God if one desires the fruits of this world or the next? Comb your heart and find out if you truly want the Lord. True desire does exist, but it is very rare.[35]

The first thing for man is to rise to God's level. In the Godman, God is fully manifested. If we become Guruman, we rise to the level of God, and we begin to see the power and spirit of God in him. We can neither visualize God nor contemplate Him, as He is formless. In the Guru, He assumes a form. Devotion to Guru then is devotion to God in him. Guru, in fact, is not the body but the Godpower working in and through that body. He is the human pole on which the Divine Power works and carries on the work of regeneration. This power neither takes birth nor does it die. It eternally remains the same.[36]

You may call Him by any name you like—Guru, Sadhu, Mahatma, Master, or anything else. When they asked Hazur what to call him, he said, "Call me brother, or think of me as a teacher, or equal to your father, but live according to my advice; and when you reach the higher regions and see there the glory of the Guru, you may say what is in your heart."[37]

To love, revere, and feel grateful to our fellowman is to love and revere God. So, too, the love for the visible

Master, our closest connecting link with God, is in reality love for the Supreme Father. It has spirituality as an end and is not idolatry. The atmosphere in which such a genuine Master moves is charged with currents of peace and love which affect those who come into contact with Him. Even letters written by or on behalf of Him carry a current of ecstasy that influence the innermost recesses of the heart. Guru preceeds God.[38] Thus God moves as an ordinary man in disguise. As a man, externally, no one can recognize Him except one who contacts the Master-Saint within. This is according to the divine science, i.e., the laws he has laid down for man's use. Externally, if one takes a Master-Saint as an ordinary man, he can derive no benefit from Him. If one accepts Him as a superman, the benefit is much more. If one takes Him as All-in-All, the benefit becomes a truly great blessing. When he contacts the Master within, he receives all and everything.[39]

Master can know everything about the person meeting him. Yet he behaves in such a manner that the others may not feel embarrassed with such an attitude, and tries to meet the humans on their own level. He sees us just as we can see what there is in a glass bottle—pickle or jam, but in his sheer graciousness tries to hide the facts, lest these actions are considered as transgressions in the ethical code. An initiate of the competent living Master carries the Radiant Form of the Master at the eye-focus, which can be detected and seen by the living Master.[40]

He is a law unto Himself and can bestow his divine blessings on any one of his own choice. But the start should not be considered as the end. It is a life long struggle and strenuous effort of the disciple which he or she is required to undergo for the growth of his or her inner spiritual illumination has to be taken care of. As a matter of fact, ever since the disciple is granted the sacred boon of holy initiation, he or she is granted a complete visa for entering the inner realms up to the true home of the Father. But there are very few who labor much and lead the life as enjoined by the Master and can progress within. Please refer to *The Jap Ji* stanza 33 in this behalf where it has been explained at length.[41]

> *You have no power to speak or be silent,*
> *No power to ask or to give,*
> *You have no power over life or death,*
> *No power over wealth or state for which you*
> *   are ever restless.*
> *You have no power over spiritual awakening,*
> *No power to know the Truth, or to achieve*
> *   your own salvation,*
> *Let him who thinks he has the power, try.*
> *O Nanak! none is high or low, but by His*
> *   Will.*[42]

JAP JI 33

Without a God-man the mystery of the soul is never realized. It remains a sealed book. The ascent of the soul to the highest regions is impossible unless one is ushered into those planes. Of course, one may be able to withdraw the spirit current within the eyes from the body, through Simran or see some light at times, but there is nothing to take or guide him upward. Many were held in these elementary stages for ages and ages, and no help came to guide them up. Some have called this stage the be-all and end-all, but they still linger at the outskirts of grosser matter and in the stronghold of the finer matter. It is here that the help of some competent body is needed to extricate the devotees from the iron-hold of the subtle matter. That somebody should be the man who has gone through the different stages of spiritual development and travelled to the Region of Pure Spirit, the Sat Naam, far beyond the hold of matter.[43]

When a Guru initiates a disciple on this path, he will not leave him until he has taken him to the lap of Sat Purush, God in His true form. After that the Sat Purush will take him to Alakh, Agam and Anami, stages of imperceptible, inconceivable and nameless God. A Guru's duty is very exacting. In truth, a Guru is God Himself. In whichever pole God has manifested Himself, that pole is known as Sadhu, Sant or Mahatma, or Master. He never says, "I am the doer," but always refers to the will of God.[44] It is God's law that nobody can reach Him except through a Master Soul. This is what is given out by almost all the Saints who came so far.[45]

Positive and Negative Powers are the two phases of Absolute, deriving power from Him. The functions of these powers are diverse—one is for the inner recession beyond the senses, whereas the other leads outward. A Master of the highest order initiates the souls into the mysteries of the beyond for proceeding back to the true home of the Father. His mission is purely spiritual based on ethical living. The Negative Power is the controlling force of this plane and demands adjustment of each farthing in accordance with the law of karma. The initiates are advised in their own spiritual interest to abide by the holy commandments to incur the least karma, and by attuning themselves with the holy Naam within to evade the load, by reposing in His will and pleasure. Every pleasure has its price—this is the law of this power. The spiritual aspirants should regulate their lives to strict spiritual discipline, and pursue such a sublime pattern of life.[46]

You are in the custody of a true Master from the very day he gives initiation. He becomes the very breath of the disciple. Baba Sawan Singh Ji used to say that from the day the Master gives the blessings of Naam, the Guru becomes the indweller, along with the soul. From that very moment, he starts forming the child with love and protection, until ultimately he takes him into the lap of the Oversoul. Until that time, he does not leave him for one minute.[47] It is merely out of his innate compassion that he rears us with his own life-breaths of the divinity in him.[48]

It is true that the Master winds up the karmas, but not just like that; he adjusts them to further the man-making of the disciples. He takes the children in his charge, but he will make them into something worthwhile before taking them home. It is his duty to clean them first; nobody packs dirty clothes away in storage. When people are initiated they rejoice and say, "We have got a Master; we have got salvation." When meeting the Satguru, you will get salvation if you obey his words.[49] The Guru may give happiness or misery, for he has to make a beautiful form from a rough piece of stone and therefore has to wind up all the karmas; but a true follower will never complain, no matter what hardships the Guru allows.[50]

The bonds or relationship between Master and disciple are the strongest in the world. Even death cannot sever them, for they are tied by the divine and omnipotent will of God. The Master remains with the disciple wherever he may be. Death and distance are immaterial in the relationship of the Master and the disciple. He is always by his side, here and hereafter.[51] He who resigns himself to the will of the Master, places himself under the Master, who hastens to awaken the divinity in him. He talks face to face with his devotee and gives him counsel in time of need. He molds the disciple into the likeness of God and makes him a living temple of the Divine Consciousness.[52] Whosoever's mind is stayed on Him with full faith He will keep him in perfect peace. There is hope for everybody. Master Power comes into the world to save sinners and to put them on the way back to God. It is for you to remain devoted to Him, and keep His commandments. The rest is for Him to do.[53]

The Guru bestows the life force—the incomparable gift. There are many kinds of gifts, but the gift of Naam is above all others, and having given it, the Master then develops it within you, because he wants you to reach the same stage as himself. He wants you to enjoy the bliss that he enjoys.[54]

So know that if you meet a true Guru, you have met the Lord. He is not only a Guru, but a messenger from God, come to take you back to Him. Go wherever he leads you. If you obey him, you will become what he is. If not, if your mind steps in and interferes, you will not be able to get anywhere near him. Those who have met a Perfect Master are greatly blessed.[55] A true Guru wants nothing from his children; he only feels grateful that another soul has become free and is returning to its own home. He has true love for the soul. [56]

No Perfect Saint has ever failed his disciples. Realize fully, this one will not fail you. Think deeply upon this rare privilege; a divine dispensation has been granted to you. Master is not the body. He is the power functioning through the body, and he is using his body to teach and guide man.[57]

So the Master affirms with conviction that this place is not the place of permanent abode for your soul, but a halfway house for a limited period, assigned to you for the higher purpose of spiritual perfection. If you will view things from this lofty viewpoint, you will find that our life so far has been as futile as anything. It is a matter of deep concern for each one of us, and we must assess the position carefully before it gets too late in the day and we are forced to fight a losing game.[58]

Without the instruction from the God-man, the Word cannot be communed with, but when this communion is had, it leads the soul to the Lord, from which the Word emanated and all our efforts have their full reward. When you, through immeasurable good fortune, find such a holy person, stick to him tenaciously with all your mind and all your soul, for you can realize through him, the object of your life—self-realization and God-realization. Do not look to his creed or color. Learn the science of the Word from him, and devote yourself heart and soul to the practice of the Word. Master is one with the Word. The Word is in him, and incarnates in the flesh to give instructions to mankind. Truly the Word is made flesh and dwells among us.[59]

Apra-Vidya and Para-Vidya

OUTER TEACHINGS, which we call *Apra Vidya*, are helpful, but one should not accept them blindly. Investigate the reasons why certain rites are performed— why the lamps are lighted and the bells are rung, and so on. If you continue your inquiries until you find some real information, your time will be well spent. To blindly perform rituals may yield a little peace of mind, but they offer nothing valid.

No matter what we do, unless we increase in awakenedness it will amount to little. Learn to differentiate. Inherit the truth, and make the best use of the untruth. Go to one who is fully awake, who has full powers of differentiation. You may call him by any name; some say Guru, or Sant, or Mahapurush, or Satpurush. Although all are man, yet Mahapurush is one who is awakened— a true man. Satpurush is he who becomes one with the Truth itself. We are all purush or conscious beings, and we are all fortunate to have been given the human form; it is a grand opportunity to realize the Lord.

Apra Vidya is a term which categorizes the outer practices: repetition of names, austerities, prayers, devotional rituals and customs, pilgrimage, alms and donations, scripture study, songs of praise, etc.—they are all connected with the mind and senses. We will gain reward from these good actions, but in doing them one's doership remains, and as long as we regard ourselves as the doers, we shall continue to revolve around this interminable cycle of birth and death. While the ego remains, both good and bad actions are binding; as Lord Krishna said . . . like gold and iron shackles.[60]

Para Vidya is to connect the soul with the Truth. Ego and attachment are consumed by the fire of Shabd; Gurumukh gets the everlasting light. This Shabd can only be received from the Guru. There is Ashabd, which is the Wordless God, but when He expressed Himself, that expression is called Shabd or Word. Through the Shabd, creation came into being, and through the Shabd, dissolution occurs. Creation, dissolution, and again creation— it all happens by the power of the Shabd. And where is the Shabd? Shabd is the earth, Shabd the sky; through the Shabd the Light came; Creation came after the Shabd; O Nanak, the Shabd is in every being. Shabd is also known as Naam, so we have: Naam is the nectar of life, it is the name of God, and in this body does it reside. When can you see it? When the senses are controlled, the mind is at a standstill and intellect is calm— then the soul perceives in crystal clearness. It is the first stage of realizing the Lord. Self-knowledge precedes God-knowledge, so when one knows who one is, by rising above the senses, one then realizes why it is said that "self-knowledge is God-knowledge."[61]

The Holy Path: Surat Shabd Yoga

THE REFERENCES to Light and Sound, say the Masters of the Surat Shabd Yoga, are not figurative but literal, referring not to the outer illuminations or sounds of this world, but to inner transcendent ones. They teach that the transcendent Sound and Light are the primal manifestations of God when He projects Himself into creation. In His Nameless state He is neither light nor darkness, neither sound nor silence, but when He assumes shape and form, Light and Sound emerge as His primary attributes.[62]

When we say the *Surat Shabd Yoga,* communion of the soul with Naam, is easy, we are using the words relatively. It is easier when compared with other forms of yoga: *karma yoga, jnana yoga, bhakti yoga, raj yoga, hatha yoga,* the traditional *ashtang yoga,* all of which call for stern and severe outer disciplines, which a common busy man in the work-a-day world of today has neither the patience nor the time nor strength nor the leisure to do with all the wits about him. The *Surat Shabd Yoga,* on the other hand, can easily be practiced by every one, man or woman, young or old, with equal ease and facility. It is because of its naturalness and simplicity that it is often termed *Sehaj Yoga.*[63]

The course of Surat Shabd Yoga, as described by Guru Nanak, is the most natural one. Even a child can practice it with ease. It is designed by God Himself and not by any human agency, and therefore, it admits no addition, alteration, or modification.[64] You think the Holy Path is an extremely difficult undertaking. Maybe so, but it is made easier by the guidance and grace of the Master. The benefits which are to be derived from this path are immeasurably great. What therefore if a little physical sacrifice is to be done to achieve this, the great spiritual end.[65] In the olden days, a man had to spend many years at the Guru's feet before he would be given anything: in these days, who can do this? The Guru must now first give something, and then the disciple learns to purify his life. You will be able to observe that the more the *Kali Yuga* (negative age) increases its force, the more grace does the Guru bestow—to save any soul.[66]

The path is straight and narrow and difficult, very difficult and exacting, but for one who is truly willing, every help is promised, and he can attain the goal in this very life; a goal that sets all other goals to shame, for beside it there are no goals at all, but empty baubles and toys, at best half-way houses.[67]

Initiation: The Awakening

IT IS THE "Word" personified or the Master Power that gives initiation, and it does not matter where the Master is at the time of initiation. Regardless of whether the Master himself is near at hand, or far away overseas, the Master Power always works. In case of distance the authorized representative conveys the Initiation instructions, generally in the morning hours. At the time of Initiation, the Master takes His seat at the Third Eye of the initiate and takes care of him henceforth. The accepted aspirants who are sincere and receptive during initiation, do have a perceptive first-hand inner spiritual experience (there is a difference between the psychic and the spiritual) at which time the spiritual (third) eye is opened to see the Light of God and the inner ear is opened to hear the Voice of God—the Creative Sound of the Beyond which has a soothing and healing effect. Occasionally an aspirant may feel for one reason or another, that the initial experience was lacking. This could be due to over-excitement and inability to discern the more subtle type of experience granted such a person in line with his background. However, in due time, this individual receives a magnified experience which erases any feeling of lack should such still exist. The Master Power from the moment of Initiation, guides and protects one, even after the end of the world, and beyond.[68]

The instruction in the esoteric teachings consists of the exposition of Simran, Dhyan and Bhajan, that is to say, repetition (mental with the tongue of thought only) of the words which are charged with the power of the Master; concentration or meditation (fixing consciousness or gaze) at the center of the two eyebrows; and linking the spirit with the saving lifeline within, ever reverberating in the form of the perennial Sound Current, the very life-breath of the Universe, of which the Master himself is the living embodiment. As soon as a devotee is able to transcend the physical body, the Radiant Form of the Master (Guru Dev) appears in the subtle plane and becomes a guiding force to the spirit on the journey into higher spiritual realms, bringing him back to the True Home of his Father. Henceforth the Master-spirit never leaves the soul, but continuously helps and directs, visibly and invisibly, directly and indirectly, in this life and the life hereafter, as the occasion may demand.[69]

With initiation and spiritual sadhna or practice, one gradually becomes aware of his shortcomings and tries to weed them out, and the more he purifies himself, the more he grows into Divine Life. As the scales begin to drop off, the true values of life become more and more apparent. The spirit gradually gets freed from the shackles of the world and is enabled to transcend the physical body and make flights into the higher regions. Hereafter, "he walks not after the flesh but after the spirit." Living in the world, he is no longer of the world. He now delights in the bliss of higher spiritual regions and not in the pleasures of the senses and sense-objects. The gift of Naam or Word comes only from a Master-soul who, by injecting his own life-impulse, befits an initiate for the spiritual journey.

The measure and speed of advance, however, depends on the individual's own make-up, the ground on which he stands, and the preparation that he may have made in past incarnations. As each one has a different background, each one has his own starting point. The seed is sown, but its unfoldment, growth and development depends on the nature of the soil in which it is planted.[70]

Each one however, as said before, takes his or her own time for efflorescence and fructification. The dormant spiritual faculties begin to quicken with life and the initiate feels within him a sort of fullness, a satiety, a blessedness. This is a gift imperishable and indestructible. It can neither be stolen nor washed away. The seed of spirituality once sown in the innermost depths of the soul must bear flowers and fruits, in the fullness of time. No power on earth can stand in the way of its growth or stifle it in any way whatever.

He who has once been initiated by a competent Master is assured, once and for all, his liberation from the bondage of mind and matter; it is but a question of time. The seed of spirituality sown in him is bound to sprout and fructify. The spirituality when awakened and the spiritual experience gained must develop, and the Master Power cannot rest contented until the child owned is reared and taken home to the house of the Father.[71]

Man has got himself so enmeshed in mind and the outgoing faculties that his release from them can only be brought about by struggle and perseverance. His plight is, in a way, similar to that of a bird that has been kept in a cage for so many years. Even if you should open the door of the cage, the bird will be loathe to fly out. Instead, it will fly from one side of the cage to the other, clinging with its talons to the wire mesh, but it does not wish to be free and fly out through the open door of the cage.

Similarly, the soul has become so attached to the body and the outgoing faculties that it clings to outside things and does not wish to let go of them. It does not wish to fly through the door that has been opened by the Master at the time of Holy Initiation, at the threshold of which the Radiant Form of the Master is patiently waiting to receive the child disciple. True discipleship does not start until one has risen above body consciousness.

It is from this point that the disciple will feel not only comfort, but will begin to experience the joy and bliss that awaits him in the Beyond. He will have as his companion the charming Radiant Form of the Master, who is ever at hand to impart the guidance that is so necessary in order to avoid the pitfalls on the way. Until this point is reached, the disciple is, as it were, on probation, but such probation that cannot be severed. It is during this probationary period that the soul will feel some discomfort. It has become so besmeared with the dirt of the senses that it has lost its original purity of heart and is not fit to be raised up out of the prison house of the body.

Even though the door has been opened, the soul is so attached to the things of the outside world that it does not wish to be free. It is only when the soul begins to regain its original purity of heart and mind that it can at last want to be free of the desires of the flesh and outward attachments. The loving Master tries to avoid all possible discomfort for the child disciple by explaining what are the vices to be avoided and the virtues to be developed in order to regain this purity.[72] Unfortunately, more often than not the words of the Master do not sink in and little or no action is taken by the disciple to amend his ways. Therefore, the Master Power must take firmer measures to bring home to the disciple the importance of the truths that have been explained in words. Hence, the discomfort that is sometimes felt by the dear ones in their day-to-day living. If implicit obedience would be given to the commandments of the Master, all the difficulties and discomforts would vanish. If a child gets itself so dirty that the only way the mother can wash it clean is by using a scrubbing brush, can it be said that the child will feel comfortable during the scrubbing process? It would only feel comfortable after the scrubbing has ceased and it is shining clean and pure.

God-realized souls are always present in the world, but in the past they were few, and even now they are very rare. Who then are the privileged ones who get to meet them? Those whose hearts are true. Those without deceit in the heart not only have the privilege of the Lord's own arrangements for meeting the Guru; with a clean heart they are able to absorb the full benefit of that meeting. The best attitude of mind is to sincerely serve in humility, and in more and more humility. *Then the Guru will come by Himself.* God Himself makes the soul hungry—and then He feeds it. There is really no need to worry about anything; simply be sincere and true to your own self. He has sent you to the right place; and He is the giver. It is a very subtle and exacting subject; what can I say about it? If a person thinks of him as Guru outwardly, tremendous change will take place. . . .[73]

All the gifts of nature are free. Spirituality is also a gift of God, not of man. Why should it be sold? It is not a marketable commodity. Knowledge is to be given away free. Do we have to pay for the sun that shines on all of us? Why then should we pay for the knowledge of God?

It is God's gift, and it is to be distributed free and freely. So no true Master will ever accept anything in return. He gives freely.[74]

Q. Please explain the importance of Initiation.

A. Initiation by a perfect Living Master assures an escort in unknown realms by one who is Himself a frequent traveller to those regions. He knows the presiding deities or powers of these planes, conducts the spirit step by step, counsels at every turn and twist of the path, cautions against lurking dangers at each place, explaining in detail all that one desires to know. He is a teacher on all levels of existence; a *Guru* on the earth-plane, a *Guru Dev* (astral radiant form) in the astral worlds and a *Satguru* in the purely spiritual regions. When everyone fails in this very life, at one stage or another, His long and strong arm is always there to help us, both when we are here and when we quit the earth plane. He pilots the spirit into the beyond and stands by it, even before the judgement seat of God.[75] The Guru's blessing is such that no matter how disobedient a child is, yet it will never come under the rule of Yam Raj again. What a concession that is! When the soul realizes, the records of Dharam Raj (another name for the Lord of Death) are burnt. The back records of the individual are transferred from the negative power into the hands of the positive power—the Guru.[76]

Q. When the inner Guru is felt, that He is leading or guiding, is this the initiation—the inner initiation? Should initiation be sought? Or the Satguru be sought?

A. Initiation from a Master on earth is required. Even those who are being guided by others, for further progress there have been cases in which they send them back. Christ and other Saints were asked when they were met inside, "What to do further?" They directed them to the Master on earth. Ask them if they can direct you further, and I think they will guide you that way. It's the same in so many cases; after all there is some government there, no lawlessness, you see.[77]

All those who are initiated into the Mysteries of the Beyond by a Living Master were destined to become His disciples. It is not a question of one choosing the path or the path choosing the disciple, but rather one of the disciple's background.[78]

In the past, the subject was very vague, for Masters agreed to give the experience only after long years of study, when one was fully prepared. Today, it can be seen immediately what spirituality is. What a magnificent blessing![79]

Meditation: All is Within

GOD IS FOUND not in books, as only statements about Him are given in them. Nor can He be found in temples made of stone by the hand of man. In these we gather together only to pray to God, or to thank Him for all that He has given. He resides within you. The body is the true temple of God. When you have understood this, then where do you go to find Him? First within your own self.[80] Withdraw from outside, withdraw from the mind and outgoing faculties and come up to the seat of the soul at the back of the eyes. Once you are able to rise above body consciousness you enter into an **awareness** of the higher order, which lies behind the reach of all philosophies and psychologies, for then you are on your way to the Causeless Cause, the Mother of all Causes, knowing which everything else becomes known of itself, like an open book. This then is the alpha and omega of the religion of soul, which begins where all religious philosophies and polemics end. Here all thinking, planning, imagining and fantasy, as mentioned in your diaries, fall off like autumn leaves.[81] The whole of this life's purpose is to become still—to withdraw from outer environments, and to concentrate. You have great strength in you; you are the child of a Lion.[82]

Satsang: To Sit in His Presence

IT IS A RARE privilege to gather together in His name to invoke His gracious mercy and to imbibe the sacred teachings.[83] Satsang is the central theme of the sacred teachings and I always impress upon the dear ones here and abroad not to miss it, as it is during these precious moments when you are near the fountain-head of bliss and immortality, that you grasp the true import of the teachings and assimilate the rare virtues of Godliness, by sitting in the charged atmosphere which is filled with His loving life-impulses. Satsang is the sacred arena where spiritual stalwarts are built. It is the pool of nectar which grants blissful God-intoxication and all differences of caste, creed, or country sink down to their lowest ebb.[84] So your purpose in coming to Satsang is to imbibe the love of God, to sit in His sweet remembrance, to unite with Him. All things past and future, all irrelevant matters can be dealt with in your own place of residence. Come, but come with the very best of intentions. Bring the remembrance of the Lord with you, and take it with you when you leave. Do not listen to others' conversation and do not talk to anyone unless it be about the Truth. You will thereby gain full benefit from Satsang—otherwise the years will pass by without any real advancement.[85] Even though you may not understand what is said, yet if you sit with full attention you will profit by it. If your thoughts are somewhere else, not only will you lose, but other people will also be affected by the impure atmosphere you are creating, for thoughts are living and possess great power. Regard the Satsang as a place of purity; do not talk or think of anything but God, and whosoever attends will be blessed by the uplifting atmosphere. We do not go to Satsang to meet our friends or to socialize.[86]

This place is a sanctuary, as you say. Sanctuary means what?—a place of sanctity. That should remain as a place of sanctity, not as a place of mirth and joy. Make it a point that those who come from outside come in all devotion and all inspiration. Don't make it a place of mirth and joy. Love—love is strong you see. When you enter, enter in obedience to the Master; then what will happen? The atmosphere will be charged. Whenever you'll enter you will have peace of mind, otherwise the atmosphere will not be charged. This place, as you were told the other day, should be a place where there should be medita-

tion and no sleeping. Also no mirth or joy, mind that;
come in awe and sanctity. If you will do it, in a month
or two the place will be charged.[87]

The easiest, the shortest and the simplest way to get
greater benefit is to lose yourself completely in the holy
presence of a Sant Satguru. This in fact is the significance
of Satsang. Swami Ji says, "O Soul, be fully absorbed in
Satsang at least this day."

What then is 'full or complete absorption' is the question? It means that while in the company of a Saint, one
should forget not only the place where he is sitting but
become wholly oblivious of the very surrounding in which
he is and dissolve his very being, losing all consciousness
except of the holy presence of the Master. This blanking
of oneself is called 'absorption'. The more one empties
himself of his worldliness and pettiness, the more he will
be filled with the divine grace emanating from the divine
presence before him. This is the secret of a successful Satsang. Excuse me, when I say that it is seldom that we get
a Satsang or company of a truly perfect Master, for such
highly advanced souls—souls one with the Lord—are
very rare indeed. They are not easily available and recog-
nizable and if by some mighty good luck we do come
across a Godman, we do not know how to derive the fullest benefit from his company or Satsang. The way to
make the most of such a rare opportunity and derive the
maximum benefit is that one should try to come to the
place of Satsang as early as possible and sit silently in a
prayerful mood, blanking the mind of all the worldly
thoughts in the august presence of the Master, inwardly

absorbing his words of wisdom. If by sitting close to fire we feel warmth and the proximity of a glacier gives a cold shiver, there is no reason why one should not be affected by the divine aura of a Master-saint whose radiation has an unimaginably long range.[88]

At Satsang there is a great charging, but you must be connected to it; it is no good just sitting there. Furthermore, your attention should be on the Master alone; even if you are thousands of miles from him physically, you can still enjoy Satsang. Naturally, there is more benefit in being completely attentive when near his physical presence, for you will get a direct charging; but no matter where you are, you will still have help, if you are receptive. Some people ask, what is the actual effect of Satsang? Well, if you tie a wild horse to a stake he will naturally make a run for it, but when he reaches the end of the tether he will be brought up with a jerk. He may try to run away several times, but will always be pulled up by the tether. Satsang has some effect like this on the mind, and after repeating a few times the inclination to run away grows less, until it eventually learns to still itself. Satsang also cleanses the bad smells which come from the habits of lust, anger, greed, etc., that is, if the person is receptive. He becomes something different.[89] In Satsang the flow of mercy is pouring into you, so get the fullest benefit from it. Weed out all imperfections, one by one; that is why I have told you to keep a diary. When the soil is weeded, it is ready for the seed to be sown, then the true growth can begin. If small pebbles and rocks are not removed, the seed may sprout, but it will not bear fruit.[90]

When you go to a realized soul to get right understanding, go with all humility, put aside *your* views. What you know, you know. While you are with him, try to understand what he is saying. Consider the level he is speaking from, and then compare your own knowledge. Many would hesitate to go to him for pride of their own knowledge. The man of prominent worldly position will not go, for he is intoxicated with his own power; and a rich man will not go, for he is lost in pride of wealth. Remember, a God-realized person cannot be bought with money, impressed by power, pushed by force. When you go to him, put aside your own ideas—after all, no one can rob you of them! We make the mistake of measuring what he is trying to say with what we already know: "We have heard that before"; "So and so said that"—etc. Brothers, he will say all this and more, for he must speak on man's level for fuller comprehension, and will quote many truths that others have said, that the seeker may find his way more easily. But the fact remains, if the seeker wants to receive, he must still his intellect for a while, and sit in all humility.[91]

I am glad you have a better appreciation of the value of the Satsang meetings, which are always inspiring, helpful and beneficial, as Master's love and grace is radiated in abundance therein, and all those present receive the life impulses from the Master Power working overhead. In group meetings, the entire congregation assimilates the overflowing grace of the Master and occasionally the Radiant Presence of the Master is experienced by the audience. Such meetings have a deep inspiring significance and, therefore, should be cherished in all loving devotion.[92]

Satsang is the name we give to the company of an awakened soul. A Satguru makes a Satsang.[93] Where would you go to realize God? Into a Satsang, where the Teacher, Sant or Master has himself realized the Truth and is competent to impart this wisdom to those present. Actually, Satsang is the medicine for that disease and pain which comes from ignorance of the truth, from searching for the answer to: Is there a God and how does one realize Him?[94] Hazur Sawan Singh Ji used to say that Satsangs served a very useful purpose as a protective hedge around the field of Simran and Bhajan, so that these vital and life-giving processes continue to develop and thrive, in spite of the otherwise busy life in the family, in society, in your respective avocations, and the like.[95] The first thing the Negative Power does when he wants to keep control over a soul is to stop him doing Bhajan and Simran. The individual finds that there is always something to lure him away from his meditation. This is his first method, and secondly he slips that question into the mind: "Why go to the Guru or the Satsang? What is the use of it?" Satsang is the very place where a turning point can be effected and an awareness of wrongdoing and wrong living is achieved, so he will try to persuade us not to go there. If you have the strength to ignore him, he will then suggest that you just go and bow down and then leave. He will place all kinds of doubts in

the mind, and instead of the fullest benefit from the Satsang, the person returns home with nothing but dissatis-
faction or the bad effects of gossiping and back biting
from other wavering individuals. These are two very
powerful weapons that the Negative Power is constantly
wielding.[96]

Similar is the case with attending Satsang regularly.
We can develop this habit by regularly going to see the
Master and attending his discourses full of Divine Knowledge. It is often noticed that persons with very poor spiritual background tend to grow spiritually by benefitting
from the radiation of the Master-Power in the charged
atmosphere.[97] O brothers, keep connection with the Satsang, and all your wrongs will be righted. Even your
earthly life will be a success.[98] The very physical body is
blessed when one sits in the Satsang.[99] Satsang serves as
a protective hedge around the holy seed of spirituality
where one enjoys divine radiation and gets clarity of vision. Missing of Satsang for devoting time for meditations
is not advisable.[100]

*Q. Would you discuss the handling of small children
at Satsang and meditation gatherings?*

A. I think for that you can detail somebody who can
sit outside with two or three of the children. They should
sacrifice their time for the good of others or mothers
should keep them quiet—any of the two things.[101]

Satsang is of the Master and every initiate is also part
of the Satsang and can contribute to the general atmosphere of the Satsang by setting an example in living up

to the teachings of the Master. Christ said, "Let my words abide in you, and you abide in me." The words of the Master are the Master, and the Master cannot be separated from His words.[102] The importance of attending Satsangs or spiritual gatherings cannot be over emphasized.[103] To attend Satsang is like having a protective hedge around your meditation; it also increases the incentive to meditate. Attend the Satsang even if your time is limited. Cancel some other appointment in order to do so, if necessary, for the benefits of Satsang are invaluable. . . . Attend the Satsang and have the advantage of a protective hedge around your meditation. I once asked Hazur Maharaj, "What are your orders regarding Satsang?" He told me, "If you are very sick in your bed, but you can move, then attend Satsang." Just note that he did not say that if you have the strength to walk, then attend Satsang. From this single instance, one can see how important it is.[103]a

Leave hundreds of urgent works to attend the Satsangs.[104]

Prayer: Your Dialogue With God

PRAYER IS THE master-key that unlocks the Kingdom of Heaven. Prayer can be defined as an anguished cry of the soul in distress or helplessness, to a Power, fuller and greater than itself, for relief and comfort. It is, in the generic and commonly accepted sense, an invocation to God or Godman (a living Master), competent enough to grant solace and peace to a mind tortured by the problems of life and life's surroundings.[105]

The instinct of love cannot come into play unless one sees the beloved. As long as we do not see God or the glory of God, we cannot have any faith in the existence of God and without this, all prayers go in vain. But Guru or Godman is the abode of God's Light and is a radiating center of the same. We can pray with equal efficacy to the Master, who is at one with God. Connected as He is with the Power-house behind Him, the Master is equally competent to grant our desires and fulfill our wishes.[106] We must go in prayer unto God or a Godman and after being able to commune with Him, we should depend on Him alone and not on any other power; for He alone is capable of drawing one out from the mighty swirls and eddying pools of mind and matter, and of applying a healing balm to the lacerated hearts torn by wild desires and temptations. He is the strength of the weak, the sheet anchor in the storm and stress of life and a haven of safety for the homeless. His glance of Grace soothes the broken hearts.[107]

All the religions are in agreement on the point that prayer at the seat of the soul wells out all the latent powers of the Godhead within and one can achieve spiritual beatitude through it. It is a connecting link between the Creator and His creation, between God and man. It is a supporting staff in the hands of a spiritual aspirant and a pilgrim soul cannot do without it from the beginning to the end of the journey, for it saves one from many a pitfall on the way and transforms the mind through and through until it shines forth and begins to reflect the Light of the soul.[108] We generally pray when we are in distress and trouble, but when we escape therefrom we begin thinking that we wrought liberation by our own efforts and thereafter do not feel the need for prayer. We must guard against such serious pitfalls. Prayer in fact is needed at every step. When in difficulty we must pray to escape therefrom. In distress, when all else fails, the thought of the Omnipotent Father gives solace to the mind. When success be in sight, then pray that you may not get elated and puffed up, and ask for God's Grace and bounty for without these we can never succeed. After the fulfillment of our desires or riddance from difficulties, we must render thanks to the Almighty for His favors. When God is the Loving Father and we cannot do without Him at all, prayer must become a part of our very being.

How many people in the world truly pray to God for the sake of God? The Sikhs have a prayer:

> *To be with the Gurumukh, to have the company of a Sadhu, to have the intoxication of the Naam; This is the true affinity in which Thy Name is remembered in the heart.*

They pray also:

> *Nanak's servant wants only this happiness;*
> *Give me the company of a Sant.*

Midst the ever-changing phenomena of the world, there is but one unchangeable permanence and that is God and God-in-action (the Holy Spirit, Kalma, Naam or Word), responsible for the creation, sustenance and

dissolution of countless universes. Why then should we
not long for, ask for and pray for that imperishable life
principle, so that we too may have "Life Everlasting"
and come to our eternal heritage, the everlasting Godhood which is our birthright. Our native home is in Sach
Khand. Ages upon ages have gone by since we parted
from the Father and we are still in exile in this world.
We must then yearn for a reunion with the Beloved, separated as we are from Him for myriads of ages.[110] Last,
but not least, prayer opens our eyes to reality and enables
us to see things in their true perspective. It gives new
values to life and gradually transports an individual into
a New World and initiates him into a New Order.[111]
With a life of prayer a person eventually rises into cosmic
awareness and sees the hidden hand of God working out
His will and His purpose which otherwise remain a
sealed book too subtle for the average man to pierce
through and peep into. The more this inner contact is
established, the more Godhead is imbibed by the spirit.
Only when a complete identification comes about does
one become a conscious coworker with Him.[112]

We cannot win God either by flattery or by vain repetitions, nor does He stand to gain or lose anything whether
we offer prayers or not. Compassionate as He is, His
grace is always at work in each and all alike, for we cannot live without it. We can, however, attract that grace
to our advantage by becoming a fit receptacle for it.
Humility and faith purify the mind and make it a fitting
instrument for God's grace. These two aids help in inverting the lotus of the mind which, at present, is attuned

with the senses. Unless we are able to turn its direction upwards, God's grace cannot directly flow into it. Prayers, humble and sincere, help in establishing a harmony between man's mind and God's grace. All that is required is a loving and pure heart attuned to His grace and the latter is automatically attracted to it. Prayer has in it a great dynamic force. It strengthens and prepares a person to face and fight the battle of life fearlessly and successfully. It is in fact, the only panacea for all types of ills. It is the key that unlocks the Kingdom of Heaven.[113]

Prayer must arise from the depths of the soul. It should not be a vain repetition of empty words with little meaning. What we pray for we must really wish for, not only intellectually, but from the very core of our being. It must churn the very soul to its depths and the music of prayer should come out and tingle—from the very nerves, tissues and fibers of the entire frame making us unmindful of everything else beside the sweet music of the soul.[114]

The secret of successful prayer lies not so much in the words we use, nor in the time we devote to it, nor in the effort that we put into it, as it lies in the concentrated attention that one may give it at the seat of the soul so as to make it soulful. The most natural form for a fruitful prayer is the yearning of a soul without the agency of words, oral or mental, with the tongue of thought. A prayer like this generates and releases such a fund of spiritual energy that all the cosmic powers are attracted, and combine together, shaping out things as well as possible. A true prayer is one continuous process, independent of form, time and place, and leads ultimately to perfect equipoise and no desire whatsoever. This, then, is the climax of a genuine prayer and here prayer itself ceases to be a prayer and becomes a state of being as one gradually rises first into cosmic consciousness and then into super consciousness, with the divine will fully revealed unto him. This is the be-all and end-all of prayer.[115]Where all human efforts fail, prayer succeeds.[116]

The Commitment: Responsibility of Initiation

THE MASTER HAS to do his job and the initiates their own: to push on with full confidence in the Master. There are too many leaners on idealistic imagination among the initiates and too few who practice. The meditation period should not be one of pretty emotional feelings only. The initiates should surrender their all to the Master and be willing to die and give up their life for God. "Learn to die so that you may begin to live." The Master knows how to deal best with it. Ours is to act well in the living present, as enjoined by the Master. If we act up to his commandments, he will never forsake us till the end of the world. But we feel, on the contrary, that after the Initiation we are absolved from all obligations, and are free to do what we may by simply putting our trust in His Grace. This attitude is a great stumbling block on the path and retards all real progress. It does not pay in the least to purposely close our eyes in self-complacency to the stern reality of the situation that places rights and obligations in equal proportion on each and every individual. We cannot pick and choose, as we may like. We must therefore guard against such a frustrated mentality and have to work our way ourselves for there are no short shrifts in the science of the spirit. It is a long and laborious process of unfoldment for the spirit and we have of necessity to take care of the higher values of life at each step if we are keen in our search for Truth. It is a steep path which if we have to tread without stumbling we must tread with our heart forever fixed on the goal and on the steps immediately before us, for there is no time to look behind; it can only make us shudder and tremble. Ignorance is the only disease from which the soul suffers. It can only be cured by knowledge and the knowledge is the action of the soul and is perfect without the senses, though on the physical plane it cannot do without the service of the senses. True knowledge only dawns on the supramental plane where physical senses can be of no avail. But until that stage of direct communion with the Radiant Form of the Master is attained, one has to take care in everything, for the path is slippery and strewn over with hidden traps that may at any moment catch the unwary pilgrim on the path. Once one slips, the golden opportunity is lost and one does not know when one may be able to get a human birth once again. When we lay too much stress on the means, viz., vegetarian diet and karmas, we should lay still more emphasis on inversion and withdrawal from the senses and put in more time for the purpose.[117]

Consider the parable of the seed given by Christ. The seed was sown. Some seed fell on the road; some fell in the thorny hedges; some fell on the rocks; and some seeds fell on the quite clear land which had been divested of all foreign matter. That seed which had fallen on the hard open ground or the road is eaten away by sparrows; the seed that was thrown on the rocks grows but there is no depth of soil beneath such seeds and, little by little, such growth fades away; and naturally, those seeds which fell in the thorny hedges will grow, but they cannot fully grow—they are retarded; and any seed which fell in the quite prepared land will grow abundantly. If you put in one seed of anything, that one will give you hundreds of seeds like that. For instance, you put one mango in the ground, and that will give a tree which will give you hundreds of mangoes. So there is abundance in nature. This parable, then, shows what? The "seed" is the contact with the Light and Sound Principle, which is the expression of Word, or Naam in the hearts of the initiates. For those who simply take it, the Negative Powers use it up because they never put in time for that, although they are given the "seed"—the seed is sown in them—but as they do not put in time at all, and they don't care, after Initiation the seed is lost. Concerning those seeds which fell on the rocks and beneath which there is little or no underlying soil, after Initiation that seed should be fed by Satsangs; for if those seeds are not watered by Satsangs, you see, naturally they fade away—they also don't grow —they come for a few days, then leave it. So that is why I tell the people, "LEAVE HUNDREDS OF URGENT WORKS TO ATTEND THE SATSANGS." Those seeds that fell in the thorny hedges won't grow there encumbered by the distracting thoughts and other kinds of hedges; they are just like those who have too many irons in the fire, they have no time to attend to these things; they say they have no time. Such people also don't grow. Only such a seed which has fallen on the quite prepared land grows fruit in abundance. So you will find that the purpose of this diary, which I always enjoin to be kept, is to weed out all imperfection from the soil of the heart. Those who keep the diary regularly, naturally they progress. If they are not progressing, there is something wrong somewhere, which is explained to you by just referring to this parable given by Christ.[118]

Spirituality, being the highest goal in life, is also the most difficult; Only those who are really in search of the Truth should venture forth to travel on this path.[119]

The Master unites us in a true relationship, which can never be broken. This relationship is with God Himself, who is manifested in the human form. It is such a relationship that can never be sundered, even after death, not to speak of during life. But we, with our poor understanding, assert ourselves with pride, ego, and low habits, desiring to be recognized. Consequently, we succeed only in heaping more misery upon our heads. What is the use of attending Satsang for so long if you are not going to change the old unwanted habits? Dry land can become green again by giving it water, but of what use is land that is watered, yet remains dead? Your attendance has become mere routine—you cannot get salvation by rote —you will not get it, you will not get it.[120]

If you knew there was some treasure hidden somewhere, wouldn't you like to dig it out? If a thief came across an unguarded house with no one to see his actions, do you think he would sleep in the night? So many say that God is within us, but even then sleep without caring. Why don't they dig out the Truth? Even if one meets someone who can help to bring out this Truth, and some understanding is given, even then one does not care to do the digging. How unfortunate is he! What can we call such an unfortunate person? If he were not conscious of the thing it would be a different matter, but if someone has shown a little of that treasure inside, and even then one ignores it, then what is to be done? The usual excuse given is, "I have no time," is it not? Do you want someone else to dig out the treasure for you?[121]

If God's mercy has been given, and the Master's mercy is over one's head, then why does it not show forth? Many people are puzzled by this. The reason is that the soul is not showing any mercy unto itself. God's mercy gave us this human form, and through it also the yearning for Him began. Furthermore, he brought the seeker to the feet of a Godman in whom He was manifested. The Godman's mercy was bestowed when he gave the contact inside. If you, the soul, do not have mercy upon yourself, then what can be done? My Master used to say, "The Doctor gave you the medicine, but you did not take it, so how can the cure be effected?" Without the soul's mercy, the seed will not fructify. It is true that the seed has been planted and will never be destroyed, but the person will have to come again to the world, even though he may not retrogress below the human form. Make the best use of the grand opportunity before you. A great part of your life is already spent. "Much has gone, a little is left; in the remaining time, do your work." You have been separated from Him for life upon life, upon life, and the Father is anxious that His chilren should now return to the fold.[122]

Self Evaluation: The New Direction

IF ONLY THE THOUGHT remained uppermost in mind: "Who am I? Where am I going?" This could change the very pattern of our life.[123] You *can* direct your own destiny.[124]. . . You are advised to draw a thick curtain over the past and just forget everything which has since passed as no amount of repentance or resentment can do it. You must start a new pattern of life.[125] This invaluable guidance is written in the sacred books, but sadly it remains there, or it penetrates only to intellectual level. We have to take the knowledge and live up to it, only then does it become a part of life. The night is a jungle —do your work in the daytime and then benefit from the night. The true purpose of having a human form is to make daily progress toward the great goal, so sit down each day and see where you are. The meaning of keeping a diary is of the utmost importance, but very few fully understand it. Remove those things which are obstructing your progress—weed out the imperfections, one by one. A strong man revels in his strength and the weaker man wonders how he got it. When a wrestler walks abroad, people turn to stare and remark on his strength. He has not achieved that overnight, but through many nights of hard exercising. As the renunciate leaves everything and goes to the woods, you can sit down nightly in your own home, forgetting the world and freeing your-self from all entanglements.[126]

If you will take one step, He will come down hundreds of steps to greet you.[127] No matter what your past has been—stop now! View the facts and start afresh. Stand still and become tranquil, or you will not succeed.[128]

The question, once again, is of earnestness. Do we really need God? Sometimes, we do ask for God. Even our intellect also, at times, feels the need for God. But does our mind want God? This is the crux of the problem. We ask for things with mental reservations—only if they are of any use to us on the physical plane. On the other hand, the mind is entirely dyed in the color of the world. It has no time to think of anything else. Mind has a great potential in it. What the mind wants, it fervently prays for it. At times, it even cries for it. God comes in only as the means for the satisfaction of his worldly de-sires. And day and night one thinks of nothing else. This is the actual condition of our mind. You can search it for yourself. Do you sincerely wish for God? No. We want Him only as a means to an end—the end being physical pleasures and comforts. Otherwise, God has no meaning for us. It is a question of demand and supply. If we actually wish God, the law of nature comes to our aid. Where there is fire, oxygen comes to its aid. All that we need is to put our tongue, intellect and mind on one level. Such an attitude increases the mind force. Where the mind force is strong, nothing can stand in our way. We must be true to our 'self' and then whatever may be wished shall be fulfilled.[129]

So decide from today onward, you see—decide what is your aim in life. We are adrift, aimlessly adrift; the result is we are just starting this way, some days ahead, some days back. Some days we proceed; some days we recede. We dig so many ditches in the earth, some five feet, some seven feet, some four feet. Water nowhere! Now all of you see the way clear before you? Then do it! Start from today; what is past is past, don't care for the past. Just don't dream of the future, too. When you are put on the way, you'll reach the goal. And what is that you have to contact? Light and Sound within you. Like the electric lifts, when you sit down, that current is there, that's all. So as I submitted before: spirituality is not difficult, it is we who have made it difficult, that's all. Simply follow it. Simple life and high thinking.[130]

The human form is the king of all the species and is the highest rung in the ladder of creation, for in this form God has placed the power of differentiation through which one can define truth from untruth and so achieve that which can be done in no other form.[131]

It does not matter if you could not live up to the holy commandments till now. Your sacred aspirations for improvement are laudable. Thus far and no more should be the motto. If you will follow this golden principle of life, you will certainly change in due course. Slow but steady paces shorten the journey. One step in the right direction under the protective guidance of the Master Power will set the ball rolling. You should please note that every pleasure has its price and every suffering has its equivalent compensation.[132]

Obedience: " If You Love Me, Keep My Commandments "

*If I may only please Him 'tis pilgrimage
    enough;*
If not, nothing—no rites or toils avail:
*Whichever way I look, I find that in His
    creation,*
None has won salvation without His grace—
*Regardless of Karmas you can discover untold
    spiritual riches within yourself:*
*If you but abide by the teachings of your
    Master.*
My Master has taught me one lesson:
*He is the Lord of everything, may I
    never forget Him.*[133]

JAP JI: 6

IF YOU OBEY the Master literally, then He will make you master of your own home.[134] Naturally the child who heeds his father's slightest wish will enjoy his pleasure. Whoever insists on his own ideas and does not want to obey, doubtless he will also get the Master's love, but the inner key will not be entrusted to him.[135] Make up your mind whether you would like to conform to the dictates of your mind or to the Commandments of the Master. The choice lies in your own hands; you are free to choose; no one else can make the choice for you. The world may condemn you who choose the Master's way. However, you need not worry because you have taken up the right way.[136]

We should exploit those qualities which will assist us to join back to God, and discard all traits which are liable to lead us away from Him. It is not difficult to realize the Lord, but it is most difficult to become a man— a true human being. One hundred times and more we bow our heads and say "yes, yes, I will do it," but in action we do just as we please. This indicates that as yet we do not truly understand the spiritual path. If you have not as yet changed your old habits, then do so at once. Make a start *now*. To have bad thoughts for others, to take sides in enmity, like a lawyer criticizing the lives of your fellow beings—would you not expect the fire to flare up within you? The Guru sees all events with a different eye, for every man sees from his own level. If you have accepted someone as being superior to you, then obey him.[137] By merely looking at a Master you will not get salvation; remember that. Just by seeing the Guru, salvation does not come, if you do not love the Satguru's words. Do whatever the Master says: follow his advice, obey him and become receptive to him, for the soul gains strength through receptivity. The work which may seem impossible just now will become easy. All sins are burned away in the company of a true Master, and from a true Master you can receive the precious gift of Naam. The Satguru is so powerful, that not only the disciple gets the benefit, but those who love the disciple will also gain His protection. This has been proved by historic spiritual record.[138]

There is less hope for those who pay obeisance to the body of the Master, as compared with those who pay

obedience to the words which he utters. For them, emancipation is definite, sure and certain. We should obey and
pay respect to the words that the Master utters. Then
we are sure to go back to the home of our Father.
Those who only pay obeisance to the Master outwardly
and do not live up to what the Master says, there is yet
time. The time factor is a necessity.[139]

To abide by the teachings of the Master is just like
treading a razor's edge. The more you walk on the edge
of a razor, the more it will cut your feet. What does this
mean? The more you abide by the teachings of the Master, by the sayings of the Master, the more you have
to tear up your old name and fame, what you are, whether high or low. You have to care only for the Master.[140]
So the first difficult thing on the way to devotion to the
Master is that you must abide by what he says, irrespective of whether the world praises you or not. It may be
possible that he says something that does not appeal to
your intellect, but what is your duty? When the officer
in the field orders "fire" what will the soldier do? He
must fire. The Master will never say anything which is
not becoming. It may be that you do not understand
what he says at the time, but he has some noble purpose
behind it for your betterment. That is why it is very difficult to follow the orders of the Master.[140a]

The ABC starts from where?—when you obey the
the orders of the Master. What does the Master say? He
says, "Keep your life pure—For a while, leave off from
outside and introvert within—Rise above body consciousness—Come into contact with the God into Expression

Power, the Light and Sound Principle within you—Then rise above the astral and causal bodies. You will realize what is meant by "I and my Father are One." You can then rise further into the Super Conscious state. This is the ultimate goal."[141] So brothers, obey my direction, do your meditation even if it be a little, increase whatever experience you have been given. See into each action of your daily life, and keep a diary. Do not leave off your Bhajan and Simran. There is a remedy for mistakes, but there is no remedy for disobeying, and the road is long for such people. Those who have Naam will definitely reach God, but it will be a long journey for whosoever disobeys the instructions. You have to do it whether in one birth, two or four, so why not now? Remember that the disciple who always has his face turned toward the Guru, draws the Guru's attention. If you keep someone in your heart, you will reside in theirs.[142]

All creation is in God's control, just as a powerhouse controls all other machinery. He who is in charge of the powerhouse will tell you that not a single piece of machinery can move without his orders. Those working under him say, "Be careful not to disobey his orders, otherwise a limb might get chopped off in the machinery." His wishes are like standing orders and cannot be erased. So God is called by the names Shabd or Naam or Word. That which we term the Controlling Power is His wish or order, or you can call it the Will of God. "Through the Shabd all happiness is acquired, and through love of the True Naam." Soul is a part of God, just as it is a part of the Shabd. When the soul becomes one with God, it becomes full of bliss. "If ye long for eternal happiness, surrender thyself to God." Go under the protection of that Power which is perpetually vibrating.[143]

One will go on coming and going until one surrenders one's whole being to the Guru; and this means living in accordance with his wishes, thinking as he advocates. The keeper of the intellect is the Guru. Maulana Rumi Sahib prays to God, saying, *This intellect will turn my face from You; Keep your control on it, and I am saved— otherwise I am lost*. It does not take much time to spoil the milk! The intellect is like that. If your mind obeys the Guru one hundred percent, you will know then who the God is. Don't let your intellect interfere in the slightest fraction with what you know is right. He who is willing to obey him without a question will receive the treasure. Naam's perpetual song, precious jewel of the Lord, is in the Sadhu's keeping. You can also say that God has handed over His treasure to the Master. Then? The Guru places it before him who takes his words as truth. To find a Guru who can do this is the height of good fortune. Without good fortune, the Satguru is not met.[144]

If one has found a true Master, who is attuned to the Lord and is His mouthpiece, and obeys Him in all things completely and absolutely, he will surely destroy the hydra-headed serpent of the ego and reach his heavenly home one day. There will be moments in the course of such love when one, judging from one's own limited understanding, doubts the validity of the Master's instructions, but such moments are only tests to make our self-surrender more complete and more secure, and he who passes through these tests successfully, will one day radiate with the glory of God.[145]

To obey, and to surrender oneself, are two different things. Being obedient to the Guru's wishes does not mean you have surrendered yourself, although he who has surrendered is naturally obedient. But if you have surrendered you will not think of why and what, you will just do what he says. *I have given Myself unto Your reckoning, so do what You will.* When Hazrat Ibrahim's slave was asked where he would like to sleep, what clothes he would like to wear, the slave replied, "Sir, you have bought me, whatever you wish I will do." This is what surrender means. It is a very difficult step to take, for hundreds of doubts enter the mind.[146]

If you ever come to know what a Guru is, then there is nothing left to learn. The Guru teaches this with love, with persuasion—after all, they are his children! If a child is covered with filth, he cannot kill it. Under the influence of the mind, the manmukh has little understanding; he does not obey the Guru, he does not live for the Guru's pleasure, but he is concerned with his own will. The reason? He has little or no connection with the Shabd. When a person gets the connection, he should keep it intact and not break it! Only then will all the virtues come, without effort. The precious attribute of true humility will grow in his heart. Just listening to the Shabd is a treasure of all virtues.[147]

For how long will you try to deceive your
   Guru?
Now recognize what He is.

Hiding the true facts, you think, "What does tne Guru
know? What *we* want to do is correct." You get hold of
an idea and place it above all else, considering everyone
else to be wrong—even if your Guru tells you something
different. How long will you keep this up? Make no mistake, he watches our every action, for the Guru Power
is residing within our very being. But we foolishly think
that he is not present to see us, so we can do anything
and he will not know. He entreats us to try to realize
what a Guru is. The Guru is not the physical form—he
is not the human pole but is the all-omnipotent power
of God which has manifested therein. It is accepted that
God is everywhere and sees everything. Give full attention to learn what the Guru is, and then come to
know it.[148]

From today, become a worthy sikh—worthy even to
be called a gurusikh, the beloved disciple of the Guru.
You can do this if you obey the Master's words. You will
not do it? You will *have* to do it—if not in this birth, then
in the next. Oh brothers, what is the use of coming again
and again? Why not do it now? *If this birth goes, it will
not come again in your hands, and the precious life is
wasted.*[149]

We may have been given human birth many times,
but pride and ego killed us again and again, ruining all
our good work and causing us to return to the same scene

time and again. In the past it was our ruination, and it is winning the present also. Do not obey your mind—obey the words of the Guru, which will bring you great joy, whereas obedience to the mind will give you unending distress—the mind ever gave birth to trouble. Wash anger away with love, just as your Guru does. If you refuse to understand, then nothing can be done.[150] You will just have to continue paying up for your mistakes.[151] If the Guru's initiation is followed by absolute obedience to his wishes, all sins will be washed away forever, along with all the miseries of the worldly life.[152]

Why do Masters come and what is their work? They release the soul from mind and senses and connect it with Naam. They come only for this purpose, though they go through many difficulties and work hard. Go to the Satguru and obey him. *The words of a complete Master, I tie on my heart.* Tie his words close to you—they should not enter from one ear and leave from the other —tie them securely in your heart.[153]

If one is spiritually developed in life, he or she remains so in after-life, but if one is not so developed, how can he develop after death? We have a golden opportunity now in the human body wherein we can develop to any degree of perfection and can become detached from the things of this world. When one has developed overwhelmingly in love and devotion for the Master and has advanced spiritually so much so that he or she has become detached from worldly things, he need not return to earthly life, but will proceed onward in the Inner Planes with the guidance of the Master-Power residing with him. If only the initiates would do and act as they are told, surely they will rise up into the regions of Light and Supreme Joy and meet the Radiant and charming Master face to face. It may seem difficult, but it is a practical possibility and is within the reach of everyone with the grace of the Master. Everything that is holy, lovely and good is hard, but the rewards are supremely superb.[154] Every initiate of a competent Master is destined to reach his True Eternal Home. The speed is accelerated when the disciple obeys the words of the Master. In this way great progress is made here and now.[155]

He is not to be won by words, but by deed—*if you love me, keep my commandments*.[156] If we scrupulously act up to his instructions, he will make us a Saint like himself in due course.[157]

Testing the Disciple

THE MASTERS TEST the disciples again and again, to see how much the disciple can sacrifice, how much loving devotion he has, and to what extent he still remains under the influences of mind. He who sacrifices everything for the sake of his Guru has achieved all.[158]

Time Factor is a Necessity

MAHATMAS ARE NOT made in one day. Rome was not built in a day. Man is in the make. . . . You must not be sceptic about your inner progress as it is beyond the ken or human comprehension to gauge the inner growth. The divine love of the Master is just like a spark of flame which reduces everything to ashes in good time.[159]

In the Gurbani it is written that purity of thoughts and perseverance are needed. Do you want to become something worthwhile or don't you? Hearing such words, an interest is awakened, but the work cannot be accomplished in one day. A child, learning to read, reads a few lines and promptly forgets them. He must read them again and again, but after much struggling with learning, he one day may be able to write a book. Every Saint has his past, and every sinner a future. The people who are like us today can become something tomorrow. For this, true guidance is required from one who has seen, not anyone else. The second requirement is implicit obedience to one's Guru. The Master's words are not just words alone, but are the Master Himself! Added to this, perseverance is necessary.[160] Those who are now better situated may have been like you some time back, or even worse off. They persevered and did the right thing. It gave them strength and power. You can do likewise. It is just a matter of starting anew. START RIGHT NOW. The Master is anxious to see you progress. He wants his initiates to rise to sublime heights and have their bowls filled to the brim with the nectar of God-consciousness.

But the bowls must first be emptied of the rubbish that they contain in order to make room for the nectar to be put in.

Seek only that company which is helpful to you. Discard all others lovingly and unprovokingly. You will surely make progress. But remember one thing—Rome was not built in a day. It required a huge effort in toil from hundreds and thousands of people for a very long time.

Your discipline may not have to be as severe, but you cannot have what you want so easily. You must work for it. But be sure that with a little work you will get better results. The Master wants you all to develop love and humility. These must be lived with tolerance. Spiritual Science is very definite, and whoever, even the vilest of the vile, follows it, is changed for the better. If some people who have been put on the way are not changed for the better, it is purely their own fault and not that the Science is wrong.

This is the most perfect way given out by all the Masters who came in the past. Our day to day life should be a living testimony of what we profess. This is the long and the short of the whole thing. Everyone must learn it and the sooner, the better. Reformers are wanted, not of others, but of themselves. It is better to see one's own faults and try to remove them than to pick holes in others.[101]

Karma: The Wheel That Binds

EACH THOUGHT, each word and each deed has to be accounted and compensated for in Nature. Every cause has an effect and every action brings about a reaction. Uproot the cause and the effect disappears. This has been done by the Masters who have transcended these laws, but all others are bound by the bonds of karma, which is the root cause of physical existence and the clever device of nature to maintain this existence. The law of karma sees to it that we are paid an eye for an eye, and a tooth for a tooth, in the shape of joy or suffering. It is the goading whip in the hidden hands of nature. The mind contracts karma, puts a covering on the soul and rules the body through the organs and the senses. Although it is the soul that imparts strength to the mind, the latter has assumed sovereignty and is governing the soul instead. Control of the mind, therefore, is the first step to Spirituality. Victory over the mind is victory over the world. Even accomplished Yogis and Mystics who can transcend to high spiritual realms are not left untouched by the hand of karma. Saints classify karmas into three distinct groups, as follows:

I. SANCHIT (*stored*): Good or bad deeds that stand to our account as earned and contracted in all previous bodies of the order of Creation, counting from the day of the first appearance of life on earth. Alas! Man knows nothing about them or their extent.

II. PRARABDHA (*fate or destiny*): The result and effect of which has brought man into his present body and has to be paid off in this life. The reactions of these karmas come to us unexpectedly and unperceived and we have no control over them whatsoever. Good or bad, we have to tolerate or bear this karma, laughing or weeping, as it happens to suit us.

III. KRIYAMAN (*account of our actions and deeds in the present body*): This is distinct from the above mentioned two groups, as here, man is free to do exactly as he pleases, within certain limits. Knowingly or unknowingly, deeds committed and coming under this heading bear fruit. The result of some of these we reap before we die and the residue is transferred to the Sanchit storehouse. Karma is the cause of rebirth, and each birth is in turn followed by death. Thus the cycle of enjoyment and suffering, which are concomitants of birth and death, continues. "As you think, so you become," is an unalterable law of nature, owing to which this Universe exists. No amount of integrity or genius can absolve a man so long as there is the slightest trace of karma. Ignorance of the law is no excuse, and though there may be some concession or relaxation with man-made laws under special circumstances, there is no such allowance made for this in nature's laws. Prayer, confession and atonement may give temporary mental relief but they cannot overcome karma. All karma must be wiped out completely before permanent salvation can be had.[162]

Similarly, the philosophy of karma too, has a specific place in the system of spiritual science. But it should on no account be made to induce morbidity and breed a spirit of frustration among the initiates and non-initiates. Man is the maker of his own destiny. Though we cannot alter the past yet we can forge the future as best we may. "Thus far and no further" is the deadline which the Master draws for each one of us and it should on no account be transgressed.[163] It is our past karmic evolution which moves us around under His divine will. We are bound within certain limits on account of past karma and free within certain limits. We can make the best use of free karmas to change our course to proceed on our

spiritual way.[164] Now that our fate has brought us here,
how can we make the best of the human life? We should
not sow any more seeds. Whatever happens in life due to
past actions should be borne with cheerfulness. Happiness and unhappiness will come, but one should never be
disheartened. The great spiritual leaders also go through
similar experiences, but without suffering the pinching
effects. My Master used to say, "You cannot clear up all
the thorns which you yourself have spread in your path,
but you can wear heavy boots for protection." The task
of saving ourselves from the reactions in store for us
should be seriously considered, for only in the human
form do we have any chance of rendering them inactive.
The Saints who come—forgive me, but they also leave
the body at death. They also get riches or poverty, but
they always avoid those actions which will cause reaction.[165]

> He who is of one color enjoys perpetual
>   freedom;
> He has no fight with anyone.

He has right understanding; he has full awareness of the
oneness of all life. He remains unaffected through each
passing phase, while the ripples on the surface of the
ocean of life come and go. He works endlessly, tirelessly in
this field of action—yet is above the effects of action. The
meaning of the words *neh-karma* is to do the actions yet
remain actionless, so those who cannot see the true facts
cannot become neh-karma. Only by seeing the action of
the Lord in everything can one attain this state. He is

neh-karma who is connected with the Shabd.[166] When
one has become the conscious co-worker of the divine
plan, all past actions, sanchit karmas (those in store) are
erased—finished. If the person who was tasting the actions is not there, then who is there to taste them and be
responsible? When there is I-hood, one must receive the
results of one's actions. A man may state, "I am not the
doer," but within the folds of his heart he cannot believe
this, and continues to consider he is doing everything,
thereby holding responsibility for his actions and the reactions to follow. If he becomes the conscious co-worker
of the divine plan and knows that he does only that which
God wills, how can he be burdened by any action?[167]
To be neh-karma then should be our ideal in life and this
means salvation.[168]

We are at the mercy of our actions and whatever we
do sets up an action-reaction. Good actions bring good
reactions: bad actions, bad reactions. In the *Gurbani*
(sayings of the Sikh Gurus) it is written, "Do not blame
others, but blame your own past actions." Brothers, do
not blame anyone. You got this human form as a result
of your prarabdha karmas (destiny, governing this life's
pattern); it is the good fruit of your past. Whatever you
have to give and take from the past lives must be accounted for now. You have to take from some people
and give to others. Sometimes when giving something to
a certain person, such warmth of love swells up from
within the heart, and yet another occasion one gives with
hatred and reluctance. This is reaction from the past.
Someone is rich, another poor. Some are masters, others

servants. In all, there are six things over which man has no control: life, death, poverty, riches, honor and dishonor. These are all beyond our control.[169]

Good actions will no doubt bring their reward, but you will still be a prisoner. Perhaps some will go into a Class A prison, some Class B, some Class C. Some might get the pleasures of the other worlds. Heaven and hell will come again and again, for this circle cannot be broken unless one gets out of the illusion.[170] We come into the world only to settle our old accounts of give and take. All our relationships—father and son, husband and wife, mother and daughter, brother and sister, and vice versa —are the result of past karmic reactions. It is said that the pen of destiny moves in accordance with our deeds. What we sow we must reap. We come with fate writ in our forehead: even the body itself is the result of our karmas and it is rightly said to be *Karman sharir*. It is the destiny that casts our mold. Without body there can be no deeds and without deeds there can be no body. It, therefore, behooves us to pass our days happily and ungrudgingly give what we have to and what we must for there is no escape from it. We have, of course, to be careful not to create new relationships and sow fresh seeds. This is the only way to get out of the abysmal depths of the karmic ocean.[171]

To expect that after initiation the affairs of the world would so change that bitter things will never come your way, is a mistaken idea. Ups and downs do come here as a result of the reactions of one's own doings. They have to be faced and squared up. If we were to run away from them, the debts will remain unliquidated.[172] We have been joined to our family and relatives through God's will and the prarabdha karmas, and we should accept the conditions joyfully. Only he who truly knows, willingly pays his way through life. Who knows how many difficulties are due to our unpaid debts?[173] If you have sucked anyone's blood now, in the next birth, he sucks your blood. On the surface it may seem to be, "he is doing wrong to me, he is a tyrant, he is cruel," but who knows what is the reaction of the past?[174]

I am sorry for your personal affairs when you feel hurt and confused. The present earth life is chiefly based on the reaction of past karma which determines pain and pleasure, health and sickness, honor and ignominy. However, a well planned and disciplined life based on spiritual beatitude goes a long way in offering new vistas of peace and harmony. Ups and downs are the normal features of earth life and should be considered in the spirit of their being passing phases. The golden principle of accepting the weals and woes of life in a spirit of mental stability and equilibrium, being in our best spiritual interests, should be followed cheerfully. An initiate's life, just like a bank going into liquidation when each farthing is to be squared up and paid off, is for releasing the soul from past karmic debts. If you will accept all events in this spirit of right understanding, you shall be more positive, happy and cheerful. The decrees of heaven are subject to no error. Yet divine dispensation is invariably flavored with mercy. A spiritually developed person would surmount all difficulties of material life by merging his or her will in that of the Lord.[175] When Masters come they do not disturb the prarabdha karmas, although in one way they do: they start giving food to the soul. To feed the physical form we have to eat and drink. To strengthen the intellect we read, write and think. All these words are food for the intellect. The soul is fed only with the Bread of Life, which is the experience of the Beyond. With such food the soul becomes very strong, and though unhappiness and sorrow may come it will not have so much effect. If there is a thorny road to travel and one puts on heavy boots, then one will not feel the thorns. Say there are ten people, and they get beaten up physically. One of them is very weak, and after a slight beating he collapses. The others admit they were beaten up, but did not feel it so much. Similarly, if the soul is strong, happiness or unhappiness may come, but will not have any drastic effects.[176]

Q. *Can we overcome past karmic impressions?*

A. Karmic reactions which are in fruit you cannot; just have strong boots on to save you from the pinching effects of the thorns. For as man has to die, he will die, he must die. So karmic reactions of the past which are in fruit, they cannot be stopped but you can have such a position where they won't pinch you.[177]

Q. *Is there anyway we can know if our actions are paying off an old debt or if we're starting something new?*

A. Rise up to the causal plane, not before.[178]

Q. *If an initiate because of his karma has to come back again, how soon will that be?*

A. If he is initiated by a competent Master—first question; and if he is following His commandments, living up to what He says; regular in his devotion to practices, sees Light and also hears the Sound Principle, so much so that he has cut off *all* desires from outside—such a one is not to return at all. He will progress further later on. And those who have done little or nothing, then they will have to come back, but not below man body. Again they will get further guidance and go up. And those who have got very strong love for the Master, so much so that all their desires have been burnt away, such a soul won't return, they'll progress from there onward.[179]

No initiate can take the karmic load of others. It is only for the gracious Master Power working on the human pole of the Living Master who can liquidate karmic debts under His divine will, and none else.[180]

Turning from the Path

THE WAYS OF MASTERS are often misunderstood, through lack of spiritual growth.[181] If, having got the double blessing of the human form and the Satguru, you throw away the chance by disobeying him, what will happen? Those who live on another's earnings go under the law of give and take or illusion; if you offend or harm anyone, you reap the reaction of that and under the same law you will be born there where the offended person is born, that the account may be accurately balanced. *Wherever your attention is, there will you reside.* Who knows when you will again get the human form?

Fire consumes even green wood as well as the dry, and everyone must go sometime. If you spend your days losing everything but saving the invaluable treasure given to you, then your work here will be successful.[182]

There are various factors which lead to doubts and scepticism when the dear ones leave the path or go astray. The chief being lack of steadfastness and implicit obedience for the commandments. The stress on initial experience is given simply for testing the competency and genuineness of the Master as to whether one can have first hand inner experience of Holy Naam on Initiation. If one has the experience, may be less to start with, more can be expected by regular practice in due course. Perfect discipleship is a rare blessing which evolves in very few who not only work assiduously for their spiritual progress but surrender their all at the holy feet of the Master. It is perhaps much easier to meditate regularly, abide by the dietary regulations and observe other outer disciplines, but to inculcate a sense of complete self-surrender is most difficult.[183] Disobedience results in being consumed perpetually in the fire of senses, not only in this life, but hereafter also.[184] Remember, he who breaks the wall of the Guru's orders will never realize the inner knowledge. He may get a little inner experience and help, but he will never become perfect.[185] You were asked to develop these further by giving regular time to meditation with love and devotion, which are the keynotes for success on the divine way. In not living up to these instructions, you lost a chance to secure the Master's guidance, which is needed at every step.

Thus in obeying the dictates of one's own mind, if one finds fault with the science of nature, you can see for yourself how far it is justifiable. The mind has to be settled on the way.

So many of the cases of failure in meditation are due to want of accuracy in the method, lack of love and devotion, not following the proper diet, mixing in other methods or exercises. All of the lapses come from the disciple. This is the way of being born anew and to enter the Kingdom of God. "Learn to die so that you may begin to live" is what Christ taught as well as all other Masters. You are fortunate to be put on the way to God.[186]

The Lord, sitting at the human pole, makes it possible for the soul to overcome all negativeness. In the *Gurbani* it is asked, what is the Negative Power?—I can kick it out or remove it altogether and replace it. The records containing the words of the great Masters have an authoritative truth in them, for only the Masters (or anyone else on whom they may shower grace) see the true state of affairs. The Negative Power has no standing, unless with the approval of the Positive; but we are misguided, foolish people who sometimes allow ourselves to be drawn away from the true Guru—forgive me, but this happens. No matter what difficulties come, no matter what your condition may be, never leave hold of the Guru's hand—for your own sake. It is a natural law that you will go to the stage which your Master has reached.[187]

To forget the Master is to lose his protection thereby

giving an opportunity to the Negative Power to pin you down. Nevertheless, the Master Power is not going to forsake you in midstream, He has mighty protecting hands. The seed of spirituality sown by Him at the time of initiation must germinate sooner or later. "None can destroy this seed." But if you do not prepare the soil conducive to its germination now, you will have to be reborn, undoubtably as a human being, to accomplish the task, for the seed sown by a competent Master must germinate and sprout fully. But why delay and prolong your torture?[188] Why not put in time, grow now, and finish this returning? You come into contact with the Light and Sound Principle within and by progressing you are intoxicated with that. That has more bliss in it. We get more enchantment and bliss inside and naturally we are withdrawn from the outside things. Such a soul can never return, and lives in and is kept in the Beyond after the death of the physical body. Such souls have to progress there too, but this takes a longer time as compared with the time it takes in the physical body. So it is always better to develop here, the more you can, the most you can, so that you can straightaway go to that higher plane to which you have developed here. So tell them all that I wish them to progress. They have gotten, by the grace of God, first-hand experience at the time of Initiation. If anything goes wrong, it is due to the result of these things as I have explained.[189]

What makes one stray from the golden Grand Trunk Road of Spirituality after finding the Godman and having sacred Initiation from him? It is the ego in humans which debars them from spiritual illumination. It can be annihilated only by stern spiritual discipline and a sacred schedule of holy meditations together with deep reverential humility. Sometimes uncongenial environments do affect the spiritual progress of the dear initiates, who should always pray for right understanding and divine grace.[190]

Without doubt, there is none equal to the Guru. He who starts seeing another as equal to his Master, HIS SOUL BECOMES AN ADULTERESS.[191]

Q. An associate made up her mind to leave the Path. Why does this happen?

A. Because she is under the control of the mind; she is led away by the mind. When you come to a Master, as Christ said, "Satan wait." If you say, it is alright to let Satan come forward—then you must delay your progress.[192]

You reach home with the Master, not with the mind, which will lead you away from the Path, from the Master. It will find fault with Him: many things which are truly speaking your own faults, the colored spectacles you see through. And those who consider that they have become something, they are also led away by mind, you see. Mind, as I told you, is a very wily friend. It will always try to lead you away from the Path, from your Master, from God. So mind is a disciple of the Negative Power, you see. It is working to take you away from the Path; from God.[193]

To Invoke His Grace

The lowly became high through God's grace,
And through His grace the sinking stone
was made to swim accross.

O NLY GOD'S GRACE made this sinking stone swim across, so there is hope for everybody. There is a great wealth to be gained through *Gurubhakti*—devotion to the Guru. You have to earn your reward through using whatever he gives you to start with. So the first step should be through Gurubhakti.

> *One whole lifetime of Gurubhakti is required,*
> *And in the next life you will get Naam.*
> *The third brings salvation,*
> *And the fourth takes you to your True Home.*

If you do Gurubhakti in one birth, in the next you will get Naam, the third will bring salvation, and in the fourth you will arrive in Sach Khand, your true home. All these stages can be had even in one span of manbody, with the grace of the Guru. All Masters have sung the praises of Gurubhakti.[194]

He tells us that God loves anyone who tries to adopt His own attributes; so we should find out what they are, and also inculcate them into our being. If there is a vacancy in a certain office, and the man in charge has good talent in handwriting, he will naturally be more attracted to those applications which have been written in a good hand. So if we desire the Lord's pleasure, we should adopt His attributes. But how can we know what they are, when no one has seen Him? We can only observe His attributes as they are demonstrated in the Guru, who is the Word made flesh —God manifested in human form. Whatever God's attributes are, the Guru will have them. By loving the Guru, and placing all our attention on Him, we can imbibe all virtues, and those very virtues will then manifest in us. As a man thinks, so he becomes. If one goes on thinking of some depraved person who has broken away from God and all things God-like, one will become like that in a short space of time. The Lord's love is inate in whomsoever He has manifested Himself. *God's attributes can be seen when you see the Guru.*[195] So we should go to the Master with very clean hearts, with love for Him, with all due deference for Him. Then naturally, He will give His own Self to you. So this is how we can develop love for the Master, for the God in him. The attributes that He has developed in him, you should try to develop in you. What are they? He wants love, no show, strict obedience to what he says. Once he says something, obey him. Obey him literally. While developing these things you will all the time be having the sweet remembrance of the Master within and also outwardly. It is for the Master to see what he has to give. He has come only to give life. He has no other business. He is Life, Light and Love. He can give you these qualities only when you have become receptive and there is nothing that stands between you and Him. The attributes of God are reflected in Him. If you just adopt those attributes in your own life, then you will be loved by the Master and by the God in Him. As Christ said, "Those who love me, will be loved by my Father, and whom my Father loves, I manifest myself to Him." All Masters have said the same thing.[190]

Your loving and humble supplications to the Master are noteworthy. Such like prayer coming from the depths of the heart does invoke the divine grace and mercy. It is only when one realizes his insignificance and helplessness that God extends more grace to the child disciple. The true disciple is one who implicitly obeys the Master's commandments.[197]

Everyone is a precious personality and must have his due reward. Everyone has been endowed with great potentialities which can be developed by making proper use of Master's grace.[198]

> *True is the Lord, true His Holy Word;*
> *His love has been described as infinite.*
> *Men pray to Him for gifts, which He grants*
> *   untiringly.*
> *When all is His:*
> *What can we offer at His feet?*
> *What can we say to win His love?*
> *At the ambrosial hour of the early dawn,*
> *Be you in communion with the Divine Word*
> *And meditate on His Glory.*
> *Our birth is the fruit of our actions;*
> *But salvation comes only from His Grace.*
> *O Nanak, know the True One immanent*
> *   in all.*[199]

References

1. *Sat Sandesh,* April 1972, p. 5
2. *Morning Talks,* pp. 150-151, '70 ed.; pp. 192-193, '72 ed.
3. *Morning Talks,* p. 152, '70 ed.; p. 194, '72 ed.
4. *Morning Talks,* pp. 152-153, '70 ed.; pp. 194-195, '72 ed.
5. *Sat Sandesh,* August 1972, p. 5
6. *Morning Talks,* p. 153, '70 ed.; p. 195, '72 ed.
7. *Morning Talks,* p. 151, '70 ed.; pp. 193-194, '72 ed.
8. *Sat Sandesh,* December 1973, p. 14: Circular 27 p. 11
9. *Sat Sandesh,* February 1970, p. 10
10. *Sat Sandesh,* August 1969, p. 10
11. *Spiritual Elixir,* pp. 69-70, '67 ed.; vol. II, pp. 69-70, '72 ed.
12. *Spiritual Elixir,* pp. 70-71, '67 ed.; vol. II, pp. 70-71, '72 ed.
13. *Spiritual Elixir,* pp. 72-73, '67 ed.; vol. II, pp. 71-72, '72 ed.
14. *Sat Sandesh,* January 1970, p. 13
15. *Morning Talks,* p. 61, '70 ed.; p. 79, '72 ed.
16. *Sat Sandesh,* January 1970, p. 7
17. *Spiritual Elixir,* p. 292, '67 ed.; vol. I, p. 205, '72 ed.

18. *Sat Sandesh*, March 1971, pp. 5-6
19. *Sat Sandesh*, March 1971, p. 11
20. *Prayer*, p. 84
21. *Sat Sandesh*, September 1972, p. 20
22. *Prayer*, p. 85
23. *Prayer*, p. 86
24. *Prayer*, p. 87
25. *Sat Sandesh*, March 1969, p. 3
26. *Prayer*, pp. 40-41
27. *Sat Sandesh*, October 1971, p. 4
28. *Spiritual Elixir*, p. 24. '67 ed.; vol. ii, p. 122, '72 ed.
29. *Sat Sandesh*, April 1970, p. 4
30. *Sant—The Master* (circular), p. 6
31. *Sat Sandesh*, December 1973, p. 5
32. *Sat Sandesh*, March 1972, p. 19
33. *Spiritual Elixir*, p. 209, '67 ed.; vol. i, p. 122, '72 ed.
34. *Sat Sandesh*, March 1972, p. 21
35. *Sat Sandesh*, March 1971, p. 14
36. *Sat Sandesh*, March 1969, p. 3
37. *Sat Sandesh*, October 1971, p. 16
38. *Spiritual Elixir*, p. 209, '67 ed.; vol. i, p. 122, '72 ed.
39. *Spiritual Elixir*, pp. 214-215, '67 ed.; vol. i, p. 128, '72 ed.
40. *Spiritual Elixir*, p. 28, '67 ed.; vol. ii, p. 28, '72 ed.
41. *Spiritual Elixir*, p. 32, '67 ed.; vol. ii, pp. 32-33, '72 ed.
42. *Jap Ji*, pp. 117-118, '64 ed.; p. 157, '72 ed.

43. *Spiritual Elixir,* p. 202, '67 ed.: vol. I, p. 115, '72 ed.
44. *Sat Sandesh,* March 1970, p. 13
45. *Simran,* p. 10
46. *Excerpts from Letters to New York Satsangis,* p. 25
47. *Sat Sandesh,* September 1970, p. 9
48. *Sat Sandesh,* May 1969, p. 3
49. *Sat Sandesh,* September 1970, p. 15
50. *Sat Sandesh,* February 1972, p. 9
51. *Spiritual Elixir,* p. 208, '67 ed.; vol. I, p. 121, '72 ed.
52. *Spiritual Elixir,* p. 217, '67 ed.; vol. I, p. 130, '72 ed.
53. *Simran,* pp. 3-4
54. *Sat Sandesh,* September 1970, p. 9
55. *Sat Sandesh,* November 1971, p. 32
56. *Sat Sandesh,* September 1970, p. 19
57. *Spiritual Elixir,* p. 234, '67 ed.; vol. I, p. 147, '72 ed.
58. *Sat Sandesh,* December 1973, p. 10
59. *Spiritual Elixir,* p. 218, '67 ed.; vol. I, pp. 131-132, '72 ed.
60. *Sat Sandesh,* July 1971, pp. 5-6
61. *Sat Sandesh,* July 1971, p. 5
62. *Crown of Life,* pp. 144-145
63. *Spiritual Elixir,* p. 15, '67 ed.; vol. II, p. 15, '72 ed.
64. *Simran,* p. 10
65. *Excerpts from Letters to New York Satsangis,* p. 57
66. *Sat Sandesh,* July 1971, p. 28
67. *Sat Sandesh,* August 1970, p. 23; Circular 17, p. 4

68. Initiation Circular
69. *Naam or Word*, p. 275
70. *Naam or Word*, p. 278
71. *Naam or Word*, p. 279
72. *Excerpts from Letters to New York Satsangis*, p. 81
73. *Sat Sandesh*, February 1972, p. 11
74. *Sat Sandesh*, December 1969, p. 30
75. *Spiritual Elixir*, p. 52, '67 ed.; vol. II, p. 52, '72 ed.
76. *Sat Sandesh*, July 1971, pp. 30-31
77. St. Petersburg Darshan, December 4, 1972
78. *Excerpts from Letters to New York Satsangis*, p. 83
79. *Sat Sandesh*, December 1970, p. 13
80. *Morning Talks*, p. 187, '70 ed.; p. 238, '72 ed.
81. *Sat Sandesh*, September 1970, back cover
82. *Sat Sandesh*, April 1972, p. 5
83. *Spiritual Elixir*, p. 111, '67 ed.; vol. I, p. 24, '72 ed.
84. *Sat Sandesh*, July 1970, pp. 19-20; Circular 22, pp. 2-3
85. *Sat Sandesh*, February 1971, p. 3
86. *Sat Sandesh*, February 1971, p. 4
87. Anaheim Farewell Talk, November 1972
88. *Sat Sandesh*, July 1968, p. 11
89. *Sat Sandesh*, October 1971, p. 5
90. *Sat Sandesh*, December 1970, p. 11
91. *Sat Sandesh*, June 1972, p. 9
92. *Spiritual Elixir*, p. 90, '67 ed.; vol. I, p. 2, '72 ed.
93. *Sat Sandesh*, October 1971, p. 5
94. *Sat Sandesh*, October 1970, p. 2
95. *Sat Sandesh*, December 1971, p. 22
96. *Sat Sandesh*, October 1971, p. 4

97. *Spiritual Elixir*, p. 74, '67 ed.; vol. II, pp. 73-74, '72 ed.

98. *Sat Sandesh*, December 1971, p. 14

99. *Sat Sandesh*, July 1970, p. 20; Circular 22, p. 3

100. Letter to an Initiate

101. Santa Clara afternoon talk, November 17, 1972

102. Circular 66, p. 2

103. *Sat Sandesh*, April 1970, p. 25

103a *Sat Sandesh*, November 1973, p. 14

104. *Sat Sandesh*, October 1971, p. 22

105. *Prayer*, p. 1

106. *Spiritual Elixir*, p. 219, '67 ed.; vol. I, p. 132, '72 ed.

107. *Prayer*, p. 14

108. *Spiritual Elixir*, p. 245, '67 ed.; vol. I, p. 158, '72 ed.

109. *Prayer*, p. 66

110. *Sat Sandesh*, September 1972, pp. 18-19

111. *Prayer*, p. 58

112. *Prayer*, pp. 58-59

113. *Spiritual Elixir*, pp. 127-128, '67 ed.; vol. I, p. 40, '72 ed.

114. *Prayer*, p. 43

115. *Spiritual Elixir*, p. 246, '67 ed.; vol. I, p. 159, '72 ed.

116. *Spiritual Elixir*, p. 247, '67 ed.; vol. I, p. 160, '72 ed.

117. *Sat Sandesh*, March 1970, p. 25; Circular 3, p. 4

118. *Sat Sandesh*, October 1971, p. 22

119. *Selections of Letters From Master*, p. 2

120. *Sat Sandesh,* February 1971, p. 4

121. *Sat Sandesh,* March 1970, p. 12

122. *Sat Sandesh,* November 1970, p. 8

123. *Sat Sandesh,* April 1972, p. 9

124. *Spiritual Elixir,* p. 114, '67 ed.; vol. i, pp. 26-27, '72 ed.

125. *Excerpts from Letters to New York Satsangis,* p. 78

126. *Sat Sandesh,* April 1971, p. 14

127. *Sat Sandesh,* November 1970, p. 19; *The Way of Love* (circular), p. 2

128. *Sat Sandesh,* September 1971, p. 23

129. *Sat Sandesh,* March 1969, p. 10

130. Cincinnati Talk, Vernon Manor, Nov. 4, 1972

131. *Sat Sandesh,* April 1972, p. 6

132. *Excerpts from Letters to New York Satsangis,* p. 42

133. *Jap Ji,* p. 93, '64 ed.; pp. 121-122, '72 ed.

134. *Morning Talks,* p. 151, '70 ed.; p. 194, '72 ed.

135. *Sat Sandesh,* December 1970, p. 9

136. *Message on Baba Sawan Singh Ji's Birthday,* July

137. *Sat Sandesh,* February 1971, p. 6

138. *Sat Sandesh,* October 1971, p. 8

139. *Morning Talks,* p. 59, '70 ed.; p. 77, '72 ed.

140. *Morning Talks,* p. 130, '70 ed.; p. 166, '72 ed.

140a *Morning Talks,* p. 131, '70 ed.; p. 168, '72 ed. 20, 1968

141. *Morning Talks,* p. 61, '70 ed.; p. 79, '72 ed.

142. *Sat Sandesh,* October 1971, p. 6

143. *Sat Sandesh,* March 1970, p. 12

144. *Sat Sandesh,* December 1971, p. 31

145. *Sat Sandesh,* August 1970, p. 20; Circular 17, p. 2

146. *Sat Sandesh,* September 1972, p. 20

147. *Sat Sandesh,* July 1971, pp. 29-30

148. *Sat Sandesh,* February 1971, p. 5

149. *Sat Sandesh,* September 1972, p. 24

150. *Sat Sandesh,* February 1971, p. 12

151. *Sat Sandesh,* February 1971, p. 31

152. *Sat Sandesh,* September 1972, p. 22

153. *Sat Sandesh,* October 1971, p. 6

154. *Spiritual Elixir,* p. 303, '67 ed.; vol. I, pp. 216-217, '72 ed.

155. *Spiritual Elixir,* p. 300, '67 ed.; vol. I, p. 213, '72 ed.

156. *Spiritual Elixir,* p. 96, '67 ed.; vol. I, p. 8, '72 ed.

157. *Sat Sandesh,* April 1969, p. 9

158. *Sat Sandesh,* December 1970, p. 8

159. *Excerpts from Letters to New York Satsangis,* p. 75

160. *Sat Sandesh,* March 1970, p. 6

161. *Spiritual Elixir,* pp. 91-92, '67 ed.; vol. I, pp. 3-4, '72 ed.

162. *Man Know Thyself,* pp. 12-14

163. *Sat Sandesh,* March 1970, p. 24; Circular 3, p. 3

164. *Spiritual Elixir,* p. 42, '67 ed.; vol. II, p. 42, '72 ed.

165. *Sat Sandesh,* February 1970, p. 7

166. *Sat Sandesh,* July 1971, p. 28

167. *Sat Sandesh,* February 1970, p. 9

168. *Spiritual Elixir,* p. 75, '67 ed.; vol. II, p. 75, '72 ed.

169. *Sat Sandesh,* February 1970, p. 7

170. *Sat Sandesh,* January 1970, p. 13

171. *Sat Sandesh,* January 1969, p. 8

172. *Spiritual Elixir,* p. 119, '67 ed.; vol. I, p. 32, '72 ed.

173. *Sat Sandesh,* April 1971, pp. 30-31

174. *Sat Sandesh,* December 1972, p. 7

175. *Excerpts from Letters to New York Satsangis,* p. 54

176. *Sat Sandesh,* January 1970, p. 15

177. Fort Lauderdale Talk, December 7, 1972

178. Cincinnati Talk, November 3, 1972

179. St. Petersburg Talk, Sandpiper Hotel, Dec. 4, 1972

180. *Excerpts from Letters to New York Satsangis,* p. 56

181. *Sat Sandesh,* September 1970, p. 11

182. *Sat Sandesh,* February 1971, p. 11

183. *Excerpts from Letters to New York Satsangis,* p. 27

184. *Sat Sandesh,* June 1971, p. 32

185. *Sat Sandesh,* December 1970, p. 9

186. *Spiritual Elixir,* pp. 140-141, '67 ed.; vol. I, pp. 53-54, '72 ed.

187. *Sat Sandesh,* October 1971, p. 9

188. *Sat Sandesh,* April 1968, p. 12

189. *Sat Sandesh,* October 1971, p. 23

190. *Spiritual Elixir,* p. 10, '67 ed.; vol. II, p. 10, '72 ed.

191. *Sat Sandesh,* December 1970, p. 10

192. Fort Lauderdale Talk, December 8, 1972

193. Cincinnati Talk, November 3, 1972

194. *Sat Sandesh,* March 1970, p. 15

195. *Sat Sandesh,* February 1972, p. 8

196. *Morning Talks,* p. 248, '70 ed.; pp. 316-317, '72 ed.

197. Letter to an Initiate

198. *Spiritual Elixir,* p. 298, '67 ed.; vol. I, p. 211, '72 ed

199. *Jap Ji,* p. 90, Stanza IV, '64 ed.; p. 118, '72 ed.

SELF-INTROSPECTION
&
MEDITATION

.

THE TEACHINGS OF KIRPAL SINGH
Volume II

SELF-INTROSPECTION
&
MEDITATION

*Compiled and selected from
the writings of Kirpal Singh
by Ruth Seader*

SAWAN KIRPAL PUBLICATIONS

Preface

from *Seven Paths to Perfection*

A TINY SEED contains a mighty oak in its heart which can blossom forth into fullness by proper nourishment and protection. All young and tender saplings do need hand-watering, periodical weeding, fertilizing and protective hedging against the stray wayside cattle so that the saplings are not harmed. In due course of time the tree grows into full maturity, providing shade and shelter to the wayside travelers and becoming a source of help and inspiration to others. Exactly in the same manner, the Holy Seed of initiation thrives best in a rich and fertile soil formed of high ethical values and loving compassion. A divine stir by the Living Master of the soul in man is a happy start for the long spiritual journey ahead. Seekers have been therefore advised to do self-introspection which helps in developing fertility and in germinating the divinity to full bloom. The seven basic requisites enumerated in the prescribed self-introspective diary* aid immeasurably in covering the entire field of ethics, and help a lot to invoke the Divine Mercy.

KIRPAL SINGH

* see following page

At the end of the day each initiate is requested to recall the number of failures in thought, word and deed, in the various columns of the self-introspection diary which is shown below.

DIARY TO BE MAINTAINED FOR SELF-INTROSPECTION FOR THE MONTH OF ———— INITIATED ————

for disciples of His Holiness Sant Kirpal Singh Ji Maharaj

OBSERVE	FAILURES	1	2	3	4	5	6	7	8	9	10	11	12	13	14	15	16	17	18	19	20	21	22	23	24	25	26	27	28	29	30	31	RESULTS AT END OF MONTH
(1) AHIMSA (Non-violence)	In thought																																(1) How far are you withdrawn from the body?
	In word																																
	In deed																																
(2) TRUTHFULNESS	In thought																																(2) What you see inside.
	In word																																
	In deed																																
(3) CHASTITY	In thought																																(3) What you hear inside.
	In word																																
	In deed																																
(4) LOVE FOR ALL, HATRED FOR NONE, IRRESPECTIVE OF POSITION, WEALTH OR LEARNING.	In thought																																(4) Any difficulty you have in meditation.
	In word																																
	In deed																																
(5) DIET																																	
TOTAL																																	
(6) SELFLESS SERVICE	Physically																																
	Financially																																
TOTAL																																	
(7) SPIRITUAL PRACTICE (Time devoted in) 1. Repetition of names 2. Contacting Sound Current																																	
TOTAL																																	

NAME ———— ADDRESS ————

HELPFUL FACTORS: 'Service before self' - Attend Satsangs - Love for the Master - Implicit obedience to His commandments - Self-control & Discipline - Humility - Sincerity & Longing.

Table of Contents

BOOK ONE

SELF-INTROSPECTION

Self-Introspection

Importance of Keeping the Diary

IF WE COULD learn to obey and keep the diary, we would become gods and goddesses.[1]

It may be that he knows his condition; he reads, he thinks, he attends Satsang, he makes resolutions, but always falls back into the old habits again and again. This is why I have advised keeping a daily spiritual diary. It is a method of self-introspection which I have introduced after much deep thought on the subject. If you would only keep it . . . even send it to me blank! How many months would you go on sending it blank? The benefit of this is a moral upliftment—this is a very sweet way of explaining it.

With time, methods change. In olden days, clothes were washed by thrashing them against rocks, and nowadays we have got to the stage of dry cleaning, without the use of water. Masters have used many ways through the ages, trying to induce an awareness in men of their way of life. Those who are not following this Science correctly never keep diaries.[2]

Spiritual diaries have been prescribed after careful thought, and with deep purpose. Daily self-introspection must be kept up, and through this you will be able to see for yourself how far you are coming out of the senses'

influence. With the Satguru's mercy one gets a little connection with the Light and Sound Principle, but if the
life is not kept pure and chaste, the curtain of darkness
will obscure the Light again. You must be regular in
your meditation to maintain the Light; there are important reasons behind the keeping of diaries.[3]

The diary is meant for one's personal use and helps to
bring out many of the hidden underlying weaknesses to
the surface so that one may begin to see them and try
to remove them one by one, and with their removal life
becomes pleasant and spiritual progress is accelerated.[4]

The diary is planned to be a personal thing for the
information of the Master and a helpful and sweet re-
minder for the initiate not to deflect from the right Path,
and also to help him to progress from day to day by im-
proving, and if there is no improvement, to ponder and
reflect why this is so. It is a very useful thing.[5]

Initiates have been given self-introspection diaries,
which they should maintain regularly and scrupulously.
By this means they will be, at least, remembering the
Master's enjoinders during the day. If they don't keep
the diaries they will simply forget to act up to what they
have been told . . . so this is one good of keeping a diary.[6]

The diaries show how much time you put in and how
many places your heart is attached to outer things in one
form or the other. Devotion requires purity of heart.
Purity of heart requires that no other thought should
strike in your heart other than of the One whom you
love. If there is no other thought in your heart for anybody else and it is vacant from outward attachments,

then God is there. Devotion starts when you detach your heart from the outward things and attach it to God or to the God-in-man. This is developed by coming into constant contact with Him. The ABC starts by regularity of devotion to your spiritual practices.[7]

So those who are not keeping diaries must maintain them. I always again and again press this point. Those who are not maintaining diaries will fail constantly. In due course of time, their whole heart will be attached to the world. Outwardly they might appear to be very devoted, but they are really devoted to the world.[8]

Those who do not maintain the diary will lose valuable ground in making steady spiritual progress. In time, they will cease to apply themselves to their spiritual practices and in consequence the virtues stressed on the diary form will be observed less and less.[9]

If some of the dear ones desire to maintain diary for self-introspection (before initiation) such like dear ones will eventually benefit from the Holy Path.[10]

Self-Introspection and Man-Making

THERE ARE basically two stages to be gone through before the struggling disciple rises above body consciousness and begins to enjoy the spiritual disciplines and to firmly tread the Path of Spirituality. The first stage is where the disciple has little or no knowledge of self-introspection and is in a state of abysmal ignorance. The second stage is when the disciple begins to realize that he has innumerable faults and failings which must

be corrected before he can hope to rise above body consciousness, at which state this Path really begins.

This second stage, which is for most a long drawn-out
struggle with lower tendencies of the mind, is known as
"man making." Spirituality, or rising from the lower
realms of existence to higher realms of untold bliss and
harmony, is not difficult. It is the "man making" which
is difficult. There is no specific time limit for this second
stage. It all depends upon the disciple's aptitude for self-
discipline, obedience to the commandments of the Master, and developing a love for Him. It is the self-assertive
ego which is the last obstacle to be conquered, and this
cannot be done until the soul begins to come into its own,
has some glimmerings of its true nature, which has the
result of developing in the disciple a natural humility.
This is not to be confused with an attitude of servility,
mind you. True humility has strength, but is nevertheless
not self-assertive. Although the gracious Master Power is
ever at hand to help the disciple in this struggle, it is
something which the disciple must go through himself.
Nobody else can do this for him. You have been put on
the way and have been given some capital to start with,
which still exists with you. A seed has been planted in
you which one day must surely fructify and you have as
your constant companion the Master in His subtle form
of Light and Sound. He is also quite capable of manifest-
ing to you in His charming radiant form when you have
learnt to rise above body consciousness.

It is not reasonable to expect to attain to the higher
planes without first perfecting yourself to a great degree.

As in worldly studies, in which it is not unusual to spend twenty years or more to obtain the necessary qualifications to fit yourself for a career, so even greater is the time and effort that must be put in by the disciple before he can be made a fit vessel to receive the truths of his own soul and of God. It is a very odd outlook that some have: to expect self and God-realization in a short time and with little labor, while the same people are willing to toil for years to obtain the pot of porridge that is all this world has to offer.[11]

In no other expression but the human form can a soul realize God.[12] The gods and goddesses are anxious to get the human form, and it means only that the human form is the highest in all creation due to its great spiritual possibilities.[13]

I would stress the importance of self-introspection, for which the maintenance of the diary has been prescribed. A keen vigil and careful living is an essential helping factor for inner progress. A disciplined life by having complete control over the senses, which feed the mind, which in turn overpowers the soul, should be cherished. The inner divine links of Light and Sound are most helpful for controlling the senses. If you will follow these divine principles, the inner change of life will follow automatically. Truth is above all, but higher still is true living.[14]

Adopt a righteous way of life and be content. You may have certain desires, but stop there; don't increase them. Then reconsider the desires and where they will take you. What lies ahead, and what will you take with you? We are hurrying, scurrying through life; we are not even conscious of what we are doing most of the time. So the Guru advises us to handle all our affairs with tranquil serenity.[15]

When one undertakes to reach a certain goal in any field of human activity, it is necessary to take stock of one's progress from time to time. It is only through such stock-taking that one can become conscious of one's shortcomings and errors, eradicate and uproot them and plan out future progress. Having put our shoulders to the wheel of the Great Master's Cause, it is necessary that we should, in like manner, review our activity and achievement, from time to time. Without such self-analysis and self-criticism, no real advancement is possible and it was to encourage this practice and make it a daily habit that, in the case of individual initiates, I insisted (and continue to insist) that they maintain a daily record of their thoughts, words and deeds and of the period of meditation. What is necessary for us as individual initiates is even more necessary for us as members of a large movement.[16]

One must first think of the result before doing or even contemplating any deed.[17]

Fear of God is the beginning of wisdom and a danger foreseen is half-avoided. One who is forewarned, is forearmed.[18]

Everything will be given to you in due course of time if you follow His behests and live up to what He says. Every day you are given tasks which are intended to help your spiritual growth. Unfortunately, most people look for a very special assignment to be given to them by the Master personally before they accept it as a task from the Master. They do not see that their day-to-day dealings and behavior with other people in their work, the responsibilities they have to assume in their other mundane duties and how well they fulfill them, are all tasks given by the Master. If you watch closely your reaction to situations that confront you in life you cannot but be aware of how much you have grown spiritually. This is the most important part of spirituality as far as the disciple is concerned. He must first complete his course in "MAN-MAKING" with full honors before he can be given higher tasks to carry out.[19]

Every thought, every word and every deed, good or bad, leaves an indelible imprint on the mind and has to be accounted for. Hence the necessity for right thoughts, right aspirations and right conduct, all of which constitute the hedge around the tender sapling of spirituality.[20]

What constitutes desire? All conceptions in the mind are desires. So, be desireless. You will have noticed that when an obstacle blocks the achievement of one's desire, anger arises. Then there is pride—"I must have this (or do this), otherwise I will be belittled in the eyes of others." One can accept pride as being the basis of all sins, for it turns into I-hood. He recommends us to leave off perversity, or stop being obstinate. Always be sure to listen to the other person's point of view—you may find that what he is saying is correct. Perversity just binds a person more; there is no room for expansion. Dogmatic knowledge of books, for instance, which might be right or wrong, should be discarded. It goes without saying that all attachments should be broken away—you must finish up the give and take—you must leave the body and all its environments. If an obstacle comes between you and your desire, it grows even stronger. Just put a large rock in the middle of a fast flowing stream and you will create two things: froth and noise. When a man is angry he cannot speak softly, and finally he froths at the mouth. If you do get the thing you desire, it turns into attachment. There is only one cure for all this: Only after seeing your true self can you realize the Lord.[21]

Millionaires will leave their millions behind, those who have mud huts will leave them, this body did not come with you and will not accompany you when you return. Yes, you will take your actions with you.[22]

Is any thing else required to become reunited with the Lord? *Sadachar* (righteous living) is most essential. The mind that is running amuck in bad outer influences must be brought to heel; only then can any real progress be achieved. Our greatest obstacle is that the soul is under the mind's control, and mind in turn is under the senses' control. So release from this bondage is hastened by living righteously.[23]

We receive impressions from outside through the eyes, ears, the tongue, by smelling and by touch. So we must have self restraint. Such a man only can progress from day to day, by regularity and also by self introspection.

This is most important. Your very soul, the outer expression of which is called attention or *surat*, if engaged outside, makes it impossible for you to see within.[24]

With all this right understanding, what develops? Right thought, and furthermore right speech, and out of that right actions will follow.[25] If you can do this; if you can conquer the self and surrender it at the Feet of the Master; if you can learn to see Him working through all things; if you can accept the fact of your own limited vision; if you can undertake a ceaseless and zealous watch over your thoughts and deeds, weeding out all evils and imperfections—then you shall not only win salvation yourselves but enable others to do likewise. Your example shall shine like a torch in the darkness, and men, even those who may first oppose you, will turn to you for guidance and help. You will find a new sense of peace surging through you, a peace that does not depend on the absence of outer disturbances, but is an inner state of mind that stands unshaken even in the most tempestuous situations. And this same quality shall enter not only your individual lives, but the larger life of the great spiritual movement of which you are a part.[26]

Attachment

THE HUMAN BODY is the temple of God. In order to attain super-consciousness, one has to withdraw from all the physical attachments. So long as we remain identified with external objects, we cannot assume a subtle form.[27] All Masters say that when you have got a man-body, the highest thing is to attach yourself to God. Wherever you will be attached, there you will go. You have been coming to the world again and again. The reason is because you are not attached to God, otherwise you would have gone to God. So keep your diaries and eliminate all foreign thoughts from your heart. Our heart is at present divided. It should have no other thought except of Him to Whom you want to be devoted.[28]

So generally, what do we do? We get something to start with and fritter it away by being attached to outside. The father will be pleased with the child who has made the best use of what has been given to him. If he becomes an honest man to be relied on, he will be given more and more. We find people who say, "We were very well off before, but not now." But why not now? We have made beggars out of our own selves. So we have to be careful. Self introspection is most necessary. Those who do not keep it, their capital will be dwindled away.[29]

Now you see how important it is to maintain self restraint. Make use of something when you want it. Now you are dragged irresistably to outside things. You have to live in the world quite detached. When you want to use one faculty, use it. When you want to leave it, leave it. It is not so with you now. For that purpose, you are given a contact with the Light and Sound Principle within you. When you get more bliss there, your outward attachments will be cut off.[30]

A man who is really detached from the world is not affected by it. Renunciation truly lies in the fact that we are not tied to the world, to anything outside. A man who has got love within him, love of God, is attached to God so much that all other things leave his mind, he is not attracted by anything else.[31] A heart that is not attached to the world never thinks of worldly things. One who does not show failures under the different headings and who has a pure heart, then God must sit in it. He is already there, but He will become manifest.[32]

Self-Control and the Importance of Being Self-Centered

So THE IMPORTANT THING is to first learn to handle your outer environment, consisting of your domestic and/or working life. We are to be judged by our actions and not by our words. It is from the abundance of our heart that all actions result, whether physical, emotional or intellectual. The mind is an index and reflecting mirror and it truly depicts one's inner state. A measure of success of how well you are succeeding in handling your outer environment will be a gradual awareness that you are becoming the master of your own thoughts. It is to achieve this success that I introduced the self-introspective diaries. How many really keep their diaries properly? Very few, if any, I am sorry to say. If the diaries were to be taken advantage of, you would see a change in your behavior, your mode of thinking, and, consequently, you would progress spiritually by leaps and bounds. The purpose of the diary is to reflect your own inner state, so that you know where you stand. It is a tool, which if used properly, will chisel you into a receptacle fit for the manifestation of the Master within you. You should put just as much devotion and attention into keeping your diary as you put into your meditations.[33]

Unfortunately, few, if any, have any idea of what

keeping the diary really means. As time passes, their entries become a mere matter of form, and the whole purpose behind keeping the diary is lost. We are asked to maintain the diary in thought, word and deed. How many of us really do so? The majority just react in thought, word, and deed to the stimulus of the moment, in other words, instinctively. The truth of the matter is that we must become consciously aware of every thought that passes through the mind; we must weigh our words before we speak and not speak idle words as a mere reaction to the situation that confronts us. If we are able to make some progress in this regard, then we will be far on the way to controlling our self. This in essence, is the practice of Raja Yoga. Only when we have advanced far in the practice of living the life demanded of us (as implied in the keeping of the diary), will we become fit enough to reap the fruits of the practices of the Surat Shabd Yoga.[34]

One can gauge his or her spiritual progress by the measure of *conscious control* that he or she has over his or her thought patterns. One who has in some measure achieved this control will not be swayed or upset by outer conditions, stresses and strains that his environment may place on him. *If one cannot rise above, be in full control of, and handle with ease the circumstances of his outer environment, he will never be able to succeed in the way of Spirituality.*[35]

To gain control of one's being, to bring one's whole life under that perfect control, to help oneself to cut away from outer attractions, requires self-introspection. Start by consciously controlling a small fraction of your life. You will be able to succeed if you are also enjoying a little inner intoxication of Naam. All Masters say there is no success without meditation.[36]

It is we who give power to the mind. It is we who give power to the outgoing faculties. It is we who see good or bad outside. If we become self-centered, we may make the best use of our outgoing faculties however we like.[37] Unless you become self-centered, you cannot avoid the influence of others.[38] We derive effects from outside and wherever our attention goes, we are affected by the radiation of those with whom we come in contact. If they are pure, that's all right. If not, you get their radiation.[39]

Victory over the mind is victory over the world. You have been granted the yardstick for measuring your spiritual attainments in the form of an introspective diary, and you can surely judge things for yourself and see how far you have advanced on the Path.[40] Man-making precedes spirituality. Unless and until you become the master of all the five senses, appreciable inner progress cannot be made.[41] *Control all Kama (desire), anger, greed, attachment; This play is loved by the Lord.* Kam attacks through the eyes, anger through the ears. Attachments come through embracing. Rise above all these, and you will gain connection with the Truth.[42]

The recurring failures in various columns of the diary shows that you remain too much engrossed in worldly affairs, which should be reduced by keeping yourself immersed in the divine grace. Silence, solitude and serenity should be cultivated by living a life full of spiritual disci-

pline as enjoined by the Master. You can cut short unnecessary engagements and wild pursuits by keeping your
spiritual goal in the forefront. A well regulated life earns
rich dividends.[43]

Every action has a reaction. Every act of omission or
commission has an appropriate penalty. We cannot escape from sin as long as we consider ourselves as born of
the flesh, for flesh is the root cause of all evils in the
world. Until a spirit learns to leave the sensual plane at
will, enjoyments and distractions do thrive like a bay
tree.[44]

Every day brings in a new life full of vast opportunities. You must not apprehend any fears whatsoever and
instead try to harness your faculties for attaining the
goal of spiritual perfection. Take and accept life with all
its vissicitudes in easy terms of joy and bouyancy. Just
face the situation bravely with mental equipoise and stability. The tree of life reared in storms yields more of cool
shade and rich fruit. Failures should serve as stepping-
stones to success. It is persistent effort which overcomes
all difficulties.[45]

Change Your Ways

O MAN, it is the time now to discard your old, dis-
reputable habits and adopt new ones. Habits are
formed by repeatedly doing the same things, so we should
first unravel all the bad actions: lies, hypocrisy, cheating,
criticism of others, enmity, avarice, malice, backbiting,
and various others. If you do not intend to change these

ways, what is the use of attending Satsang? *Your steps are forward, but your mind is retrogressing.* Satsang is the means of making us into something beautiful, but not by merely repeating God's name. Change your habits now into good ones, for habit turns into nature with time. Cast away all negative thoughts, and instill positive ones in their place. If a person does wrong, forgive him, and he in turn should forgive your misdeeds.

In the Koran, it is written, *Even God has no thought for him who has no inclination to change.* How can we expect other people to show excellent examples? If we ourselves would change, the whole world would change with us. It is a message for all. One of the worst habits is that of criticizing others. All virtues exercised in righteous living are good, but that of *ahimsa-parmo-dharam* (non-violence of thought) is the highest. It can become a daily habit, for it lies inherent within us all, and although other thoughts are there, yet consciously or unconsciously it is working and will rise to the surface one day. That is why you are told frequently in Satsang that the past is past, forgive and forget, and do not make a foundation of bad thoughts or there will undoubtedly be reactions. You will be the loser, for again you will revolve on the cycle of births and deaths. So with love the Masters encourage their children to change their habits while there is still time.[46]

Man is a conscious being and has been given the faculty of discriminating right from wrong. Where man falls short in this discriminatory ability, he has the golden opportunity of approaching some Master who can give guidance and right understanding on the subtle points of his behavior and actions. The sacred books that have been written by the Master cover every facet of Spirituality and should be studied with a view to clarify how one should act in daily life. Other literature has also been issued on the same subject and the booklet entitled *Seven Paths to Perfection* should be carefully read by you for the purpose of knowing the ennobling virtues to be developed as opposed to the failures to be avoided, which are given on the diary form. You may take the virtues given in this booklet and the failures to be avoided as given on the diary forms, to be your blueprint for living; the rest is up to you. This blueprint can be successfully applied to any situation that may arise in life and as such, there is no need to write to the Master on every situation when a little self-honesty and application of common sense will show you the right course of action.[47]

You should know it for certain that you are divine in all respects and are the master of your destiny which is full of higher potentialities. You are simply to make exertion to change for the better, and firmly stick to your resolutions. All else is to follow of itself, as the Gracious Master Power is at your side to extend all feasible help, grace and protection.[48] The more one aspires to weed out the imperfections by daily introspection, the more serene bliss and grace come from above. Patience and selflessness are ennobling virtues. Right understanding is the basis of all happiness.[49] You should not worry about past or new Karmas. If at every moment you are consciously watching your behavior, a calm consideration will replace a blind instinctive reaction to certain situations in life where the choice lies between committing a lapse in behavior or avoiding it.[50]

They should guard against the five deadly sins of desire, anger, greed, infatuation and vanity, and develop instead the virtues of truth, chastity, non-injury, universal love, and selfless service.[51] The paths leading to worldly enrichment and to God lie far apart. One can take either of the two, as one may like. The mind is a single entity linking the body with the soul at one end and the body with the world and worldly riches at the other. Thus one has of necessity to choose between the two alternatives. Once the die is cast, one has perforce to apply oneself steadily to reach the goal whatever it be.[52]

In short, the sincere and conscientious aspirant will reorient his entire mode of life, in eating and drinking, thinking, acting, feeling, etc. He will gradually weed out of his mind all irrelevant and unhealthy desires, until he gradually attains the state of purity and simplicity that marks the child.[53]

Make a wave of receptivity from heart to heart—this is the way to realize the Lord. Become even a little receptive and the Master in you will restrain you when you are in danger of going wrong.[54]

The dear ones should have their lives well disciplined and carefully regulated in the larger interests of their spiritual progress. One thing at a time and that too with single-minded attention and devotion. That is keeping the house in order. A kind thought will attract all

the kindness of the universe and contrarily a vicious idea
will create a vicious circle by accepting all vice in the
universe. A mango sapling will attract all the sweetness
of the soil whereas if a pepper seed is sown a little apart
it will attract all its bitterness; both the plants will flour-
ish with the varying elements of Mother Nature, yet on
the same soil. One is full of all sweetness and the other
of all bitterness. That is the Eternal Law. Human heart
is the soil in which good and bad thoughts are the seeds,
which when sown carefully are sure to be grown gradually by honest and correct cultivation. You are to choose
the best virtues for acceptance and inculcating in your
life, when you can expect a bumper crop in due course.
You are free to some extent and can benefit from this
limited liberty by hard work, right living and regulated
discipline. Just learn to implant lofty ideas in your sub-
conscious mind and feed them with the waters of self-
confidence, determination, diligence and adaptability.
Stick to your guns. Never stoop low, never and still never.
Stand aloof with your sublime principles of life which
will stand by you in the hour of need.[55]

Hence it is, that mystics of all traditions have been
untiring in their stress of the need for absolute self-
surrender. It was this cross of sacrifice of the self, the ego,
of which Jesus spoke when he exhorted his disciples to
bear their cross daily. For in every little act, word, or
thought, the ego is seeking to dominate us and if the
seeker is to triumph over it, he must be prepared to
crucify it every moment.[56]

To fall in sin is manly, but to remain there is devilish.

One falls often, no doubt, but one becomes a good rider only after many a fall. But don't lie down and remain wherever you fall; that is bad. In the Koran it is written that God will not change any people who have no thought to change themselves. Where there is a will, there is a way. Keep your aim before you always, and work for it; then you will be sure of success.[57]

Success in spirituality is not the difficult task which most of us take it to be or make it to be; but it does require patient self-purification, a watchful introspection, a careful weeding out of all undesirable elements present and a pruning of outspreading ramifications; and above all, timely tending and nurturing of the tender spiritual sapling as it sprouts from the soil of the human mind. This work hangs on the shoulders of every one of you and I am sure that you are fully alive to your responsibilities and obligations in this behalf.[58]

Until one can love, *obey* and transform one's life, the gift of the Master remains as a seed locked away in a steel vault that cannot sprout and grow to fruition.[59]

Time Factor

MIND IS A SLAVE to habit, and is forcibly led astray by it. Find for yourself what habits are obstacles in the way of truth. Get rid of them by and by and fill their place by good ones. For instance, anger should give way to calmness and avarice to contentment, and so on. By continued application, mind will give up bad habits. But note that mere theory of a thing does not help, unless a thing is actually done. Mind is very powerful. At the time of deliberation, it makes promises but does not care to fulfill them when the occasion arises. To control it is not the work of haste; it requires years of patient perseverance. So long as it does not take pleasure in the internal music, it must fly out to worldly pleasure. Apply your mind with love and keen interest to the spiritual exercises, without any false apprehensions. One day you will get complete control over your mind and senses and find it is a great blessing.[60] But the time factor is a necessity, patience is a necessity, perseverance is a necessity. It will not happen in one day.[61]

The Need for Prayer and Effort

PRAYER AND EFFORT go cheek by jowl. We pray to God for what? For the success of our endeavors. Should we wish for a thing, we must try for it, and alongside our efforts to achieve it pray that God may grant it. Prayer is just the last weapon and a sure one that comes to our aid. *Where all human efforts fail, prayer succeeds.* As a bird cannot fly on one wing only nor a chariot move on one wheel, so effort and prayer must go together if we want success in all our ventures. One of them by itself can achieve nothing. As long as a person is not fully Divinized, or in other words does not become a conscious co-worker with the Supreme Power by understanding His Will, he cannot do without endeavor, for God helps those who help themselves. A mere prayer without endeavor seldom bears fruit. Just take the instance of a boy who is late for school. If he were to sit down on the roadside to pray, he would be running against time. If he wants to gain time, he must run and it is possible that even if he be late his teacher may forgive him because of the effort he has made to reach there in time. To have a ruling passion for an objective and to work hard for achieving the same is the right type of prayer in the truest sense of the word. Effort should be combined with prayer, for mere lip service to reach the goal will not help much. In all sincerity one should pray and indeed the very striving for a thing with heart and soul is the greatest prayer and is bound to fructify. In all trials and tribulations, one must try to rid himself of his weariness and pray to God that He may help him in his endeavors. This is the only right attitude. If, in spite of this, you fail in your endeavors, then take that failure as coming from God for your good.[62]

The Master-Power overhead is always aware of His children's needs and yearnings and He acts in their best interests. All errors must be weeded out one by one, and when the child-disciple is doing his or her best to eradicate these errors, all necessary help comes from within. This effort may take a long time, but it must and will come about, and much earlier for those who are lovingly and faithfully devoted to the Master.[63]

A mere confession of sins and shortcomings in prayer does not avail anything. If we think that by mere confession our sins can be washed off and we can once again indulge in them freely we are wrong. Such an attitude, far from being a saving force, keeps us perpetually down in sins. Redemption is the gift that comes either from God or the Godman who specifically comes for the benefit of sinners. Our job is just to understand his commandments and to keep them scrupulously, leaving the rest to him.[64] Apart from the work of returning the lost souls to their Source through joining them back to God, the Masters have no other purpose in the world.[65]

A keen desire to improve spiritually coupled with earnest efforts brings in radical change in the thought pattern of the initiate and the entire life undergoes change for the better. You should be more steady, humble and polite in your dealings.[66]

The loving disciple is always prayerful and repentant for his or her trespasses and lapses committed consciously or unconsciously during the day.[67]

Beg from the Lord and the Guru their Divine Vision, complete self-surrender and the gift of Naam. Pray also to be saved from the evil tendencies of the mind and the senses. Being Omnipotent, He is capable of granting us all these boons. Besides this, the seekers may pray for the gift of happily resigning to His sweet Will. We have no good qualities in us. Being ignorant and of low mental caliber, we are not well versed in religious ceremonies, etc. Therefore, oh Beloved! have mercy on us. Bestow on us the capacity to sing Thy praises and to remain happy in whatever be Thy Will.[68]

Purification: Repentance, Forgiveness, and Abstention

PURIFICATION: Purity of body, mind and soul is the most important factor in winning the love of the Lord. It may be considered in three different stages—Repentance, Forgiveness and Abstention.

REPENTANCE: Nothing under heaven is perfect and each one of us has his own weaknesses. Sin has come to man as a heritage from Adam. Mind in man is the agent of the Negative Power, and it misses no opportunity to tempt man against God. In daily life we slip at every step. Our best resolves turn into airy nothings when temptations assail us. Unaided, we cannot possibly escape from the cunning wiles, subtle snares and wild clutches of Kal or the Lord of Time, i.e., the mind. It is only the saving arm of the Master that can protect us and rid us of its terrible onslaughts. But every time that we fall a prey to temptations we must realize our weakness and sincerely repent for what we have done.

FORGIVENESS: Repentance, though good in itself, cannot alter the past. Each act of omission or commission leaves its indelible impressions upon the mind and singles us out for its reaction or fruit. In this way countless Karmic impressions go on accumulating day in and day out, making additions to our *Sanchit Karmas* (a vast storehouse of unfructified actions). Nobody can escape from this tremendous load which has a far-reaching effect, extending sometimes to hundreds of lives and over.

Is there no remedy, then, to burn away the powder magazine before it blows us up? The Saints tell us that there
is a way and a sure one indeed. Prayer for forgiveness is
a positive weapon in the hands of a sinner. There is hope
for everybody including the sinners. Saints come into the
world to save the sinners and the lost. An association
with a Master-soul goes a long way in liquidating the
Karmic account. While He forgives in His Saving Grace
our daily lapses, He at the same time enjoins abstention
from repetition of the same. "So far and no further," is
their admonition. "Go and sin no more," was the usual
advice with Christ and Master Sawan Singh too, who
used to advise his disciples to make a halt wherever they
were and to sin no more. The past actions can be washed
off, provided we refrain from sowing any more of the
dragon's teeth.

ABSTENTION: While repentance and forgiveness help
us in escaping the effect of Kriyaman or day-to-day acts,
we have yet to guard against future repetitions. No puri-
ficatory process can help us through unless we put a stop
to the incessant round of the Karmic wheel, which gains
momentum from our every act.

At times a magistrate may award a lesser penalty for
a crime but that may not ennoble the criminal. In the
dispensation of the Master, there is always the stern admonition which is so necessary an element in keeping a
person on his guard. Like a Master-sculptor, he has to
chisel hard to bring shape and form out of a formless
piece of stone.

In brief, it is necessary that we must first of all mold

our life according to the instructions of the Master, and feel a genuine delight in thinking of Him. Secondly, we must understand His Will and pray for those things that are to His liking; and thirdly, we must learn to accept smilingly His decrees whatever they be.

Last, but not least, love is the soil on which life thrives the most. Lover gives and never takes favors. If one tries to live a Godly life, all God's favors automatically flow down to him. One who loves God need not ask for any favor. It is enough for us to dedicate our very life to Him and become His bound slaves. It is up to Him to treat us as He wishes. To live in His Holy Presence is its own reward and there can be no reward greater and richer than this.[69]

How to Do Your Diary

WHEN AT THE END of the day, you recall your failures in thought, word and deed, in which direction will your mind be turned? Naturally, it will go to the One who has asked you to keep it. So keeping the diary is also remembrance of the Master; you are saying something to Him. If you remember Him, then, He remembers you, and, in time, you will develop receptivity to Him wherever you may be. There can be no true spiritual progress without receptivity, and the daily maintenance of the diary with full attention and a true yearning to be freed from the lapses which are recorded therein goes a long way to developing this receptivity.

In the Christian religion, I understand that those who

wish may make a confession of their lapses before a priest. They may go once a month or weekly, but generally not more often than once a week. But by keeping the diaries, you are making a confession every day. Let your confessions be honestly and openly recorded in the various columns, so that you know where you stand and can take rectifying action. The best and easiest way to cure your ills is to yearn to be free of them and, as mentioned above, to have sweet remembrance of the Master at the time you are filling in your diary.

Last and just as important as the foregoing, keeping the diary should not be allowed to stagnate into a mere recording of failures, which tends to become mechanical if done with little or no attention. The true purpose of putting these failures down in front of you is to make yourself aware of them so that they may be weeded out. To weed them out, it is not sufficient to cut off one or two branches; you must uproot the cause. Once you become aware of a failure, you should be able to trace it to a certain situation, and this situation will help you to identify the cause of the weakness in you which has to be eliminated. By and by, the very cause of the failure will drop off by itself.[70]

Now as to the lapses or departures from the right way, as you call them: the mind, as you know, works in subtle ways—too subtle for an ordinary man to detect and then to detect rightly and in time before the mischief is done. It is from the abundance of heart that all actions, oral as well as physical, proceed. We have, therefore, to be mentally alert about our thought-waves, so as to be able in time to mark their ebb and flow and then by-pass them by the process of concentration, forgetting all about the mind and the mental states, including even the pure mind essence which gossamer-like envelops the soul. . . . It is the memory of our experiences in the distant past and in the living present that constantly and irresistibly follows us at our heels and since we have not yet learned to keep aloof and above them the lapses occur in spite of us. The enumeration process is just the first step to be cognizant of our doings, which we are likely to overlook in our self-righteous assertiveness. . . . Thoughts are to be watched which precede actions. It is a slow yet steady process of gradual improvement for which an all-out effort is necessary. A well disciplined and spiritually regulated life is very much essential.[71]

The Lord is not an innocent child, to believe anything you wish; He sees the true condition of your life, inwardly and outwardly.[72]

Personal awareness of the transgressions of the holy commandments and immediate confession by way of inner repentance are all helpful measures for inner growth and receptivity. However, recalling and counting such lapses at the close of the day and jotting them down on the diary forms has its own benefit when you regret such deeds and feel inspired to work for improvement.[73]

Pride and ego do not let us progress—when we make mistakes we will not admit them.[74]

The diary forms are divided into seven categories. The first six categories deal with the failures to observe the virtues indicated by the heading of these categories, while category number seven is a record of the time spent in spiritual practices. In the first six categories, you are to enter the number of times that you fail to observe the virtues indicated, in thought, word and deed. For example, if you fail in "Non-violence" in thought, word and deed, four times in one day, you are to enter this figure in the column provided under the day on which the failures occurred.[75]

It is not necessary to write a confession to the Master every time you commit a misdemeanor. The Master Power is quite aware of the lapses of His disciples and wishes only that they become aware of these lapses and not repeat them. Let your confessions be honestly and openly recorded in the various columns on the self-introspection diary. This is the sublime principle behind the correct use of the diary form.[76]

If all initiates give a proper study to the books and Circular Letters and also attend the Satsang, there should be no need for them to write to the Master with any question or problem, the solution of which already lies at hand. All initiates should understand that to write to me on any problem or question but delays the answer, which could otherwise be known within a short time by following the advice given above. In my Circular of June 13, [1969] I advised the initiate who had some problem or question to which he required an answer, to sit quietly in a receptive mood, thereby attuning himself to the gracious Master Power within him. Then he would surely receive his answer and have full confidence as to what course of action he should take.

If any initiate feels that he must have some outer guidance on the Teachings, he should discuss his questions and/or problems with the Group Leader or Representative of his area.

However, there is one very important point that must be born in mind by all, whether initiates, Group Leaders, or Representatives. This is, that Group Leaders and Representatives are there purely for the purpose of giving out the theoretical side of the Teachings and arranging facilities whereby the initiates of their group or area can meet together for Satsang. Group Leaders and Representatives are not to be used as crutches for the initiates to lean upon. Nor should the initiates look to them for any purpose but to help them in understanding the Teachings. In other words, initiates should not look to them for spiritual guidance in any shape or form, as this is the function of the Master. If an initiate looks to a Group Leader or Representative for spiritual guidance, he automatically places a blockage in between himself and the Master, and his spiritual progress will suffer in consequence.[77]

The diary forms should be a true reflection of your own inner state. The failures made should be as an open self-confession of the shortcomings which stand between you and the Master. Similarly, devoting regular time to the Spiritual Practices is an indication of the positive growth. If you live up to the sublime purpose behind the keeping of the diary, you will progress from day to day, and achieve your goal in this lifetime.[78]

Ahimsa

AHIMSA OR NON-INJURY to all living creatures, and more so to fellow beings, by thoughts, words and deeds—the injunction in this behalf being: "Injure not a human heart for it is the seat of God."[79] It is an ennobling virtue that brings each one to par with his or her fellow beings and ultimately leads to the principle of the brotherhood of man and the Fatherhood of God. The cultivation of this virtue demands a broad development of toleration towards all, irrespective of their shortcomings and failures. To radiate the grand principle of the Family of Man on the divine ground of loving and compassionate desire for the well-being of all, costs very little but counts very much. A heart full of divine compassion is the abode of all virtues.[80]

I would like to impress upon you particularly to give up thinking ill of others. While you do not make the enemy your friend, you will have no peace within. Your sleep state will be full of restless dreams. If anyone thinks or speaks of you in an aggressive way, do not follow his example, otherwise his thoughts will react upon you. If a wave of water hits a hard surface, it will bounce back, but if it strikes something resilient, it will be absorbed, like the action of a sponge, and there will be no violent reaction. One curse is given, but on its return becomes many. If it is not returned, then? It was one, and remained one. Again, we remember Farid Sahib saying, *The whole world is sounding, and you are also dancing*

with it. It is better, with a cool head, to try and read between the lines to discover why the person is acting so
antagonistically, and then take action accordingly. You
will save yourself from degradation this way. To think
or speak of a person badly, to tell lies or cheat, to be
hypocritical, indulging in backbiting and other ill-becom-
ing traits—these are all degrading to the soul. Keep your
hearts pure, and as God is in everyone, try to see only
the best in all. Whatever duties have been given to you
by God, perform them with love, and if others are shirk-
ing their duties, appeal to them with love, and pray for
their better understanding. Then, leave them to the Lord.
If we always remember that the God we worship is in
all men, we would not even allow a single brother to go
hungry.[81]

Jesus always preached the two cardinal virtues:
(1) "Love Thy Neighbor as Thyself" and (2) "Love
Thine Enemies." Does that mean that it is out of timidity or weakness that one should love and forbear one's
enemies? No, there is something moral and divine that
lies at the root of such an attitude.[82]

So, love the sinner but hate the sin.[83] Purity mainly
lies in not thinking evil of others, in thought, word and
deed.[84] If you think good of others, you will radiate good.
If you purify your mind you will purify the minds of
others.[85]

Never hurt anybody. We hurt others by thinking ill
of them. We think ill of others, we scheme. This is wrong,
as thoughts are very potent. When you think ill of others
that reacts to them like a telegraphic wire. You may not

be telling anybody anything but if you think of them, radiation is there.[86]

When one thinks evil thoughts or commits an evil deed, it strengthens the forces of evil. Those who desire to belong to God should feed the sacred fire with the fuel of pure thoughts, good words and noble deeds. This will burn away all else except God and Master.[87]

If you have any bad thoughts for anyone, stop them, and if anyone has wittingly or unwittingly harmed you, forgive and forget. There is no other cure. If you cannot forgive the misdemeanors of others, your progress will stop, for forgiveness and justice are different. Forget justice, and develop the virtue of forgiveness. Keep your heart clear; do not think badly of anyone, even if they have deliberately harmed you.[88]

Any time you feel overtaken with unloving thoughts towards anybody, you should resort to the Simran of names and think of the Master. You should develop the Christ-like attitude.[89] So the foremost thing is, not to think evil, speak evil or hear evil of others.[90] If you will cast out evil thoughts about others, all are friendly.[91]

There is no evil in the world. If it appears to be evil, it is due to the smoky or colored glasses that you are wearing on your heart or mind. You will find that if you think in the way that I have just told you, then naturally you will have respect and love for all, even for your enemies. They might think otherwise of you, but if you have thrashed out every evil thought within you for everybody, you will see with that angle of vision, which the Master gives you, that it is all the manifestation of

God; then naturally, everybody will be beautiful. You will see this beauty even in your enemy: A perverted view is only on account of smoky glasses.[92]

Become the seer and see the Lord at work in everything.[93]

We should learn to forgive and forget which is a golden principle of life for attaining peace and harmony so very much helpful for having a calm and contemplative mood, which, in turn, will bless us with successful meditations. He who forgives is twice blessed. Taking revenge is cowardice, but forgiving the lapses of others is an act of virtuous nobility. The initiates are advised to take the stock of their *karma* every day before retiring to see whether during the course of their working day, they have incurred anybody's displeasure or have wronged anybody. If so, they should repent and pray for Divine Grace. Similarly, if others have in one way or the other done any harm to them, that should be forgiven in the name of the Master. There is a very good example in the Bible, where it is said that before one stands for prayer, he should forgive the lapses or shortcomings of his brother who has wronged him, so that the Father in Heaven may condone his shortcomings. Evidently, we must inculcate such a sense of forgiveness by daily practice. We must forgive all who have wronged us before we depart from this earth-plane, which will be helpful for our soul's progress on the inner planes.[94]

If someone makes a mistake, forgive him. But people prefer justice to forgiveness. Remember this, that with justice, the heart is never cleansed. Outwardly a person may be emphatic that he forgives; but in his heart he wants to strike out at the offender and cut the very roots of him. If you have no compassion in the mind, how can you honestly say you forgive?[95] To *forgive and forget* is what one must practice in thoughts, in words and in deeds so that they may become a part and parcel of daily living from day to day. Love knows no criticism, no imposition, no boasting, no reflection on others' short-comings, but works in a constructive way to cement all in one loving fold of the Master. Love beautifies every-thing.[96]

We must all learn to look within and not without. It is far easier to see a mote in another's eye than to see a beam in one's own.[97] We must reform ourselves before we can reform others, but unfortunately we are always anxious to reform others. We should weed out all im-perfections one by one by self-introspection and this will bring peace all around. Love beautifies everything and if we learn to love everyone, all our imperfections can be washed away, especially by loving kind words.[98] Kind words imbued with humility don't cost anything. If you have that attitude in life, I think ninety percent of your troubles will be avoided.[89]

The place where fire burns becomes heated first and then transmits its heat to the atmosphere around. So is the case with fire or anger. An imagined or supposed wrong keeps rankling in the mind like a thorn. When one cannot bear its intensity, one bursts forth into flames of hatred and contempt (begins abusing right and left), loses his balance of mind, and like a canker keeps emitting a malign odor that virtually goes on polluting the atmosphere around. Most of the injuries and wrongs are the outcome of our own process of thinking, and such thoughts breed countless others, multiplying in geometrical proportion. We can get out of this vicious circle only by changing our attitude towards life. Why sacrifice our natural equanimity for mere trifles, for passing bubbles and vapory nothings that are things of no consequence? Instead of brooding over these supposed and imagined wrongs it would be better by far to contemplate on the higher aspects of life, the divinity within and the divinity without, for this world is verily of the divine and divinity resides therein.[100]

You will gradually have greater control over your feelings and emotions, such as vanity, greed and lust, and develop instead virtues of humility, contentment, chastity and love. You will give up your habit of judging others and start adjusting yourself to their weaknesses and shortcomings, either by overlooking or affording constructive help to them. By this adjustment, you will bring much sunshine and happiness for yourself as well as for all those around you. If you think with a calm and cool mind, you will realize that most of us have not become perfect as yet.[101]

In this vast creation, everyone is gifted with an individual perception. The heredity, the environment and the teachings inculcated, all combine to make one what he is. We cannot blame anyone for thinking differently in his own way. Everyone has his own temperament and his own way of thinking. They must differ and they do differ vehemently. There is no help for it. It is, on the other hand, the sign of sentient life. We must not therefore on that account cross swords with them. Even if in their ignorance they, at times, may talk ill of the spiritual teachings and use harsh words, they cannot help it. But that should not disturb the true seekers after Truth. We must be polite and gentle and even humble in our conduct. Bandying of words does not help. We may try to remove misunderstandings, if any, sweetly and gently, but not in an antagonistic spirit. It is advised that individual persons (including representatives, group leaders and other old and new initiates) should not enter into any sort of discussions or disputes with any religious bodies, circles, faiths or sects, etc. If any such bodies do enter into such things, they may be directed to refer to the Master for an appropriate reply.[102]

A close view of the problem would show that ordinarily we are neither worried nor irritated when everything goes in accordance with our wishes. No sooner do we fancy that our interests are thwarted or feelings are injured, than a chain of reactions starts, resulting in violence in thought, word or deed, according to one's physical, mental or moral make-up.[103]

We aim to realize God, that God which is in all beings, whom all worship as One, though He may be given many different names. He is the great Controlling Power which keeps all souls in the body; when He withdraws, we also must leave. When a person truly understands these facts, how can the question of hatred for others arise? Whom will one hate? Out of right understanding, true thoughts and actions develop and follow naturally. God is in everyone—if you know that someone is unhappy or in need, go and help them. If they are hungry or thirsty, share whatever you have. Because of God, do service to His children. This does not mean bondage, but rather it is a helping factor. Bondage lies in forgetting Him and tying oneself to the world and its environments.[104]

"Where there is compassion, there is religion. Where there is greed, there is sin. Where there is anger, there is negation. Where there is forgiveness, there is the Lord Himself."[105]

Truthfulness

To crown all these virtues, come truth and good living. One should in the first instance be true to one's self. The trouble with most of us is that our mind, tongue, and actions do not move in unison. We have one thing in the mind, another on our tongue and still another on our hands. "To thine own self be true, and it must follow as night the day, thou canst not then be false to any man" (Shakespeare). You are in the body; God, the controlling power, is also in the body. If you are true to your own self, you have to fear none.[106] One who does not deceive the God in himself will surely not deceive others either. Before we can deceive others, we first deceive ourselves, and it means that we do not believe in His Omnipresence, otherwise we would not do these things.[107]

Truth is the greatest of all virtues; true living is greater still. We must try to lead a neat and clean life in the temple of the Holy Ghost and not defile it by falsehood and lusts of the flesh thus turning it into a money changer's den of the devil. [108]

So one should imbibe first the virtues of Truth. Lies, cheating, deceit, hypocrisy, showing something different on the face from whatever is in the heart—these things increase the corruption inside. Keep these facts in mind, for he who has no ill will against anyone will say what is true. His tongue will be sweet because he has no intention to hurt anyone's feelings, but rather speaks frankly for the sake of right understanding. Who speaks the truth without fear? Either an established enemy or a true friend, although the enemy may make a mountain out of a molehill because his intentions are dishonorable and he exaggerates. A true friend will never broadcast one's shortcomings, but with love will try to explain where you are going wrong, with your interests at heart. Imbibe the virtues of truth, and with love encourage better understanding in others. And what is more important, do not fail in your own good intentions and principles because of hearsay or rumors. Some tongues are led by selfish motives with little respect for truth. There is a purpose behind everything, which may be obvious or hidden. Do not therefore be a puppet to the tunes played by others; you will do harm to yourself.[109]

When a person tells one lie, then one hundred more lies must be told subsequently, to cover up that one.[110]

Truth does not mean simply speaking truth but it is a

righteous mode of life. Truth is above all, but higher still is true living. Our actions should be exemplary so that they show and denote that we belong to a noble school of thought, based on Truth, Piety and Love.[11] As God is Truth, we must practice Truth in all our dealings. If Truth resides in every heart, it must manifest itself in life and action.[112] Remember that actions speak louder than words. If you cultivate the habit of speaking truth, people around you will act likewise. Thoughts are more potent than words and even stronger than action.[113]

The Truth of Truths resides in the innermost recesses of the human soul and needs to be dug out, unearthed and freely practiced in all our dealings. The True Sound-Principle is the source of all life and it is only by contacting It on the Divine Ground that we become truly truthful and our life can be molded on the pattern of Truth. By practicing Truth and living in Truth, one gets clothed in the love of the Lord and freely extends love to all and sundry.[114]

Chastity: Brahmcharya

BRAHMCHARYA or life of Chastity: It includes continence in thoughts, words and deeds. We must not cast covetous eyes on others nor entertain impure thoughts within, for "Chastity is life and sexuality is death." If we want to tread the Path of Life Eternal, we must be chaste and clean both within and without.[115]

You should please note that mind is the inert force yet driven and channelised by intellect when the sense organs are made to function for gratification. It is the inner urge of the mind lying latent which arouses the intellect to seek enjoyment in sense objects, and unless the reservoir of this sub-conscious mind is depleted of carnal desires and passions, by prolonged discipline and meditations, it is difficult to overcome the lower pulls. Desire is the root cause of all suffering. Listening to the Holy Sound Current with rapt attention and practicing prolonged meditations on divine light shall bless you by ridding you of these desires. Self control leads to true happiness. Like a bird, desire finds a place while perching in the senses, seizing the thoughts, polluting the intelligence, finally bringing ruin to the spiritual aspirant in the mire of degradation. A pleasure which is bitter at the beginning but sweet at the end is worth our cherishing. You should try to imbibe these truths in all earnestness to arrive at definite conclusions for adaptability.[116]

The fake allurements of sensual gratification usually end in frustration. Carnal desires are seldom satiated by indulgence. Spiritual discipline and renunciation of stumbling impediments by careful consideration preceded by repentance, is helpful for spiritual progress. Infatuation breeds indulgence, whereas abstinence and renunciation bring in serenity and sobriety. You should know it for certain that mind is a very useful servant but a very bad master. It is the good grace of the Master that the child disciple is reminded by the gracious Master Power working overhead to follow the right course and those who abide by His instructions are blessed with success in evading the temptation and this monkey mind cooperates with them for their spiritual progress. Contrarily, those who fall a prey to the allurements and do not heed the divine counsel are hurled down into the abyss of degradation, and the same mind runs wild in that direction. So you understand the basic necessity of following the sacred impulse from the gracious Master Power in entertaining sublime thoughts.[117]

Through passion, the soul can fall very low. The seat of the soul is high, between the eyebrows. And the seat of passion? Well, everyone knows where that is.[118]

Lust attacks us eighty percent through the eyes, fourteen percent through the ears and the remaining six percent mainly through touch. So how to maintain chastity? That's the point. You have just to control your attention. The mind and outgoing faculties derive their power from the soul, and the outward expression of the soul is the attention. So if our attention is riveted at the center of the soul in the body and we make the best use of the outgoing faculties, we will not be affected by what we see or hear. You might be looking at somebody but you need not be doing so with your full consciousness, even with your open eyes. Somebody might be relating long stories of vicious things to you. If you control your attention, even with your open ears you won't hear.[119]

When you look into the eyes of somebody who drags you up and helps you to forget your body, that is a criterion of what love is. That is why I always advise, "Don't look into the eyes of others except the Master's." This is the way in which lust attacks us. We are attacked by lust through the eyes. If you look into the eyes of others who are imbued with lust or other lower things, you will have the same effect by radiation. Look only into the eyes of a God-manifested man and you will be benefitted.[120]

An impersonal deviated approach or slight relaxation in the observance of ethical code of morality in accordance with the sacred tenets of the Holy Path is likely to cause harm. Normal association and company breeds attachment. But when this is flavored with divine fragrance and relished in the Name of the Master, this is bound to have much deeper impact. Opposite sex has much stronghold amongst one another when the charm and attraction involved is too much to be resisted. This results in gradual infatuation and bondage. A slight slip can cause much havoc when the dear ones are hurled down in the abyss of sensual gratification. Divine love and sex are quite opposing poles. Sex is not only sinful, but a serious impediment on the Holy Path. It is by long cultivation that one can expect some degree of success in living a clean, chaste life. This aspect of life should please be kept in view by the senior members of Satsang when they can guide the 'young buds' in their larger interests of spiritual progress.[121]

By the observance of Brahmcharya (celibacy), we not only preserve the vital fluid of life (which is an invaluable asset in the physical body and can in no way be underrated) but it positively helps one in attuning to the Divinity, already woven into the very pattern of our life but lost in the mighty swirl of the world. The lost strands of the life-giving threads—the Holy Light and Audible

Life Stream—as manifested by the Master, cannot be held for any length of time, unless we are firmly embedded in the life of chastity. A vacant mind is the devil's workshop, and hence constant repetition of the Charged Words and remembrance of the Master are counseled. These act as powerful aids and help in anchoring the mind and keeping it steadfast in the otherwise tumultuous sea of life. It should be clearly understood that no amount of intellectual attainments or sophisticated reasoning can stand by you in an hour of tortuous agony, except the gracious protection of the Master.

Again, ripe fruits retain their freshness so long as they remain on the branches, but when once plucked can only be preserved either in honey or in some high-grade refrigerators. The personal aura of the Gracious Master is the embalming honey, and His loving protection, the invaluable cold storage, where one may find hope for liberation from this ancient malady. The lives dedicated to the holy cause of God have left behind records of their precious experiences which show in abundance that there is hope for everybody provided one is earnest in his or her endeavors, and provided above all, there is proper guidance and help from a truly competent Master-soul. As every Saint has a past so has every sinner a future, but nothing can be accomplished without the Grace of the Master-power overhead. The child disciple has, of course, to keep himself busy and occupied in something useful or at least in repeating the sacred Charged Names mentally, shunning bad company and uncongenial environment—like study of obscene literature and art—

and by avoiding looking into the eyes of others, particularly of the opposite sex, and in strictly taking vegetarian diet, conservatively cooked and in strict moderation. These are some of the helping factors which, if pursued steadfastly, can bring in sure results in due course of time with the grace of the Master-power overhead.[122] One will not suppress all sexual desires, for repression can only breed neurosis and prepare the way for downfall, but he will be ever seeking to sublimate it. He will understand that nature's purpose in this instinct is to preserve the race and will channel it so as to fulfill that purpose, never making it an end in itself, a source of physical pleasure, for when it becomes that, it turns into a drug that anesthetizes the spirit and begins to defeat nature's purpose of procreation by encouraging the invention and use of contraceptives.[123]

Besides, is it psychologically possible for the human mind to detach itself completely from its normal field of experience without first anchoring itself in another and higher one? It is a universal characteristic of man that he seeks kinship with something other than himself. This is the law of his life and source of all his great achievements. The child is bound to his toys, and the adult to family and society. As in the case of a child, you may not without harm deprive him of his playthings until he has outgrown them psychologically, likewise to expect the sadhak to give up his social and family attachments without first outgrowing them by discovering something greater and larger, is to cut at the root of life. It will not bring progress but regression for the man who undertakes it as an enforced discipline only succeeds in repressing his natural desires. The result is not the enhancement of consciousness but its numbing and atrophy, not detachment but indifference.[124]

Continence is a virtue to be observed for success in all the spheres of life, be they mundane or spiritual. A clean and chaste life is a fertile soil wherein the Holy Seed of Spirituality thrives the best. It consists of restraint in thought, word and deed, as in each case the poison is injected into the depths of the mind and multiplies with the accumulated impurities of countless ages. To cultivate chastity is an uphill task that requires a long-drawn struggle through life—something very strenuous indeed. Fortunate are those who practice celibacy because they are in a far better position to follow the Path Godwards than those who are wallowing in the miserable mire of self-indulgence. A normal temperate married life as enjoined by scriptures is, however, no bar to spirituality.[125]

The Masters do lead an ideal married life and when they take up such a role, they stop such a course. So, married life is no bar to spirituality if led in accordance with the scriptures. The partners in life are advised in their best spiritual interests to observe chastity by leading a moderate life by mutual cooperation. The check marks on the diary forms are essential for the people seeking improvement gradually. One learns by self-introspection and careful living. The dear ones are not forbidden to marry or have homes. But, they should have ideal family life flavored with the divine grace of the Master Power. The young before marriage, should be asked to lead chaste lives, as chastity is life and sexuality is death. A lamp burns splendidly when it has oil within, but if all the oil is leaked away, how can there be light?[126]

It would not be advisable to live together as husband and wife by the initiates unless they are legally married. It amounts to adultery.[127] You will appreciate that in close association it is not possible to curb sensual desires and observe a life of continence and self-restraint, which in turn will affect your spiritual progress. If a man comes out of a tavern while reading the Bible, what do you think the people at large will think of that?[128]

Procreation is only one insignificant aspect of married life. From the time of conception until a child is fed on mother's milk there should be absolutely no self-indulgence. Thus, once conception takes place, there would be a break of two or more years in sexual relations. This is what the scriptures prescribe. If one has just two or three children on this pattern, he is regarded as a chaste person.[129]

Married life is no bar to spirituality, if lived according to the ethical code laid down in the scriptures. Just in a sweet loving way induce your wife to prolong the periods of abstinence to achieve the higher purpose of life and ultimately come up to the standard as prescribed by the scriptures. I hope she will be helping you in the matter. A chaste life in husband and wife is a source of health, vigor and energy to them.[130]

You should continue to meet with your obligations towards your husband in as detached a manner as is possible. The relationship between husband and wife is sacred and nothing should be allowed to come in between. Your loving patience and cooperation will help him to awaken to the higher expression of life in due course. My best wishes are with him.[131]

Chastity is life and sexuality is death. While I sympathize with you in your present situation with your husband, you should continue to meet with your obligations in as detached a manner as is possible. You should inform him on your own behalf in a loving manner that the vital fluid which he loses each time is extremely harmful not only for his spiritual and mental health, but also to his physical health. If, however, he cannot stop all at once, he should in his own interests try to practice more self restraint. With your loving help and cooperation he will be successful in this and to some extent, safeguard his physical health. Your advice to make use of the soul was appropriate. The body is the temple of God and should be made a fitting instrument to manifest the God in man and not be degraded to the practice of sensual pleasure.[132]

Unfortunately, very few people have the right understanding as to the importance of maintaining the chastity of life. It is because man is not chaste that he is under the domination of other vices such as anger, greed and attachment. If he were to control his sensual appetite, the other vices would gradually drop away. So chastity is the key not only to the spiritual life but also to success in every other field of endeavor. The pity of it is that the very people who could help their fellow man, such as doctors and the clergy, are themselves in the grip of sexuality and are hardly likely to recommend the practice of that which they themselves are a prey to.[133]

If you always think of the body, naturally you will think of the opposite sex. Christ said that husbands should love their wives as Christ loved the Church. Even husbands and wives should not think of one another as a man and a woman. They may have one duty of begetting children but that is not everything. It is mainly to have a companion in life for the purpose that both of them should reach God.[134]

Semen is the essence of our body. It is the driving force, a vital fluid. The more of it we have in our body, the more healthy we will be. One who practices celibacy is great and courageous enough to face hundreds of people single-handed. If such a man has spiritual understanding, he is a great soul indeed. Those who are deficient in this essential virtue, are incapable of any worthwhile progress. In the *Shastras* (Hindu scriptures) it is stated that to waste even a drop of semen is equal to death and to conserve it is life. Guru Nanak has also said: "Whosoever loses semen, loses everything."[135]

Q. Does loss of life fluid in sleep retard progress?

A. It does affect spiritual progress. You should avoid looking into the eyes of the other sex and resort to the *Simran* of charged names all along your vacant moments or loving remembrance of the Master, or listening to the holy Sound Current if it has become audible. Such a schedule will be helpful for the eradication of carnal desires. Besides, you should take your food much earlier before retiring for sleep, so that it is well digested. As also the hands, feet and face and also lower portion of the rectum, should be washed with cold water before going to sleep.[136] Also, you should say some prayer before retiring and sweetly keep repeating the sacred charged names and remembering the Master. If you sleep in this relaxed mood, no further disturbances will overcome you in this way, with His grace and protection. Thoughts create impressions in the mind, which seek release in sleep when the attention slips down into the body. These should be recorded on the diary forms.[137]

After all, we have to commune with the Truth which is already within us. For becoming a Satsangi (one who is linked with the Truth) you have to cease to be a *mansangi* (one who is linked with the senses). So we have to do away with our association with sensual pleasures to obtain the ultimate Truth.[138]

Who can rise above body consciousness? One who is unatttached and is not engrossed in sensual pleasures can do it. Only such a person can easily tap inside. Ethical and chaste life is, therefore, very essential. Even if the Master by his own grace lifts someone, whose life is not pure, above body consciousness, the latter will not be able to withstand it. It is crystal clear that there are two main obstacles in the way: passionate desires and anger. To lead a chaste life is not enough. We have to overcome all desires. In anger the soul flows out. Self-indulgence and anger lead to various other vices. Unless these two enemies are disciplined first, others—greed, attachment and egotism—cannot be controlled. One who succeeds in conquering all these five enemies is free from suffering. The senses derive their power from the mind and the mind from the soul. If our attention is concentrated at the seat of the soul, the senses become powerless.[139]

It is only an alert and conscious person who can cultivate chastity and can attain higher consciousness. By practicing chastity one gradually rises into cosmic consciousness. When consciousness dawns within, one is not troubled by the sensual thieves—we are being robbed by the five deadly passions. In the absence of chastity and forgiveness, a thick wall of darkness comes over the soul and we are not our own. Christ has described this state as "death of the soul." What is death of the soul? It is the bedimming of the Light-consciousness in us. Attachment to material comforts lowers our consciousness. Consciousness increases with increasing awareness. Where does this awareness come from? It comes by cultivating compassion and chastity. See how important these virtues are, but we do not pay attention to them. We have already been blessed with his grace and also with the capital of holy Naam. Is it not our duty then to safeguard our capital? We should keep his commandments instead of doing mere lip-service to him.[140]

One who has found a Master, but has not become his mouthpiece (Gurumukh), has not yet freed himself from lusts of the flesh. After having found a Master, one must develop receptivity towards him. Who is a Gurumukh? One who has no wish of his own and lives in the will of the Master. Such a person is automatically relieved of all sorts of passions. As the Master is an embodiment of chastity, chastity radiates from Him and penetrates into the disciple the moment he thinks of Him. He is full of compassion and forgives all. Only a Gurumukh can escape from all kinds of indulgences since he abides in the Word of the Master.[141]

Be true to Him Who is dwelling within you. If you practice the two virtues—chastity and forgiveness—you will find that, without much effort, you will attain higher consciousness, complete awakening and a perfect peace of mind. Thus, you will begin to radiate peace, harmony and tranquility to those around you.[142] Who are we? We have the God in us. We are all micro-gods. It is only because of our (soul's) outflow at the plane of the mind and senses that we have become degenerated. If we withdraw from sensual pleasures and divert our attention towards our controlling power, we would surely become its mouthpiece.[143]

You may go on meditating all through your life, but unless you practice chastity and forgiveness, it will not bear any fruit.[144] Chastity and forgiveness are the two basic and noble virtues of all. If we acquire these virtues, we will be successful in our meditation.[145] Now let us listen to what Sant Kabir has to say about purity of life: "When chastity and forgiveness sprout in one's heart, the invisible Lord becomes visible. Without chastity one cannot reach Him. Empty words are of no avail."[146]

From this day itself we should resolve to lead a pious and disciplined life. We should have regular self-introspection by keeping a diary. You have just to become chaste and you will find that you have developed super-natural powers of perception and foreknowledge of world events. And if such a chaste life is dyed in the color of spirituality, then the great capabilities of a person can well be imagined. As such, purity of heart and chaste life are the main prerequisites of spiritual progress.[147] Even if the person is able to find a perfect Saint who can give the disciple a first-hand spiritual experience, progress on the spiritual way is impossible unless we practice chastity and forgiveness. We should, therefore, forget the past and start leading a clean life from now on.[148] A celibate can reach his real Goal without making much effort. One who practices both forgiveness and chastity has nothing to worry about and will realize God.[149]

Chastity is the main source of all virtues. It is rare to come across a really chaste person. Nearness to such a pure soul produces a soothing effect and even his reflection causes an awakening. It is not an exaggeration. By virtue of ethical life, the body of a celibate is charged with the divine grace, tranquility and fragrance. Chastity is thus a great blessing. "Chastity brings all the treasures of the three worlds (physical, astral and causal)."[150] As you think, so you become. If your mind constantly dwells on a chaste person, you will unconsciously attract and imbibe chastity.[151]

Desire is the root cause of all our disturbances and suffering. You will become desireless by regularly listening to the holy Sound Current for some time. It is considered the tried panacea for that. It is the mergence of the soul in the Holy Shabd which grants such ineffable bliss and harmony that the roots of desire are crippled for good.[152]

Love for All

LOVE BEGETS LOVE

LOVE IS THE panacea for most of the ills of the world. It is the core of all other virtues. Where there is love, there is peace. Love, and all the blessings shall be added unto thee, is the central idea of the teachings of Christ. The entire edifice of Christianity is founded on the twin principles of "Love thy God with all thy soul, with all thy mind and with all thy might," and "Love thy neighbor as thyself." God is love and so is the human soul, being a spark from the same essence. St. John says: "He that loveth not, knoweth not God; for God is love," and, "He who loveth God loveth his brothers also." Guru Gobind Singh likewise laid emphasis on the prime need of love: "Verily I say unto thee that God reveals Himself only to those who love."[154]

Loving and selfless service to humanity is the cornerstone of all religious philosophies and no man can make any progress on the spiritual path without cultivating love within him. The seed of spirituality that the Master so lovingly sows in the arid soil of our hearts, has to be nurtured with the waters of love, if quick results are desired. We must transform the desert of our heart into a veritable garden of love full of lovely blossoms and luscious fruits. From our heart should spring an eternal fountain of love, so that whosoever comes in contact with it is drenched with love to the very core of his heart.[155]

How can love be created? First, a desire is created within by hearing about it—and then by seeing a perfect Master. Masters are overflowing cups of the intoxicated love of God, so by just seeing them the love starts awakening in us too. However, if they also give the connection with the Lord within, then one can be assured that he is on the True Path back to God.[156]

One can accept pride as being the basis of all sins, for it turns into I-hood.[157] False pride of worldly possession or pelf, assumed superiority because of spiritual knowledge or intellectual attainments, vanity of earthly things and status may turn astray the mind of the spiritual aspirant, yet in course of time all these vanish into thin air. On the other hand, a heart full of reverential humility is a fit receptacle for His Grace, a receptacle which when filled to overflowing runneth over on its own to others. For an humble person no sacrifice is too great in the large interests of spiritual development, whereas a proud person would endlessly await and even miss the chance when offered. Time and tide wait for no man. Human birth is a priceless asset granted by Providence in the ascending scale of evolution and its highest object is spiritual perfection, for which all of us are here. Fortunate are those who are spotted, singled out and initiated into the Mysteries of the Beyond, and are linked with the Divine attributes of Holy Light and Celestial Sound. It is now up to us to "make hay while the sun shines."[158]

Love is innate in our soul. It radiates and should come in contact with the Overself, called God or Paramatma.

Instead of contacting our soul with God, we have contacted it with ensouled bodies, and this is called attachment. Love is that which overflows within and you forget yourself. This is a criterion to differentiate love from attachment.[159] If love keeps you in the body, attached to the body, that is no love, but is called attachment. This is the very fine difference between the two.[160]

Love one another for the sake of the Master. If you love for the sake of the man concerned, this will stand in the way of your love for the Master.[161] So love God and as God resides in every heart, love all for the sake of the soul and the Controlling Power that keeps the soul in the body, not the body itself. Then you are saved. If you serve others from the same level, then that is the service of God.[162]

One lesson we can derive from this is that if we are devoted to God or to the God-in-man, then we must love each other. This is but natural. But any love which is colored with your personal interest or selfish motives makes you narrow minded. You would like that the person whom you love should be loved by you and nobody else. But if you have true love for God, then naturally all who love God will be loved by you. This is the vast difference between the two.[163]

So the difference between true love and lust is that true love cannot be broken even after leaving the body. This love is developed in the body but absorbed in the soul, not in the body and its environments. So this is called true love or charity. The other is called lust or attachment and there is a vast difference between the two. Love of God makes us free, makes us all joy, all happiness, all bliss. Lust or attachment enslaves us, it makes us very narrow-minded. In the worldly way, if you love somebody, you will be envious if another person shares that love, but those who love God will also be loved by you, because they love God. So the love of God gives you love for all the world over. Love of the outside things will only make you narrow-minded, close-fisted, and the result is, one lives for God, the other lives for the world.[164]

To meet with your own wishes is no love, in the true sense of the word. That love gives you bondage and slavery.[165] Love is a negation of selfishness and will only pick up good in another, rejecting other things. Humility would mean service to be done in a humble way for the sake of service regardless of the position or even recognition.[166] Trustworthiness and tolerance bring loving co-operation, and selfless efforts bless the child disciple with reverent humility which is the most helpful factor on the Holy Path.[167]

There is only one remedy for all discord and inharmony and that is Love. He who has not mastered its secret, can never hope to be received in the court of the Lord. It is the beginning and the end of Spirituality. He who understands Love and its true nature and who lives and moves by its light, shall, as two added to two make four, attain the Lord.[168]

While we are walking on the path of righteousness, we discover that we are far from being perfect. Perfection comes slowly and requires the hand of time. It does not matter to what faith one belongs, so long as we love God and our fellow-men, for our passport to the Kingdom of God is the love we have in our hearts. If we are students of psychology or metaphysics and are well versed in the laws of mind, and lack love and compassion for our fellow men, we are outside the Kingdom of God. It is what we are that opens the door of our soul to God and makes us His channel of blessing to help others.

Some people hope for a heaven in far distant skies, but heaven is a state of consciousness in this life. If we aspire to live and love divinely, we are already citizens of the heaven to come in the hereafter. For the Kingdom of God is a state of consciousness wherein we worship God with all our heart, and with all our mind and with all our strength and love our neighbor as ourselves. Religion is, therefore, a matter between soul and God, and all other forms of worship and religious observations are in vain unless we enthrone Divine love in our hearts. It is the temple of the heart in which we always keep the Light of Truth and Love burning.[169]

We have been put on the way to God because of our love for God.[170] Learn ye, therefore, to love all creatures as yourself. Live in and for the love of all and the Lord of Love shall reward you manifold in return for the sake of His own Divine Love. That is His Law, eternal and immutable. Try to cultivate a loving and a living faith in His Goodness and nothing shall stand in your way on the Path.[171]

Diet

WHAT WE EAT goes to constitute the body and the mind. "Sound mind in a sound body" is a well known aphorism. We can have neither one nor the other with unwholesome diet. A strictly vegetarian diet consisting of vegetables and fruits, both fresh and dried, cereals, dairy products like milk, cream, butter, cheese, yogurt, etc., is essential for all aspirants for Truth. We must therefore avoid meat, meat juices, fish, fowl, eggs both fertile and unfertile, or anything containing any of these ingredients in any form or in any degree. Every action has a reaction and flesh-eating involves contracting fresh Karmas and thus helps to keep the inexorable Karmic wheel in motion for we have to reap what we sow. We cannot have roses if we sow thistles.

The above prohibitions apply equally to all kinds of alcoholic drinks, intoxicants, opiates and narcotic drugs, as they tend to dull our consciousness and make us morbid.

"The body is the temple of the living God" and it must therefore be kept scrupulously clean.

Any prospective candidate for Initiation should therefore try the vegetarian diet for at least three to six months, to ensure that he or she can adhere to it when put on the Path.[172]

The observance of strict dietary regulations is very essential for steady progress on the holy Path and any transgression is liable to affect your progress. These rules should never be violated even for the consideration of guests.[173]

These are very small things but they have much effect. So a simple diet, a strict vegetarian diet with no spices, should be adhered to. Eat only as much as you need and leave the table still a little hungry. These are the things to be followed which will make you active in all your affairs, whether in meditation, physical work or anything else.[174]

The soul, as I have said before, is eternal, all wisdom and bliss. If it is all wisdom and full of bliss, then how is it possible for it to have any unhappiness in this world? For how long will it enjoy the outer tastes? We think that we are enjoying the enjoyments, but in fact the enjoyments are enjoying us. The god of food once went to Lord Vishnu [part of the triune Lord of Creation: Brahma, Vishnu, and Shiva: the Creator, Sustainer and Destroyer, respectively] and complained. "The people are eating me up brutally, without any sympathy for me!" Lord Vishnu said, "All right, if anyone eats you beyond his needs, then you eat him up." Just think; what is the cause of all disease? Indigestion. We enjoy, and enjoy, and enjoy until we are no longer capable of enjoying anything. Then the enjoyments start enjoying us.[175]

Let half of the stomach be full with food, one fourth with water and let one fourth remain vacant, so that digestion will not be difficult.

The more your stomach is clear, the more concentration you will have. If your stomach is upset, then naturally you cannot sit, you cannot concentrate. So to help you in your meditations, the stomach should be set. No overfeeding should be indulged in. Eat when you really feel hungry, not everytime putting in something. Two meals a day are enough, though you may have a little breakfast in the morning. Sometimes the Masters say that those who would like to progress more should have only one meal a day.[176] If your food is regularized you will rise up punctually in the morning.[177] Let the stomach remain partly empty. If you put more food in it than can be digested, naturally the things which are not digested will create disease. Eat as much as you can digest. Give some rest to your poor stomach. It takes at least four to five hours to digest anything. If you eat too much too often your stomach will revolt.[178] Eating habits can be corrected by careful living. You can improve by gradual adaptation and moderation.[179]

It is very necessary to distinguish clearly the ends from the means. To lay too much stress on the means is likely to make us gradually forget our objective and to become fossilized. Once we know, for example, that abstinence from all kinds of meat diet and spiritous liquors helps us on the spiritual Path, it is enough that we avoid them. But to take it as an end in itself is to miss the goal.[180]

You should be careful for your health as it is equally important to be fit and healthy for meeting with your mundane and spiritual obligations. Physical body must not be denied adequate nourishment.[181]

Your dog should not be fed on meat as it will contract Karmic debt for you. It can live on vegetarian diet all right, just as you have switched over.[182]

The initiates should, as a matter of principle, be very cautious in their food articles especially when they have to dine at friends'. It is so simple to inquire humbly and discreetly beforehand and tell your friends that the prohibited food articles are not allowed by your Spiritual Doctor.[183]

All prohibited foods and drinks should be scrupulously eschewed even in the face of medical advice, as none of these can lengthen the scheduled life-span nor are, in fact, conducive to nourishment.[183]a It is certainly a wrong notion that flesh or eggs give extra vigour or strength; on the contrary, these things flare up the carnal appetites which in the long run result in gross dissipation of energy.[184]

If one adheres to a strict vegetarian diet, that will help a good deal in having normal life, but does not necessarily result in better tempers, controlled sex life or detachment from gross thoughts, desires and actions, worldly ambitions, possessiveness, lust or greed. Kabir says, "If you leave hearth and home and retire to a secluded place and live on pure vegetarian diet, even then the mind does not leave off its base habits." Alongside such essential and positive aids, we must religiously devote regular time to the spiritual practices of contacting the Light and Sound so as to cut down the ramifications of mind, which is so very necessary for self-realization and God realization.[185]

Drugs

IT IS AMUSING to note about the Utopiates (LSD, Marijuana, etc.) for producing hallucinations. You may please note that spirituality is the science of the soul, and the soul is a conscious entity in the body. The Way back to God as offered by the Masters is one of developing inner consciousness with the aid of Holy Naam (the Word). All suchlike outer aids resulting in temporary hallucinations, as stated by you, are certainly a mockery for the divine grace. You can well understand the vast difference between having a conscious and wide-awake approach for proceeding within and that which makes recourse to these outer aids which are no less than opiates creating sensational vibrations. You will recall that the observance of a strict diet by avoiding all flesh food, intoxicants and opiates, is a basic essential for inner spiritual progress, for attaining a refined state of mind. We have to develop consciousness, the divine attribute of soul, and for the achievement of (inner) consciousness, inner and outer piety and chastity are very much needed. The drugs are equally harmful, and should be avoided, which dull the brain and cloud the mind with vague feelings of distrust and confusion. You are advised to convey this piece of right understanding to all the dear ones who are on the Holy Path and to others who seek your counsel in this behalf.[186]

Do those who take drugs such as LSD and have certain experiences—are they valid experiences?

No, no, they are hallucinations. That's the death of the soul, you follow me? The consciousness is lessened, naturally they will have to go to the lower planes. That is all this intoxication starts, it is still more death to the soul. It is deterioration. Definitely going down to beastlihood. Even a snake is conscious but there are different degrees. Man's consciousness is more. If you use suchlike things your consciousness is affected. You will have to go to the lower planes.[187]

I appreciate your kind sentiments for your friends when you wish them to progress spiritually. The so-called spiritual experiences had under the spell of drugs are misleading and are rather likely to affect your inner progress. Spirituality is a research into the realms of reality—the consciousness.[188] Drugs, opiates and intoxicants should not be partaken as these will not only affect your health adversely but shall be detrimental for your spiritual progress. You should please leave off all such drugs and learn to live without their use.[189] It is the result of drugging which has resulted in this setback when you are to suffer from serious pains.[190]

Selfless Service: Physical

NISHKAM SEVA or Selfless Service to all living creatures in sorrow and distress: If one limb of the body is in torture, the other limbs can have no rest. "Service before self" should therefore be our motto in life.[191] Service is considered an ornament to a beautiful person that adorns and elevates his or her soul to become a clean vessel for His grace. Service of any type granted at the Holy Feet of the Master is beneficial and should be cherished as whatever one does must bring its fruit in accordance with the Law of Karma. The secret of selfless service is to deny a reward or recognition of any type and on the contrary consider one's self as a humble instrument in the Divine hands which are the sustainers and protectors of all. All credit goes to the Master, yet the media of love are blessed with the superb Divine intoxication which is of supreme magnitude.[192] Selfless Service for the Holy Cause of the Master should serve as a beacon light for inner progress. It should not be a source of pride or fake ego which definitely become stumbling impediments and hurdles on the Path Divine.[193]

Selfless service is a great virtue and accordingly means some extra labor and sacrifice. It is the manifestation of love and goodness. Mind and body become sanctified through selfless service, provided it is undertaken without ego or vanity. Love knows service and sacrifice. A humble person knows best how to serve the holy cause, under the protective guidance of the Living Master. The climax of selfless service is the annihilation of the ego, considering oneself to be a humble servant of the Lord/Master, entrusted with certain duties to be carried out through him or her and deeming it to be a fortune of the highest order.[194] The little self or ego within has to be eliminated by dissolving it into service of humanity. For all are children of one God, no matter how and where situated, or in what inhibitions and limitations of one kind or another they might be living. You may have to face heavy odds, for it is an uphill task, but all adverse winds blow over. If one is able to efface oneself for a higher cause, this in itself provides a shield and a buckler to the true crusader, and helps in overcoming the seemingly insurmountable obstacles. The tougher the struggle, the brighter shines the metal within. This helps to liberate the finer instincts, until one has risen to a great spiritual stature, towering like a beacon light, shedding rays of hope and encouragement to the lone and weary traveler, shipwrecked on the stormy and strife-ridden sea of life.[195]

No one can be said to have been born for himself alone, for none can be an island unto himself. To serve the needy, sick and starving, is also a sideline, more effective than mere preaching. "Service before self" stirs and kindles embers of sympathy, kindness and love. These virtues have a great purifying effect, and clean a person of all his dross, and entitle him to the highest knowledge of divinity. "Pleasure tastes well after service," is a well known adage.[196]

Selfless service is a great reward in itself.[197]

The more one serves silently, unostentatiously, with love and humility in a smiling, eager and spiritual mood, the more quickly does he earn the pleasure of the Master.[198] When you serve others, you are serving Him.[199]

Selfless service is done in two ways. The first is physical service. If somebody is sick, go and serve him. Shall I see somebody in need, hungry, naked, poor fellow? The Masters have always been for the poor, for the needy, to console them, to raise them up to the level of every man.[200] If you attend a sick person or stand by an afflicted one, you serve the Divine Cause. Certainly you do not and cannot take away the sickness or affliction but surely you can help in assuaging the sufferings by your kindly words and deeds. Every sweet word uttered or helping hand extended to those in distress goes a long way in purifying the mind and the body. A loving heart is a fit receptacle for the Divine Grace, for God is Love.[201]

What does service to Satguru mean? Mere lip-service, saying "Ram, Ram," or merely putting one's head on His feet is no service. It is a mockery. But he who takes his Guru as the ever-present Power of God within him, lives in awe of that, and knows that Power has constant observation over all his thoughts and action, will he ever sin? Further-more, he will hold heartfelt respect for his Satguru's words—*Satguru's words are the Satguru.* This kind of devoted service will achieve salvation.[202]

If we come to a Satguru, we should do our very best to serve him—do something toward earning this rare gift he gives.[203] *Pride, force, or strength of intellect availeth nothing;* Only serve the Sadhu. You will get nothing by giving orders, offering cash, or trying to force the issue; you can only receive by true service to the Master, the manifested God in man—the Word, made flesh.[204]

Service done to sincere seekers of the divine Path is of far greater value than any other service. Helpful ways include, among other things, distributions of alms to the really indigent and the needy, giving sweets to those engaged in extraordinarily arduous pursuits in inaccessible places, nursing the sick, and helping the afflicted ones. All these qualities are great aids in the Path and should be encouraged and cultivated by assiduous practice by all means possible. One should not, however, rest content with them alone, but one must push ahead with the help of these purifying processes, on the way to freedom as enjoined by the Master.[205]

Insofar as you can, try to do no injury to anyone. Be good to all and you will be at peace with yourself and be a radiating center of loving grace around you. The prayers of others to whom you may have done good will help you. The good thoughts of others will swarm around you with a benediction. The very idea of doing good will first affect you and will draw all good vibrations from the surrounding atmosphere.[206]

A true man is one who is truthful, leads a life of continence, radiates love to all others for the sake of God residing in them, and knows giving, giving, and always giving. We never lose anything when we give. When you give love, do you find that you have less love in your heart? On the contrary, you are conscious of an ever greater power of loving, but no one can be convinced of these things till he has applied them in a practical way. An ounce of practice is worth tons of theories.[207] So by sharing with others, our self expands. At the very moment of giving you feel a little joy within. That is the compensation you get, direct. But whenever you give, don't give with the hope that you will have a return. Give for the sake of sharing with others. Sometimes we give for the reward that we will get in heaven. This is not the way; selfless giving is what is needed.[208]

Understand, the meaning and the purpose of knowledge in one single thought is *service* to all creation: men, beasts and birds, etc. The meaning of true life is service and sacrifice. So long as you want, first and foremost, to be blessed yourselves and you expect others to minister to you, you will remain strangers to the way of spirituality. When you will wish others to be blessed, you will begin to speed on your way back to God.[209]

Selfless Service: Financial

So the general rule is to earn your own livelihood honestly, in which nobody's blood is squeezed, in which undue things have not been usurped by you. God sees what you are doing. The other rule is that your earnings should be to maintain yourselves, and share with others.[210] Some part of your earnings must be given away for the good of others. History shows that one tenth of their income used to be given away by the old Christians, Hindus and others. Why? Because some part of our income might be due to our not having done our duty very honestly, even for half an hour or ten minutes. Suppose for example, you are paid for six hours work and you have not put in six hours for the job but have wasted half an hour. So whatever you have been paid for in that half hour is not yours. It has not been earned by you. This has been the custom with all Masters.[211]

But offerings should be free and voluntary and should

not be inspired by any thought of reward or be the outcome of impositions from without, for then instead of
being a source of liberation, they become the source of
bondage. Again, charity should not be misplaced but it
should be given to alleviate the sufferings of the distressed
in the world.[212]

The noblest service one can render in this world is to
help people tread on their way to their True Eternal
Home. No financial service would be too great for as-
sisting such a noble cause. But it should always be loving
and spontaneous. No compulsion, no taxation, no impositions.[213]

So the Guru will love His disciples, because it is He
Who has given birth to them in the inner way. As He
loves us, so should we love all. He won't let anybody
suffer and you should not let anybody suffer. You must
share with others.[214] Unless the riches secured by fair
means are utilised wisely and well, one is likely to go
astray and become egocentric and a slave to his ill-gotten
wealth and is unknowingly caught in the golden chains
that keep him in bondage.[215]

So by giving away, you don't lose. At the end of the
year, you will see that money has been saved in some
other way, by freedom from sickness or any other troubles that arise generally and which involve expenditure.
Our Master used to say, "All right, you give away one
tenth and at the end of the year just count. The very
money you have given has been saved where you had no
sickness."[216]

Spiritual Practices: Meditation

SPIRITUAL PRACTICES form an essential part in the spiritual aspirant's life and should, therefore, be a daily "must." The repetition of the Five Sacred Charged Names conveyed at the time of Holy Initiation, orally or mentally, is not a difficult task and carries a deep meaning. Although it looks so simple and easy at the outset, to obtain proficiency in it one needs extra love and fortitude. You will appreciate that the Holy Names carry the Life Impulse of the Master which works wonders in withdrawing the sensory currents from the body level up to the eye-focus, thus preparing the soul for the eventual inner journey on to the regions of bliss and harmony. Certain hours for meditation should, therefore, be fixed, set apart and pursued regularly and earnestly for each such repast brings in nourishment to the soul, and one is led within to the Divine Light which dispels the Darkness of Ignorance. It is like purifying the receptive vessel every day for receiving the Divine Grace. Daily meditations clear the gross dross that one gets at the sensuous level. The second important part of meditation is listening to the Holy Sound Current, the Audible Life Stream coming from the right side. It is equally an important aspect of the spiritual practices and should not be ignored or lost sight of. After initiation, it is the disciple's duty to enrich his spiritual experiences from day to day and he can certainly extend his field with the Grace of the Master to any length he may like, opening up new vistas of sublime glory and beatitude.

In short, self introspection helps in cutting the branches and pruning all that is undesirable while meditation (spiritual practices) strikes at the very stem of the tree of worldly life.[217]

God is everywhere, but He is not manifested everywhere. Why? Because our soul—that spark of the All Consciousness—is under the control of mind and senses, and through its sojourn in creation has become the image of the body and the image of the world, thereby forgetting its true self. It must just know itself, then it can have the experience of the Overself; if it does not rise above body consciousness, how can God be manifested? Do you understand this?[218] He resides with you. The body is the true Temple of God. When you have understood this, then where do you go to find Him? First within your own Self. Withdraw from outside. Withdraw from the mind and outgoing faculties and come up to the seat of the soul at the back of the eyes. When you concentrate there, your inner eye will be opened to see God within you.[219]

The Master exhorts us to realize Him in our souls, to rise in Him, losing all sense of the little ego in the living temples of our bodies. The Kingdom of God is within us. We have to recognise the Inner Man as the image of God, the physical body as the temple of God, the tabernacle of the Holy Ghost, in which the Lord makes His appearance. In these living temples we have to attune our souls with God and live in closer communion with Him.[220]

Many do say that they are soul—a conscious entity—

indweller of the human form—but have they come to
prove it and thereby know it in truth? This is my watch,
I can place it here. These are my spectacles, I can take
them off and put them here. I can take off my clothes,
whenever I wish to. But can I become separate from my
body? Can I take my body off? It is a question of how
to rise above by self-analysis; and who can give a demonstration of this scientific method? By the Guru's grace,
you come to know yourself. Only then can it happen,
and not before. When you know yourself, then like knows
the like, and God realization is the next step. So God
cannot be known by the senses, intellect, or pranas—only
soul can experience the Lord, and this can happen only
after it has come to know itself.[221]

To know our Self is not a matter of feelings, emotions
or drawing inferences. It is really one of rising above
body consciousness by self analysis to know practically
who we are. When we know our Self and come in contact with all-conscious God, that is the Bread and Water
of Life for the soul. All worldly information and outer
sciences—the libraries are full of them. If our brain becomes full of them, well, it is not bread to the soul. It is
bread and water for the intellect to grow on. So the
Bread and Water of Life for the soul is the conscious
contact with God or the Overself. These things are to be
understood and then lived. By speaking about bread,
your hunger cannot be appeased but you must have
bread to eat. That is why Christ said, "I am the Bread
of Life. This Bread of Life has come down from Heaven.
Whoever partaketh of it shall have everlasting life."

Partaketh of it—He is the Bread of Life, of course. He also says, "Eat me and drink me." What to eat? He is Word made flesh. The more you come in contact with and devour that Word, the Light and Sound within you, the more you will be eating of the Bread of Life.[223]

All imperfections will leave you, just as when you sit by a fire, all cold leaves you. By hearing the Sound Current you become the abode of all virtues. By hearing, you can determine the direction in which you have to go. By seeing, your inner eye is opened to see where you are going. Pity it is that we give little time to these things and only waste away our time in trifling things, I would say.[224] So put in more time, please, to your practices. Develop love for God within you. You will be blessed. You will have made the best use of your life.[225]

Concentration of Spirit Current

THE DEVELOPMENT of the elementary powers of spirit is, therefore, most necessary. It is the concentration of this spirit current which plays the greatest part in the achievement. If it is applied to the physical body, one gains strength. If it dwells upon the intellect, one develops great mental powers. In the same way, if spirit is made the object of concentration—spiritual life inevitably follows and supreme bliss is attained. There is an unseen nerve that connects all these centers which is called *Sushumna Nari* or *Shah-rag*. It is through this that the spirit current passes from the lowest region to that of the highest region of Truth.

The concentration of the spirit, then, is the opening process, so that the spirit may progress to higher regions. Until all outgoing faculties are self-centered or inwardly focused, the spirit does not gain strength enough to go up. There are ten outgoing faculties or Indriyas: five are the gross—eyes, ears, nose, tongue and skin through which the five others—the subtle Indriyas—of sight, audition, smell, taste and touch keep man attached to the outer world. It would thus appear that it is the constant thought of these faculties which externalizes man.

We constantly think of the world through three main sources. First, we have the eyes that visualize the outward phenomena and bring them within the mental gaze. Through the eyes we gather in no less than 83 per cent of our impressions from outside. The second source is that of the ears which pull our attention to outward sounds and remind us of things in the objective world. Through the ears we get 14 per cent of our outer impressions. The third source is that of the tongue (palate) which, through taste and speech, keeps the memory of the outward world always fresh. The remaining three per cent of the outward impressions are received through the nose and the rest of the sense organs. It is through these three main faculties that man remains constantly in touch with the outer world and is ever engaged either in receiving impressions from without or impressing others with his own thoughts. The energy of the mind is thus drained away, leaving one bankrupt. The Master tells us not to exhaust our energy. We must accumulate and preserve our energy, so that we may be able to rend asunder the various sheaths of matter which encase the self within us.

The spirit or soul is attached to the objective world outside, on account of objective impressions. Unless the outgoing faculties are controlled and the spirit is freed from the bondage of life, it cannot rise above body consciousness. The three faculties of speech or taste, sight and audition cause a constant outflow of energy through their respective sense organs. For the depersonalization of the soul, it is necessary to channelize our energy inwards and upwards through the processes of inversion and self-analysis.[226]

These organs of tongue, eyes and ears, etc., are at work in the physical frame while one is in a wakeful state and they work likewise in the astral plane when one is in a dream state. The faculties of these organs get enhanced and become powerful if one were to restrict their outward flow. It is then that one gains strength to fathom the subjective world, for without the quickening life-impulse of the soul they lie dormant.[227]

USES OF THE THREE RESTRAINTS AND THEIR PROCESS: The three restraints are to be exercised by training the faculties to work inwards. The first restraint, that of speech, consists in doing Simran or the constant repetition of the Names of the Lord with the tongue of thought. The agency of lips and tongue is not needed. The second restraint refers to the faculty of sight, and consists in contemplation of the spiritual patterns within, which open out in full effulgence. When you fix your inner gaze just midway between and behind the two eyebrows (the seat of the soul in man), you see your own light inside. That light is yours and is already there and you have to fix your inner gaze on it. Where there is the Word—Holy Naam—there is light; where there is sound, there is refulgence, for the two are inseparable. The light patterns are of five kinds corresponding to the five different kinds of sounds, which are seen and heard as the spirit ascends upwards into the five different planes. The Monduk Upanishad speaks of these as the "five fires in the head."[228]

It does not mean that we are to neglect the use of these organs in relation to the outer world. But these are to be so trained that they may become positive aids in the way of spiritual development, thus conveying a twofold benefit. The training is meant to make the mind self-centered and prevent its stuff from needlessly flowing outside. The first process, Simran, forms the basis of spiritual pursuit. It has to be continued till the goal is reached. The second and third, Dhyan and Bhajan, follow of themselves one after the other.[229]

These three restraints help in concentration to the highest degree. The first, Simran of the charged words given by the Master, brings back the mind from outside and withdraws the spirit from the body to the seat of the soul in the body. This is first sinking from the circumference of our being to the center of our being. This also keeps reminding us of the highest ideal set up before man, which is self-knowledge and God-knowledge. The second process—Dhyan—also helps in concentration and fastens the soul inside. The last process—Bhajan or listening to the spiritual music in man—carries the soul into the beyond, to the source from whence the life current or Sound Principle of the Holy Naam or the eternal song, emanates.[230]

from *Seven Paths to Perfection*

BOOK TWO

MEDITATION

Oh man! Thou hast come into the world to make a profitable business of dealing with the merchandise of Naam which never fails. But alas, thou art engaged in fruitless and bewildering things of life. The night of earthly life is nearing its end. Those who do not reach the shore now, how can they cross when dead?

Hari Naam is the essence of all religions. All religions are deeply rooted in the Naam. Verily, verily, the true study is the study of Naam, which is the Bread of Life.

He who knows how to die while living drinks Amrit, the Water of Life, which gives everlasting life. Therefore learn to die while living at the feet of a living Master. My Master, Baba Sawan Singh, instilled in me that we do really live when we are in contact with Naam, the Word, which can be given by one who is Word made flesh living on earth. Without that, there is no no life. Very great and all powerful is the Naam, controlling us in the body. We cannot live without its shelter even for a moment. Time and tide wait for no man; please do hurry before it is too late.

July 17, 1970

Meditation

The Importance of Meditation

WHENEVER THE MIND has clear understanding and is inclined toward God, then quickly sit down for meditation—do not wait for tomorrow, do not wait even a few hours, or his mood will change and again he will cheat you out of the benefit. No matter what you are doing, when mind and soul are one, sit in meditation at once. Who knows what will happen in the next minute? Such an ideal mood is rare and valuable; there should be no delaying to take advantage.[1]

The Light of life is in you; indeed you live by that very Light whether you realize it or not. Each one of you has had an experience of that Holy Light. Now you must live in constant contact with the Holy Light. It is uncreated and shadowless, eternally the same and peerless. The whole creation came into being by the same Light, and that very Light is shining in every heart. All are Divine in nature, and religion is the expression of Divinity already existing in man. The Light of Life must be made manifest in existence. Be ye a witness to the Light of Life, not only within yourself but in others as well, for the same Light shineth everywhere and there is no place where it is not. Once you discover this Light and learn to live by it, your whole existence will be changed. Love will permeate your very being and it will burst forth from the very pores of your body, transmuting all dross into sterling gold. Love, you must know, is both the means and the goal of life. Love, Light and Life are but different facets of the One Divinity.

Try to become a channel for the Divine and the Divinity will then flow through you. This is not something impossible, but it is the very acme of all human endeavors. In this world of matter one has of necessity to deal with matter. We have to make the most of the material raiment and the material world given to us. It serves a great purpose in the Divine Plan of Evolution. Matter is the ladder by which means the spirit has to rise above body-consciousness and move into the realm beyond— the realm of Spirituality—its native habitat. Learn to make the most of the means given to you and surely as day follows night, the victory shall be yours. A true Christian ought to take up his Cross daily. The Cross represents the physical body standing with outstretched arms. You have to rise above body consciousness. You have to be reborn into the Kingdom of God. The disciple must know how to die daily so as to be able to enjoy life eternal, beyond time and space.[2]

Simran and Dhyan (meditation) flood the spirit with the waters of life. Spirit comes to its own, rises in its latent Godhood and like a tumultuous mountain stream rushes headlong toward the ocean of life which is its perennial source and merges therein losing its separate identity.[3]

A True Master is not a mere human being, but has

become One with God, and as such, contains in Himself the powers of all the gods and goddesses. He is veritably the Word made flesh and blood. The one lesson that such a Master teaches his disciples is to meditate always upon the Lord, the Creator of everything, and never forget Him.[4] Be the worshipper of the Living Light—become a slave to it. Do not attach yourself to anything else, for everything is changeable.[5]

The Masters say, "Stop where you are! Look at your condition!" It is all through the lack of meditation, and the only cure is to join the soul back to the Lord. Even a little intoxication derived from steady daily practice will start to erase the taste for outer pleasures. These outer attractions are making it extremely difficult for the mind to withdraw and go inward. If we start to enjoy inner sweetness . . . *When that sweetness comes, this other flavor is not to the liking.* Naturally the sweeter taste will render others insipid.[6] The cause of all our distress can be traced to the fact that we have not been drenched in the true color of Naam.[7] But if the soul does not learn to leave the body at will, and has not derived intoxication from being drenched in the color of Naam, no amount of speech or action will achieve success on the spiritual path. Remember this fact, for it is clear and simple.[8]

Listen! Open your ears and listen! He who has made his meditation has made everything. He whose meditation is not made will enjoy no meaning in his life's achievements. There is great purpose behind this emphasis on the importance of meditation. If your daily life is not under control, try to bring it in control, or give more time to meditation and you will be able to gain control quicker. He who becomes the conscious co-worker of the Divine plan will find that his righteous life is made. Whatever he does will be performed righteously; he will not be able to act otherwise. The reason behind your failure is that you have not truly loved your Master, but have merely made a show in various ways, physically and financially, or by lip-service. There is no one who has sacrificed his mind to the Guru. Without giving up the mind, there is no success.[9]

When will you actually experience the fact that you and He are not separate and not different? When you separate yourself from matter by self-analysis. You can try by feelings, or through inferences, but both are subject to error—seeing is above all. When can one see oneself or the soul in its native clarity? Control the senses, still the mind and intellect: then the soul is seen in all its glory. He who knows himself and knows he is the mouthpiece of God—that God is working through him—he is free from illusion. Great power arises from such a condition.[10]

Do your Bhajan and Simran; release the soul from mind and senses. Bhajan and Simran are food for the soul—do not give food to the body without first giving food to the soul.[11]

Learn how to leave the body at will and transcend into the upper regions. If so, we will benefit in two ways. First, we will know how to leave the body, as we have learned to do so daily, and when death comes there will be no pain and no fear. Secondly, by traveling frequently in the higher regions and returning to the earth at will, the fear of our unknown destination will vanish and we will develop an unwavering conviction about the true life; its mystery will be revealed. It is no use waiting for death to discover the facts of life.[12] The Masters come, lift up their hands, and shout to the world, "Oh brothers, do your meditation for without it you cannot be free."[13]

The precious moments of earth-life spent in spiritual practices count creditably toward one's eventual emancipation from the Wheel. Be regularly and lovingly devoted to your holy meditations, as that is the central pivot around which the whole sacred teaching revolves and therein an all-round development of the soul is granted.[14]

The meaning of meditation is to concentrate or meditate upon one thing, so much so that all other things are forgotten.[15]

Maulana Rumi says that compared to the vastness of the worlds within, this world is not even the extent of an atom. What a magnificent abundance of life there is within us![16]

A little knowledge is dangerous. First see what is in your own home, the physical house. Go into the folds of the holy books and see what is given there. The same knowledge that I am giving you is given therein, but for the need of a self-realized man we do not understand what is written.[17] The gem of knowledge is that Sound which reverberates, and whosoever enters inside will find it. "Everything is in this house. Nothing is outside." The untold treasure of Divinity lies hidden within, yet we search for it without and so all our efforts go in vain.

Whosoever searches outwardly will lose himself in illusion.[18]

The Change of Direction

PEOPLE shirk going within. It is difficult, no doubt, but the Path lies within. What is the use of wandering outside? A travel of one inch within is better than a trip around the globe. The mind, however, does not wish to be imprisoned, although it is to its advantage. In its outward (tendencies) it dissipates itself, and gains in power only when it goes within. On account of bad habit, it clings to the external things. The idol worship, whether the idol is of stone or paper, is the invention of mind.[19]

The world is a mere nothing—a place full of illusion and wrongdoing—valueless with no virtue, a place where the darkest deeds are carried out. What is there here that can hold any real value for either the soul or the mind? Make it understand these realities for at present it is strongly attached to all the falseness of the world and it simply has to turn and face the truth to become attached to something higher. If the soul does not leave the senses, how can it transcend the body? If it does not transcend the body, how can it realize what it is? It is a straightforward matter, requiring no special philosophy to understand. Where the world's philosophies end, there religion truly starts.[20]

So long as the heart is the focus, the mind continues generating thoughts—wool-gathering, and the individual is impressionable to circumstances. When the focus of attention has been raised to the eyes, and the mind has entered within, then the mind ceases generating thoughts and is running within instead of outside. The individual then is necessarily unaffected by external circumstances or changes.[21]

The mind often exerted his strength, almost wrestler-like, and said, "I will not do this!" But again and again he was tempted and overcome by the senses. We all make strong resolutions, but when it comes to keeping them we fall down. Swami Ji is quite openly revealing our own condition—these are our very own cries of anguish, and the promises we make to change tomorrow—that to-morrow which is in the Negative Power's hands, and never comes. Everyone is in the same boat and crying out the same cry; so look within yourselves and see what you are doing with your precious lives. Why not start the good work now? The mind is very wise, it is no insignificant thing. Like a magistrate, his thoughts are wise, and he observes that with all his efforts there is still no freedom, only defeat. Some people are dragged in passion, some are roasted alive in the fire of attachment, some are caught in the nets of ego and pride, stiffly and proudly strutting their way through life. The whole world is in this terrible condition.

I want to leave all enjoyments;
Just seeing them I am helpless.

There is so much attraction in the outer enjoyments that the mind ignores its wisdom and is rendered too helpless to fight. When a cat sees a mouse, it cannot resist it. So what happens? We say, "Let us enjoy now and face whatever the consequences when they come." We are usually aware of our follies to some extent, but too late.[22]

Mind is no small thing, and is not easy to conquer, but we should start by changing its direction. While its face remains turned toward the worldly things, the soul will be worldly, but if it turns around and faces the soul, the soul will become spiritual. We must turn round.[23]

When you are fully convinced that the fountainhead of peace and harmony is within and that you have the key and the means to tap within, you should not let the precious moments pass without deriving maximum spiritual benefit. *You are simply to decide and then act.*[24]

The Need for a Guru

ALL THE INSTANCES known to history show that no one has ever progressed to the highest conscious self-awareness without the help of a Master. It is rather a fundamental law that no one can snap or pierce through the inner veil without the active help and guidance of a Master Soul. If anybody can do it by himself or herself, let him or her try and see if he or she can do it. When one does not hesitate in learning a thing which one does not know in this world, why should one have any qualms in one's search for something that belongs entirely to spiritual worlds within. Even if as a result of some reactions of past lives, one may have some experience of his own, he will still require Someone to guide him to further progress on the Path. All those who have been put on the Way should, therefore, carry on their meditations lovingly and devotedly so that they may progress within, from day to day, and enjoy the sweet internal bliss.[25]

Outside experiences differ in various countries, but inner experience never. He may be defined as one brimming with Spirituality and above the life of the senses. He has freed Himself from various sheaths of grosser and finer matter, and He has seen the All Truthful with His spiritual eye. He is competent to develop the spiritual possibilities lying dormant in man. He is charged by God Himself with the Magnetic Force. He is the mouthpiece of the Eternal. He has in Him the Refulgent Light of the Infinite, and He is competent to light the lamps of others.[26] So it is only by the grace of a true Master that one can be guided away from the dark edge of these powerful senses—for a while. *With indescribable strength the mighty Guru pulls the attention.* And inside is the Ever-Existent Lord, described as Naam.[27]

Shabd

THERE WAS great beauty in the Shabd. It had a music that was beyond any music created by man and which drew the soul towards Itself. It was forever calling the spirit towards its Divine Home and though it was not heard by ordinary men, yet those who had developed, through practice and the grace of Satguru, the capacity of inner hearing, could hear its melody every minute of the day, now growing stronger as the mind focused itself at one point, now dimming and fading away as one's thoughts scattered in various directions and attention was dissipated. It was Shabd that was the true anchor of the seeker. It was the conscious power that had brought everything into creation and it was also one's real Master —the Shabd Guru—for the Satguru in his human form was its physical manifestation.[28]

Shabd brings in untold blessings. It is the powerhouse of all energy or force in whatsoever form, from pranas down to electricity and magnetism. Every form of life is the manifestation of Shabd. All that is, is of Shabd and nothing is that is not of Shabd—life-current pulsating in and out of space. Those who commune with Shabd and live in and by Shabd are verily the children of the Supreme One, the life of life and the light of light. Shabd is the very "Bread of Life" which comes down from Heaven for all those who hunger after righteousness, and the very "Water of Life" for those who thirst after Self-knowledge and God-knowledge. True love, wisdom and power are the greatest gifts that one gets by basking in the sunshine of Heaven's Light.[29]

Surat and Shabd are naturally related to each other. Shabd is characterized by Light and Sound principles, wherewith the mind gets stilled and the spirit, freed from the clutches of the mind, is irresistibly drawn by the Shabd and is taken to her native homestead from where the Sound Current is emanating. On the other hand, those who take up practices involving pranas, cannot go beyond the frontiers of pranas which extend to the mental or astral heaven as *Chidakash* is known to be. But a Shabd yogin can go freely, openly and honorably to wherever he likes, because Shabd pervades everywhere without ever any limitations, and reach the true home of his Father.[30]

The particular sounds that have an upward pull are five in number, as stated by the various saints, and may be apprehended through their Grace and contacted in their company. Such sounds carry with them the effect of the spiritual planes from which they proceed and in turn produce the same effect on him who comes in contact with them. They have their own heavenly melodies, the rapturous strains of which depersonalizes the soul by freeing it from the chains of mundane life.

Whoever comes near the fire, gets warmth, no matter whether he does so of his own accord or not. So the Holy Naam or the Divine Song cannot but influence you when you come in contact with it, whether you will it or not and are in time or out of time. The Power of God cannot but influence you, should you get in touch with It.

The outer music has a marvelous effect on all living beings. It shakes off the grievous burden of the oppressive sorrow and unrest under which one incessantly groans, and drives away all thoughts. It washes away the dirt of everyday life by its melodious tunes and captivates the soul. It withdraws the mind from the tumultuous hubbub of the objective worlds. It concentrates the mind, naturally, without having recourse to any fabricated methods. Music, indeed, has ever been the art of saints.[31]

These spiritual sounds are aids on the spiritual path. A competent Master, at the time of initiation, gives full

instructions on how to differentiate between them from
plane to plane, as well as how to catch hold of them on
the onward march to the highest spiritual realm. Herein
then lies the need for a Master Soul, for He is the inspirer
of Hari Naam—the Divine Word, in the depths of one's
soul. Without Him, the Eternal Song ever remains a
shrouded mystery with no access thereto. As Music personified, He is competent to manifest it, make it audible,
and thus lead one to the seat of the Almighty.[32]

If one could discover this audible life-stream within
oneself, if one could discover its lower reaches, one could
use it as a pathway leading to its source. The currents
might at certain points enter gorges and rapids, but nevertheless they are the surest way on the upward journey.
Be a range however unscaleable, the waters will have cut
a path and carved a passage, and he who will avail himself of their guidance would never fail to find a way. And
since this Naam or Word current springs from the
Anaam or the Wordless, he who holds firmly to It will
inevitably reach the starting point, transcending plane
after plane of varying relativity until he arrives at the
very source of name and form, thence to merge into That
which has no name or form.[33]

Ever since the child disciple is led to the Living Master
and is linked with the Holy Naam within, the incessant
flow of grace and protection is extended in abundance.
The faithful and the loving develop receptivity and
assimilate the same to enrich their lives and they become
a source of inspiration to others. The celestial manifestations within are the result of the grace of the Master

and in no way may be claimed as one's personal effort or
endeavor, however good they may seem to be. Yet it is
of great importance to strictly abide by His commandments, thus invoking His mercy and blessing. It is not the
inner experience which determines the spiritual progress,
but the basic personal attitude of serene living of the
child disciple, which proves his or her worth. Truth is
above all, yet higher still is true living. A man is best
known by the company he keeps and by his actions. The
spiritual development is steady, continuous, unabated,
harmonious and ceaseless from the moment one is linked
with the Holy Naam. The gaps of hushing silence creating an intense longing and pangs of separation for the
Master and Holy Naam within the innermost recesses of
the heart are happy preludes for a big leap forward. The
cumulative efforts of the sincere devotee will one day
open the flood gates of celestial glory, much to his or
her gratuitous joy.[34]

Without the stabilizing force of Naam, the soul remains diffused in the world, subject to the constant agita-
tion of the mind. Passion and anger have the same results. If an obstacle comes between us and our desire,
whether apparent or concealed, then anger arises, followed by envy, criticism, backbiting, enmity, petty squab-
bling and other things—we drift from one bad habit to
another. And all this is due to lack of substantial meditation.

Even if a little was done with deep sincerity, some intoxication would be enjoyed. *When this Nectar comes,
other wine seems tasteless.* Having tasted the real Nectar

of Life, one will leave a thousand tasks to sit and enjoy it. Every free minute will be put to use; one will readjust one's life to make more and more time for meditation. When people are asked why they do not meditate, their excuse is that they have no time. Forgive me, but there is never any time for this precious work, although the "true disciple" is always ready and willing to attend to the worldly pursuits. We are not faithful to our Bhajan because we have not had enough inner experience of Naam.[35]

"There is no way without the Shabd to leave this pot of clay;" and it lies within each being. When the connection to Naam is made, it then must be increased. It is the treasure of the two worlds: Physical and spiritual. *When you meet the Sant, brothers, value the True Naam; This treasure of life remains here and hereafter.* It is potent in both phases of life.[36] With repetition or Simran, you can achieve single-pointed concentration, and with concentrated attention—Dhyan—you will come to a standstill; but Shabd is the only power to take you up into the Beyond.[37] With kind thoughts I wish you to engage with all your mind and soul in the service of the holy Word and the holy Word will take care of you.[38] "Service of the holy Word" simply means that you commune with or tune yourself to the holy Sound Current which is the life of our life, the very first principle of Godhood or God-in-action, as it has to be contacted, absorbed in and comingled with. A dip into it is a dip into the Ocean of All Consciousness and purifies the soul of myriads of karmic impressions lodged in the mind throughout the countless ages. This then is the service to the holy Word or the Holy Ghost which manifests as the Divine Light and Divine Sound.[39]

The sovereign and the most potent remedy to wash the mind clean, say all the Masters, is by communion with the holy Word—the God-in-action power creating and sustaining all that is visible and invisible. To be in tune with the music of the soul is to cut asunder and to sunder forever the knots which at present bind the material body with the conscious soul, imprisoned in the body with countless fetters.

Guru Nanak says in the *Jap Ji*: "When the hands, feet and the body are besmeared, they are washed with water; when the clothes get dirty and polluted, they are cleansed by soap; when one's mind gets defiled by sin, it can be purified only by communion with the Word."[40]

The holy Sound Current growing more powerful at times denotes His constant protection to you and an invitation for proceeding ahead within under His guidance. You should listen to it so devotedly that your entire self is merged in it and let it transport you into the Beyond to taste the higher Bliss.[41] Bhajan is imperative to right living, for the true meaning of Bhajan is to go within and rejoin the Lord—nothing more or less.[42]

Whoever sits before a God-realized person in all sincerity, in His company will come to understand what the Shabd is, and what is the true gain from the Guru.[43]

Benefits of Communion with Naam

YOU WILL appreciate that when attention is completely riveted within at this thinking center, and all the
stray thoughts controlled by mental repetition of the
charged Names, an overwhelming inner warming comes
of itself from above, which multiplies in abundance and
then inculcates a gradual accelerated devotion for the
holy meditations. A well tilled and nicely ploughed field
will bring forth a rich harvest when watered with the
waters of loving devotion and humble supplication.[44]

Naam keeps the mind and body in a state of equipoise.
Peace reigns supreme in its devotee; the ramifications of
mind are done away with forever. All lusts cease to have
their hold on the mind. The brain gets a soothing balm.
It puts an end to wasteful hurry, and with it go all nervous tensions and mental strains and stress. Naam gives
one immunity from all bodily and worldly pains and troubles. By withdrawing the attention within, the mind is
stilled and the soul is freed of all mental conflicts. Even
the sense of egotism itself—the most ancient malady—
loses itself into airy nothing and with it, the perpetual
dance of coming and going out of the world comes to an
end. The process of transmigration of the soul is but the
natural concomitant of the self-assertive will or egoism.

Guru Nanak says: "Whenever one asserts the little
ego, 'I,' as doing things, one assumes the unending role
of an ever-active agent responsible for his actions and is
caught in the intricate net of transmigration."

The elimination of egoism is, then, the only remedy for

liberation from the unending cycle of births and deaths. It is a clear test of the spiritual current diffused in the world. All labor undergone for total self-effacement is an effort in the right direction. It is called disimprisonment of the soul from the facts of life or disenfranchisement from all that is worldly. In a word, the secret lies in depersonalizing the soul of all that is personal in it, for then one strikes at the root of all evil. The many recipes for this losing of the "I-consciousness," which flood the world today, fail to gain for us the goal of liberation. For with such methods, the ego feeds itself and grows from strength to strength and is not effaced. Unless one becomes a conscious co-worker with the divine Plan, he cannot become selfless.[45]

The Sound Current, Soul and Master are all one. Your growing interest in its listening brings you nearer to the fountainhead of this bliss. It feeds the soul and strips the mind of its age-old dross. Past karma is wiped out by its rapturous listening with the grace of the Master. The initiates are invariably stressed the importance of listening to this Divine Sound so as to be free from the reaction of present karma, which they have to contract while meeting with their legitimate duties, in accordance with their fate-karma.[46]

The load of karmic debt gets lighter by listening to the holy Sound Current even if it is in its lowest links for it holds the keel of one's barque steady on the stormy sea of life and saves it from running aground among shoals, sandbanks, and submerged rocks. But one must strive to catch higher Sounds for it is the latter that exert a powerful pull upon the soul by following which one is led to eventual liberation. These higher sounds can, by loving devotion and practice, be easily differentiated and communed with by the grace of the Master Power which is ever ready to extend all feasible help to the aspirants on the Path.[47]

Desire is the root cause of all disturbance and suffering. You will become desireless by regular listening to the holy Sound Current for some time. It is considered the tried panacea for that. It is the mergence of the soul in the Holy Shabd which grants such ineffable bliss and harmony, that the roots of desire are crippled for good.[48] . . . Be sweetly absorbed into the hearing of the Sound Current. It cleans the mind, purifies the heart and elevates the soul.[49] Those who meditate on Naam not only succeed spiritually but in worldly attainment also.[50]

When the soul gets a connection with the Greater Consciousness, it gains strength and refreshment. If one removes the attention from the body and goes up, the body gets perfect rest. The law is that if one gets true sleep for just a few minutes, it is enough. For those who travel on this Path, reduction in sleep is a very frequent occurrence.[51]

One never feels ill after meditation. The result of sweet and accurate meditation is the reverse: one feels peaceful and serene. The time that is at our disposal now is very precious. Lest one regrets having wasted it, it is better to use it to its fullest extent. To such people, inner help comes as oxygen comes to help fire.[52] The holy Naam is the panacea for all ills—physical, mental and spiritual. Medicines do help for refining the physical body, but a harmonious life full of sublime piety is only possible by regular and faithful meditation.[53]

Those who have access within can read their fate easily. It is an open book to them.[54] It is during the sublime moments of meditation when the child disciple is attuned with the Infinite to benefit from the incessant flow of Divine Grace, and it is then that the rare boons of right understanding come in increasing measure.[55]

So long as we are covered by mind and matter we cannot see reality. When you have thrown off these coverings you will be able to read others correctly at a glance. Every individual is working under the influence of mind and is blind. Mind is the snake in our body which bites us always. Under its influence we do actions and our actions are the cause of our endless struggle here causing births and deaths. This snake-mind is charmed when it catches the Word. It is attracted by the sweet Sound of the Word, hearing which it is rendered motionless and the soul is released from its bondage. Nanak says that there is no other way to conquer mind except by the practice of Sound Current. And so long as mind is not conquered there is no getting in. The mind functions through ego. The soul is free when mind tastes the Word and no other taste satisfies the mind for any length of time and otherwise sooner or later the mind gets dissatisfied and begins to look for something else. Only when the Word has been tasted the mind finds complete satisfaction.[56]

There is an instance in Lord Krishna's life, when he

jumped into the River Jumna. There he saw a huge snake with a thousand heads. How did he control and overcome that snake? By playing the flute. The mind can only be controlled with the inner Sound; there is no other way. Outer things may still it for a while, but they can never control it. Many holy men in the past have lost everything through the mind. By contact with the Word and the company of the "Word made flesh" the power of the mind can gradually be overcome. If you sit at the feet of a perfect Master, you will enjoy the benefit of the radiation, for his attention is under his own control. There you will become absorbed in the stillness and forget the world for a while.[57]

True renunciation within comes through communion with the Shabd alone. Nature with all her evanescent charms ceases to have attraction for the renouncer. By renouncing everything, one penetrates into the all-pervading spirit. His attachment to matter is ended. Thus, no more births and deaths await him. Hereafter the life of the senses and the glamour of the world fascinates him not, on his way to the Lord.

Detachment in attachment is also attained only with the aid of Shabd. Whatever he does, he does with the sense of duty with no attachment to the fruit thereof. The root cause of misery lies in the fact of one's attachment. We are caught by whatever we do—in our inability to detach ourselves from everything. We must reserve the power to remain detached from all things, however precious they may be, or however much one may yearn for them.[58]

When once the life-stream becomes audible, one never feels lonely; for he hears its reverberations wherever he may be, at home or abroad. The Voice of God keeps reminding him of the true home of his Father. The practice of the Sound Principle rids one of all troubles and afflictions, the five deadly passions, the lusts of the flesh and of the mind, leaving the soul in pristine transparency, detached from all that is of the world and worldly. Shabd is the supporting staff both in the journey of this life and of the life hereafter. With the experience of transcendence beyond the confines of the body, he becomes fearless of death and when the allotted span of worldly existence comes to an end, he throws off, once and for all the mortal coils of the flesh, as easily and happily as one does his old and worn-out garments, and is freed from the cycle of births and deaths and goes openly and honorably to his home in heaven. The practice of and the communion with the Word brings in the heaven's light and one feels divinely blessed. It gives intuitive knowledge of the self and of God and one experiences within himself the integral realization of the soul, as one common life principle extending everywhere, in and around him, without any barriers and limitations of time and space for all life is one, from eternity to eternity, irrespective of so many forms and patterns through which it may manifest. The moment one rises into the Timeless, he himself becomes timeless. This in fact is true meditation and true devotion leading to the true love of God and His creation, his own self expanding and coinciding with that of his Creator.[59]

*By communion with the Word one can attain
the status of a Siddha, a Pir, a Sura, or a
Nath;*

*By communion with the Word, one can under-
stand the mysteries of the earth, the supporting bull and the heavens;*

*By communion with the Word, the earthly re-
gions, the heavenly plateaux and the nether
worlds stand revealed;*

*By communion with the Word, we can escape
unscathed through the portals of Death;*

*O Nanak, His devotees live in perpetual ecsta-
cy, for the Word washes away all sin and
sorrow.*[60]

*By communion with the Word, one can attain
the powers of Shiva, Brahma and Indra;*

*By communion with the Word, one can win
esteem from all irrespective of one's past;*

*By communion with the Word, one can have
yogic insight with the mysteries of life and
self all revealed;*

*By communion with the Word, one can acquire
the true import of the Shastras, Smritis and
Vedas;*

O Nanak, His devotees live in perpetual ecsta-

Siddha: A man endowed with super-natural powers. *Pir*: A Muslim
divine or a spiritual teacher. *Sura*: Gods. *Nath*: Yogin—an adept in
yoga. *Supporting bull*: (dhaul), it is the fabled bull, supposed to be
supporting the earths and heavens. *Shastras*: The philosophical trea-

*cy, for the Word washes away all sin and
sorrow.*[61]

*By communion with the Word, one becomes
the abode of Truth, contentment and true
knowledge:*

*By communion with the Word, one gets the
fruit of ablution at sixty-eight pilgrimages;*

*By communion with the Word, one wins the
honour of the learned;*

*By communion with the Word, one attains the
state of Sehaj;*

*O Nanak, His devotees live in perpetual ecsta-
cy, for the Word washes away all sin and
sorrow.*[62]

*By communion with the Word, one becomes
the abode of all virtues;*

*By communion with the Word, one becomes a
Sheikh, a Pir and a true spiritual king;*

*By communion with the Word, the spiritually
blind find their way to Realization;*

*By communion with the Word, one crosses be-
yond the Limitless Ocean of illusionary
Matter;*

*O Nanak, His devotees live in perpetual ecsta-
cy, for the Word washes away all sin and
sorrow.*[63]

tises of the Hindus. *Vedas*: The earliest books of human thought.
Sehaj: This term refers to the state, when the turmoil of the physical,
astral and causal worlds with all their enchanted panorama, are transcended and the Great Principle of Life is seen within.[64]

Helping Factors

You would have true knowledge, if you transcend the sense knowledge. Enter the inner silence, and this silence will become vocal. With longing in your eyes enter within from without. This is the central message of every True Master. In your own house you will see Him. Therefore, I would request that you gaze longingly into your heart, with silence in your heart, with silence in your soul, and with no thought of this world or the next. The grace of God will descend on you and the gaze will grow into a glimpse and He will reveal Himself to you, and you will see Him within yourself.[65]

You will please appreciate that it is the constant thought of worldly pursuits which has been the cause of present human birth, and for attaining liberation from the cycle of birth and death, the very thought pattern is to be revolutionized by replacing it with divine thoughts. Loving remembrance of the Master and repetition of names serve as very helpful factors for having the withdrawal of sensory currents from the body below, when the inner process of contemplation on the divine lights and eventually the charming Radiant Form of the Master commences.[66]

Sitting in sweet remembrance of the Master is exactly what the words imply. There is no technology involved in it. It is simple enough—a feeling of deep-seated love naturally created within or a longing. The quiet solitude of a place can be helpful to meditation. Service to the beloved Master is one of the potential factors that help to cleanse the vessel of a person, and it is a powerful aid in getting within. To go within is the first and foremost duty of a disciple, and this can be achieved through the grace of the Master which in turn is hastened by the disciple living a life of love, service, and meditation, for they are linked and co related to each other.[67] Wherever you are, you can at best serve the Master and the best service which earns His pleasure is sincere meditations. An example is better than precept. This is the best dedication and has its own unrivaled reward.[68]

You should try to forget all about your mind and I-ness. It is simply your harping on it and feeding its ego by constantly thinking about it, which disturbs you. You must know that regular meditations replace the vicious qualities of the mind with virtuous ones and gradually culminate in rising above vice and virtue both. Go placidly amid the noise and haste and remember what serene peace and harmony awaits you within during meditations. Such an attempt shall bless you with profound joy and bliss. Nurture strength of spirit to shield you in all spheres of life. Never feel disturbed with imaginings.[69]

You must know it for certain that the life of an initiate is fully controlled by the gracious Master Power for his spiritual progress. Those who relish to meditate regularly and inculcate a keen sense of self-abnegation by surrendering their will to that of the Divine Will of the Master enjoy perpetual bliss and harmony. Whatsoever comes to your count is a blessing in disguise and should be accepted cheerfully. AVOID HURRY AND WORRY. Instead just learn to do one thing at a time and that too with single-minded attention and devotion. All bliss and joy lies in the concentrated attention at the eye focus and if you will develop this technique, your entire life will be changed and dyed in the color of divinity, with the grace of the Master.[70]

You need not dwell much on your personal character or impurities of mind. It amounts to self-pity. You will please appreciate that by watering the seedling at the roots, the plant thrives most and blooms in abundance. The holy Naam is the tried panacea for ills of mind. Although it is a very happy augury to be conscious of one's shortcomings, undue apprehension sometimes breeds morbidity which hampers progress. The conscious contacts with divinity within revolutionizes the thought pattern of the child disciple and he sees everything in much clearer perception. Slow and steady wins the race. Your job is to be implicitly obedient and humbly dedicated. It is for Him to reward you for your efforts. Patience is the noblest virtue but is the fruit of very long cultivation. Just learn to live in the living present and with undivided attention and devotion. You should train your mind in such a manner that when you do anything required of you, there is no hurry, compulsion or resentment from your side. You will find that it will be helpful to you in all your spheres of life including meditations.[71]

Depression and despair breed in egoistic hearts. If you will inculcate a keen sense of humility by self-abnegation and effacement, you will enjoy more ineffable bliss and harmony. Humility is the sheet anchor with the dear ones. It is an adoration of the Saints who work in this physical plane by keeping their divinity hidden from the public gaze. How safe and sublime it is to work humbly on behalf of the Master, by rolling on all credit to Him. You are a personal testimony of the sacred truth that when you work for the Master for channelizing the divine grace, how graciously you are compensated. The golden principle of attributing all success to the Master Power and failure towards your own personal weaknesses to be overcome gradually, should be followed lovingly. Ego is a human element. It is annihilated very slowly by meditating on Sound Current and Light Principles. Gradually it will dawn upon you that you are a doll in the hands of divine powers dancing to His bid.[72] Complete surrender to His Will and Pleasure is the surest and safest way for inner inversion and the journey on to the realms of pure bliss and unalloyed harmony.[73]

It is quite natural and logical, just as one goes up in an electric elevator unaided and without effort, similarly the soul currents are withdrawn to the eye-center.[74] With a calm mind sit in exercises. Trikuti is in the mind range. When the attention catches and follows the Sound Current the mind is dormant and out of action; at all other times when the attention is off the current the mind gets the upper hand.[75] You need not struggle for staying at the eye focus when you withdraw quickly. You have simply to relax fully, repose joyously and resign to the divine will and pleasure of the Master and go into the Beyond. The innermost deep silence of the heart coupled with a burning anguish of the soul will invoke more divine grace.[76] You must silence your thoughts during meditation. The silencing of the intellect is the last nail in the coffin. You should not wish to have one thing or another. Simply sit at the door and wait. The sublime silence is best and easily achieved by lovingly and humbly reposing in the gracious Master Power to grant and bless whatever is deemed fit. That benign power is incessantly with you and is quite aware of your earnest efforts. But so long as you are conscious of your actions, you stand in your own way and when you lovingly eliminate yourself, He will manifest to you in the form of celestial manifestations of Divine Light and holy Sound Current. It is something like inviting someone to enter the room while you are blocking the way by standing in the doorway.[77]

He or she is not to presuppose things or visualize results, for those will follow of their own accord. We have but to sit in loving remembrance, with steady gaze fixed in between and behind the two eyebrows, and do mental repetition of the Five Holy Words, without any exertion or strain on the eyes, or on the forehead. Ours is to be an attitude of passivity, for the Doer is one and only One: the Master, who is the best judge for the time and measure and manner of each step on the path.[78]

The meditation practices should be an easy, natural and enjoyable process, wherein you could sit for extended hours. So please try to avoid such faith-shakes as will distract your thoughts from the Path until you have progressed sufficiently and grown strong within so as to become immune to receiving unhelpful impulses and be able to radiate your own loving thoughts and impulses. This is a period where one has to be very vigilant. So please carry on in faith and regularity. The Master Power is over your head extending all feasible help.[79]

So when you sit in meditation, forget the world, and let the Guru alone be before you and you before him— there should be nothing else. When our Muslim brothers sit for prayer, they spread a prayer-mat in front of them to remind them that there is nothing between God and the devotee. Sit for practice in this way and you will not even be aware that you are withdrawing. This is the true way to realize God—to travel across the ocean of life.[80]

Some succeed in performing their spiritual disciplines in the prescribed manner in a short period, others do not for want of the conscious control of the mind and the outgoing faculties. This is why it has always been stressed to weed out all undesirable traits and habits, and to replace them by the opposite ennobling virtues; and for this, the maintenance of the monthly self-introspection diary is mandatory. The more you progress in man-making, the more your mind and senses will come under your conscious control.[81] The more you will try to eradicate the weaknesses in you and lovingly attend to Simran, Dhyan and Bhajan, the richer will be the extent of your experiences within.[82] Purity of life is essential for fruitful meditations.[83]

When the mind needs no other thing except the Master, He Who is always within draws the veil aside and appears. So it is a question of developing an intense desire for Him. This desire is aroused by meditation and by sweetly remembering Him in one's heart to the exclusion of all other things.[84]

Regularity

TO BE AN INITIATE is not enough. One has to be devoted regularly to meditation and develop from day to day. Lack of spiritual progress and remaining away from contacts where such inner progress is likely to be nourished, is apt to bring about a negative attitude under uncongenial influence.[85]

Hazur Baba Sawan Singh Ji said: ". . . no matter in what circumstances one finds himself and what new problems one is facing, a devotee should not miss his Bhajan. He may give only fifteen minutes or even five minutes to it daily, but he should be on it without a break.[86] Spiritual meditations are the food for the soul and should not be missed. A day put off backs your progress considerably. These practices should please therefore be performed faithfully, regularly and sweetly. They are designed as a first step to take your soul up above your body inwardly to the Radiant Form of the Master, who will then guide you and take you further up, step by step, till your goal is reached. Thus you will see the difference between the rituals performed within the domain of the body and senses and those that take you above the body consciousness.[87]

Spiritual inheritance counts greatly for everybody's inner progress, yet earnest and persistent efforts put in under the protective guidance of the Living Master never go in vain and in due course of time bring in much fruit and that too in abundance. You should know it for certain that everything is being recorded behind the veil, and the gracious Master Power is fully aware of your innermost aspirations.[88] Each bit laid up for spiritual discipline counts creditably toward your inner progress. The cumulative result of your devotion will bring forth very good results in due course and at the proper time, with the grace of the Master.[89]

You should always hie on your Holy Path irrespective of worldly gains or losses. You will appreciate that after all everything is to be left behind at the final hour of death, and only the Holy Naam will accompany us into the Beyond. You know very well the supreme importance of regular meditations. The more you are developed while living here, the more of the inner journey is covered in the Beyond. Know it for certain that you are here in this mortal world only for enjoying the rare bliss of Holy Naam. God and Master (God in man) first; all else secondary.[90]

Try to do one thing at a time. If you exercise discipline in all of your affairs, your progress will not be retarded by any amount of extra responsibilities you may have. Try to put in regular hours undisturbed by any thoughts of the material things about you.[91] Proficiency demands persistent and earnest efforts.[92]

When He gives you something, increase it through daily meditations. We do not like to do it and say we haven't got the time, but remember you have to die for yourself; no one else will do it for you.[93]

It is said that those who do not do Bhajan will never be free from misery: lethargy will constantly torment them. They are always lazy. When does this procrastination come and when does it go? For the negative work he is all attentiveness; while waiting on the Naam, he slumbers. To gratify the senses, he is wide awake and ready—even at midnight. But for Bhajan . . . "not now, we will see tomorrow." This is mainly due to his regular association with outer enjoyments; he has inclination toward them. He has done little or no Bhajan to speak of, has not drunk deep enough to enjoy its sweet nectar, and therefore feels disinclined. With lethargy, procrastination becomes the thief of time . . . "Not just now, wait awhile . . . we will do it tonight, no, tomorrow morning . . . let us just finish this work, and then . . ." The tragic result? If you put off the moment, the other moment which one imagines will be more opportune, will never come. If one becomes lazy, then laziness will induce sleep. If your meditation is not fruitful, how will you know what is inside? Even when at initiation through the mercy of the Master something is seen within, yet a man will start thinking it is all imagination. This is how the mind hoodwinks us, with the result that the soul recedes into the enjoyments and scatters its attention.[94]

Whatever the matter, however preoccupied with outer duties, the disciple must find some time every day—be it ever so little, for Bhajan. Only through maintaining the link with Shabd can anything be gained and once a disciple has strengthened the link through constant practice the inner music flows in incessantly at all hours of the day becoming a clarion-call forever inviting within and deftly lifting him like a silken robe from off the thorns of earthly desires.[95]

Get the full benefit of meditation, and increase it day by day. The more you increase it, the nearer will you advance toward your goal. If you refuse, the day will come when you will be filled with regret for the lost opportunity. It is all a very simple matter of fact, and outer show of respect will achieve nothing. Learn to obey implicitly —this is the secret in a nutshell.[96]

Create New Habits

MIND, like fire, is a very good servant but a bad master. It has got one of the best attributes which can be harnessed for spiritual benefit. It relishes to run into its grooves of habit, and if you will do some acts regularly at the fixed hour every day for some days continuously, you will find that a habit is formed, and it finds pleasure in doing the same thing automatically. So when the mind is diverted towards spiritual practices, by undertaking meditations at the appointed hours for some time regularly, you will find that the same mind which resents inversion will relish it, with the grace of the Master. The divine manifestations granted by the Master are superbly charming to entrap it, when it will leave aside its vicious attributes.[97]

Grow the nails of regularity. An army without a commander will end up in chaos, so we must command our lives with regularity. If you are employed somewhere, you go there daily at the proper time without any trouble, and for meditation we should adopt the same attitude and sit daily at the regular time. Sadly, we are adrift; sometimes we sit, sometimes we don't. If we were truly regular, we would find that if we should happen to have a day without meditation, we would feel ill at ease, as though we had missed something. If possible, there should be a room in the home set aside for God's remembrance alone—you would find that the very atmosphere of that room would remind you of Him.[98]

The very early morning hours are best suited for meditation, as all thoughts subside during the night's rest and the food has been digested.[99] Rise early every day, and do your meditation.

> *Rise before sunrise, and repeat the Naam;*
> *All negative effects will be mitigated, O Nanak.*

Early morning is the most beneficial time for meditation.

> *Supreme oneness of thought upon the True*
> *Naam is had at the ambrosial small hours*
> *before dawn.*

So rise early and shake off all feeling of sloth. Go into the remembrance of Him even if you are lying down— even at night, or when resting. Go to sleep with the same thought, so that the very remembrance of Him will be the very beat of your pulse. When you arise in the morning, be awakened—have a bath or wake yourself by any means, but be really awake when you sit down for meditation. With these habits, even in sleep your meditation will continue, and when awake, even then you will have that meditative attitude all day.[100]

The quiet solitude of a place can be helpful to meditations. Service to and for the beloved Master is one of the potential factors that helps to cleanse the vessel of a disciple and aids in going within. To go within is the most important part of the sacred teachings, and this can be achieved only through the grace of the Master, which in turn is hastened by one's living a life of love, service and meditation. Thus they are linked and co-related to each other.[101]

No one is nearer to you than your Master. There is no need to run to mountains, though quiet surroundings do help in peaceful meditation.[102] If you have noise in your own place, you may find some monastery or church nearby where you can have more peace and quiet to carry on your meditations.[103]

In the future we should learn a lesson and not destroy the purity of our surroundings by our sinful actions—especially those places meant for meditation. Swami Vivekananda said that if we repent the sins we commit in the worldly places, God will forgive us, but He will never forgive the sins which are committed in holy places. So when you go to a sacred place, keep your thoughts pure and turned toward God alone.[104]

The Light and Sound are so efficacious that if absorbingly attended to, the mind will be stilled. You may say some prayer before your meditation creating an aura which would serve as hemming all around you and you will feel the presence of the Master to your great joy. Please remember that mind itself is inert and takes life from spirit, which, when attuned to the inner manifestations, becomes calm.[105]

Spiritual Background Plays a Part

SPIRITUAL evolution is something personal and each one brings with him or her past background to progress, all under the protective guidance of the Living Master.[106] All is dependent upon the background, the earnestness, the love and devotion that a person will put into the spiritual practices. The divine treasures are for all, whether rich or poor. Master's loving help accelerates progress.[107]

Is the nature and extent of our spiritual growth or advancement beyond the tenth door determined by our past lives? Yes—in a way it is determined. A man is in the making. One who passed primary class will get admission to the next grade. One who has just been put on the way will take his or her own time. However, there is no hard and fast rule about it. The one who has been put on the way progresses more by regular devotion of time to meditations with full faith than one with a different background who is not regular in his meditations.[108]

It is incorrect to think that spiritual progress cannot be had for at least five years. Those who are not ready, are neither led to the gracious Living Master nor are they initiated into the Mysteries of the Beyond. Those who are initiated get some experience of Light and Sound to start with. However, progress does vary according to the past background and because of this some may progress rapidly and others lag behind. But there is sure hope for everybody. It is a simple, yet arduous schedule which is made much easier by the grace of the Master.[109] Even if He gives a little at the beginning, then there is hope for much more; and whatever He gives, protect it with your life.[110]

Time Element for Development

"ONCE ONE meets a competent Satguru, one learns the complete inner way and launches on the spiritual journey," Baba Ji would say. "There is then only the liquidation of give and take that limits its flight. The soul is not then pure enough to catch the Divine Shabd and must be first freed of all karmic reactions. The Satguru must free it from the chain of karmas in this life itself so as to safeguard against the necessity of taking further births for their repayment."[111]

You need not feel sceptic over your restricted inner progress but try to be more accurate and earnest. It is inner longing of the soul and intense loving devotion which blesses the child disciple with fruitful meditations. You will grow gradually in due course.[112]

There should be no clutching on your part to have one thing or the other. Simply sit in an attitude of humble supplication, having full confidence in the competency of the Master to grant you that which is in your best interests at the time. It is up to Him to give and not for us to demand.[113]

Matter and mind are subject to change, but there is
no change in spirit. Mind is not such a thing that can
be switched off and on at will. It cannot be taken away
from its routine course, in spite of one's best efforts, in
a day, or a month, or a year. It is a life's struggle. Those
who have conducted this struggle or are engaged in
struggle understand what it is to struggle with the mind.
Look at the coarseness of the mind. It is son, daughter,
wife, husband, parent, wealth and property, attachment,
greed, lust, anger, pride, and what not. It is attached to
the outside world with ropes, double ropes, triple ropes,
and many-fold ropes. It has been held by these chains
so long that it does not feel the irksomeness of these
chains. To the caged bird the captivity is the normal run
of life.[114]

You should not be skeptical about your inner progress, as such an attitude impedes progress. Please rest
assured that everything is being recorded carefully behind
the veil, and all your earnest efforts stand to your credit
spiritually. Thought is the keynote to success. It is the
thought pattern of the initiate which is changed gradually when he or she feels overall protection and guidance
from the Master Power in all spheres of life.[115] Everything that comes to you in the divine dispensation is
invariably right for your spiritual progress.[116]

Patience and Perseverance

THE SECRET to success on the Path is practice, more practice and still more practice.[117]

Your complaint that the mind wanders during exercises is the complaint made by almost every practitioner in the early stages. The mind feels pleasure in roaming at large and does not like to give up its liberty until it has attained to higher pleasure in exchange for its present enjoyments. But constant practice will force it to give up its former habits.[118]

Just see how simple and easy it looks, but it requires much perseverance and steadfastness for attaining proficiency on the Path. You are simply to maintain a reverential silence within for enjoying the full fruits of the Divine Grace, which will manifest itself in great abunddance. Please note that if you call at the door of some rich man and await regularly for some days continuously, he will one day surely ask you the purpose of your daily calls on him. It is but a worldly example, and if you mentally wait at the celestial door of the Divinity, accurately and with firm patience and all humility, don't you think that He will respond to your supplications? Most surely He will. You just wait patiently and see within.[119]

So I wish for you to tread the Path having full faith and confidence in the Master, and above all, be grateful that you have been accepted for Initiation in this difficult age we are living in. Persevere, persevere, and persevere again. Perseverance combined with full faith in the gracious Master Power working overhead will one day remove all obstacles, and your cherished goal will be achieved.[120] But the time factor is a necessity, patience is a necessity, perseverance is a necessity. It will not happen in one day.[121]

Simran

SIMRAN of the basic names of God has an inevitable influence on the mind. It leads to Dhyan, making the spirit forgetful of the world and worldly objects. In meditation nothing but concentrated Simran remains and from the great and deep silence of the heart (Hriday Kamal of the Saints; i.e., the Divine Ground behind the eyebrows) there issues forth a ceaseless Sound Current, which helps in pulling the spirit up, leading to the withdrawal from the body (without of course breaking the silver cord) and guides the spirit in its journey into various spirit realms. The luminous form of the Master always remains with the spirit helping and guiding it at every step. This Sound Principle is the link between God and Man and in this way an indissoluble bond and relationship is established between the Creator and His creation.[122]

The repetition of names at intervals has a significance as stated above. It is a safeguard against the untoward and impeding factors which beset the Path, and helps the sensory currents from the body below to withdraw to the eye center without any strain on the part of the child disciple. The attention should be riveted penetratingly into the middle of what you see before you. If the repetition of the names mentally is done constantly, the attention will be divided. The gaze should be fixed constantly, and repetition done at intervals, simply to guard against any negative effect and help the process of withdrawal from the body.[123]

The basic names of God have the power to dispel the forces of darkness that may meet and assail a spirit on its onward journey. Simran of these names helps the soul both in the physical plane and supra-physical plane, one after the other. Hence it is imperative that Simran be done of such names as the Master Soul enjoins, for they are charged with a tremendous spiritual power which negative powers can hardly put up with and from which they flee as from an enchanter driven. Immortal and everlasting as these words of the Master are, they bestow life everlasting to the soul in which they sink and take root.[124]

The sacred charged words carry the life impulse of the Master and their repetition with deep faith and single-minded devotion, feed the soul with gradual consciousness, and leave behind indelible impressions over it. Even if you fail to see anything within during your meditations, you should resort to faithful Simran, which will be like tilling the soil, to be prepared for the bumper crop of Spirituality, which will be watered well with the gracious mercy of the Master, and the Holy Seed of Initiation will fructify in due course.[125] As soon as mind begins to roam away, stop it by Simran (repetition).[126] Be strong in your Simran; it will remove all difficulties. You will

become bold and fearless. You will see within so many
rivers, mountains—you will cross them by flying over
them. Simran will enable you to fly over them.[127]

Withdrawal: Rising Above Body Consciousness

THE ABC STARTS where all philosophies end. It is a
matter of seeing, of rising above body consciousness,
of experiencing for one's self. The highest aim is to rise
into God consciousness. That will come only when you
know yourself, who you are. You are not the man-body,
you are dwelling in the man-body, the highest rung in
all creation. We have to make the best use of it and that
is: how we can be out of it. For this purpose, Masters
always advise us to rise above body consciousness. "Learn
to die so that you may begin to live." You will have the
right spectacles to see through if you do this. Everything
will appear in its right perspective. This is why all Masters have said: "Know thy Self!"[128]

The withdrawal of sensory currents from the body below with the aid of repetition of the charged names or
listening to the holy Sound Current as coming from the
right side is the normal feature of meditations. You may
understand it more clearly: suppose there is a roof with
a hundred stairs and unless you cross all the hundred
steps, you cannot reach the top, even if you reach the
ninety-ninth. You are under the roof and not on its top.
As you approach nearer to the roof, you have more and
more light. Similarly, the withdrawal of the sensory
currents up to the eye-focus demands complete cessation

of outgoing faculties and focusing the inner attention at the center between and behind the two eyebrows.

The sacred process is to be undertaken in a state of effortless effort. If you are completely riveted within at the eye-center and are not watching the process of withdrawal, you will find that you will be completely withdrawn with little or no effort on your part, without any feeling, just as a hair is taken out of butter. When you are withdrawn completely or even partially, you may see into the middle of what you see in front of you, and the intellect should be stilled for the time being when the inner vision will open.[129]

If you do your practices accurately, you will rise above body consciousness. The body is not you. You will begin to have experience of the Beyond. You have to leave the body. This fate awaits everybody and there is no exception to the rule. But with all that, we are afraid of death. Death is only a change, just as the sun sets on one side of the world and rises on the other. Similarly, we leave this physical world and rise into the Beyond. This is a practical question, and if somebody gives you a demonstration of rising above body consciousness, you should develop it from day to day. If you just have that angle of vision by rising above body consciousness, you will always be conscious in knowing that this is not your home. The Home of the soul is the Home of our Father. We are fortunate in having the man-body, in which we can go back to the Home of our True Father. This cannot be done in the lower orders of creation. The man who learns to die, to leave the body at will, gets everlasting

life, never to return. All glory and beauty lie within you.
The astral planes are more beautiful than the physical
one. The causal plane is still more beautiful, and the
spiritual planes beyond are the most beautiful of all.
Those who have experience of the Beyond would naturally like to go there, but they are bound. Even the Masters are playing their role. They want to go back, but
they are bound by order. They have to carry on.[130]

In meditation, when you rise above body consciousness, the body gets complete rest, and your consciousness
increases. When you resume the body, it is recharged
and gets a fresh lease on life.[131]

You are fortunate to have been taught how to take up
your cross daily so as to rise above body-consciousness
and be reborn into the Kingdom of God which is within
you. Learn to stay longer in the Beyond and enjoy the
bliss of the Kingdom of God within you.[132]

Guru Dev: Radiant Form of the Master

ONCE THE MIND has been brought under control and
it no longer doubts and wavers, "Then the Radiant
Form of the Master appears within. There is no difference between it and the physical form. It is like a reflection in a clear mirror. So long as the glass is not clear,
nothing can be seen reflected."

The mind was indeed a glass, which when sullied by
the muck-flow of worldly attachments blurred and hid
everything, but the moment this film was cleansed, it
imaged the Universal in itself.[133]

The term Guru Dev, therefore, signifies the self-luminous form of the Master, which is free from and far above his physical body, and which the spirit actually perceives with its inner subtle Light. When the spirit comes face to face with the astral Master, all doubts vanish and its labors get the crowning regard—the *summum bonum* of life.

This subtle form disengaged from the bodily form of the Guru is termed Guru Dev. It is self-luminous and lustrous with Light extending over miles and miles. Satguru or the Master of Truth is the Power of Truth or God that works through both Guru and Guru Dev. With roots firmly embedded in Sat, or Truth, he directly derives his inspiration from the eternal and unchangeable permanence, Sat, hence is known as Satguru.

Guru Dev meets and greets the spirit as it crosses the border lying between the physical and subtle regions by passing through the stars, the sun and the moon, spoken of in the Vedas as Devian and Pitrian Margs (Paths). This astral form is exactly like the physical form of the Master, but much more beautiful, luminous, and magnetic. Guru Nanak refers to this illuminated path, thus:

The Luminous Form of the Master is won-
drously enrapturing and enchanting. Only a
perfect Master can manifest this to a spirit.

This lustrous form of the Master always accompanies a spirit in the various planes, ending with Sach Khand or the Home of Truth. When His luminous form descends to the focus of the eyes, a devotee has nothing more to strive for. Herein lies the devotion of the devotee.

Half his success has been achieved, and hereafter the Master's astral form takes over the charge of the spirit with full responsibility for leading it to the final goal. Even the Saints also adore this form and derive ecstatic delight from it.

The manifestation of Guru Dev depends purely on the grace of God and one's special merits in one's progress on the spiritual path.[134]

There is hardly any need to imagine or visualize the Master's Form while engaged in *Simran*. Any such attempt is likely to scatter the attention. Then there is another danger in doing so. What form you conjure up, will be a make-believe, a projection of your mind and not reality. When one is initiated the Master resides in the initiate for all time. What is already inside will automatically come into view when you get in there fully and completely, though it may take quite some time to adjust yourself to the new surroundings, unknown before. God manifests of Himself more fully in some human form in which He is working without any visualization.[135] It is really a happy day for an initiate to meet his or her Radiant Master within. The enjoining by the Master of regular meditations and stressing the need for living a life of love and purity are intended to make the way clear for the initiates. It is not their efforts alone that will bring them success in their uphill task, but the loving and willing surrender and faithful repose with which they sit and obey the commands.[136]

Once the soul had won access to the Master in his Radiant Form within, its major task was over. The rest was a matter of time. It could of course be taken directly to higher planes by the Satguru, but he worked out the progress gradually for else, as was the case with an insistent Pundit, the shock and strain of it would be too great.[137] When you join the Master inside, you will be able to perceive all things, from the beginning to eternity.[138] The Master talks with His disciple face to face in all the planes and gives him wise counsel in times of need.[139]

A disciple should never be content until he or she contacts the Master within, face to face, in His Luminous Form and talks to Him as one ordinarily does without. You should gather up all your thoughts to gain this end as early as possible, for then alone all your worries will come to an end.[140]

Difficulties in Meditation

Why is it so difficult to hear Shabd?

SHABD IS reverberating in all Universes seen or unseen. The human soul and Holy Shabd are of the same Divine Essence. Those who develop their Inner Consciousness by regular, faithful and accurate meditations can listen to this Heavenly Melody any time they choose to do so. The novices do feel some trouble in focusing their attention at the eye center and controlling their vibrations and thoughts carefully. Besides, those who speak much and waste their precious energy in idle and loose talk cannot listen to this Heavenly Melody. It is the inner single-minded devotion and attention which grants this rapturous listening. Practice undertaken with

perseverance and steadfastness invokes Divine Grace and
the initiate can listen to the holy *Shabd Dhun*.[141] It is the
scattered attention of the initiate which does not allow
him to hear the holy Sound Current. Besides, the overwhelming attachment to worldly pleasures and sense
gratification stand in the way. The Living Master is Love
Personified, and as such, loving devotion to Him is the
factor which makes for better inner contact of the Audible Life Stream. It is rather the tendency of human mind
which does not relish being chained and as such it requires some discipline to be observed for having an inner
conscious contact of the celestial melody. At the outset it
is indeed difficult but by regular practice the soul feels
an innate affinity with the Sound Current, when inner
bliss is experienced with the grace of the Master.[142]

*Q. Why does one put off practicing Shabd when it is
so very essential for spiritual progress?*

A. Human mind is fashioned as such by Providence
that it resents silence and stillness at its center—back
between the two eyes. It is an agent of Negative Power
attached to each human soul and relishes externality. It
does not relish introversion. Besides, it is fond of sensuous
pleasures, which cannot be eschewed easily. It is the
gracious protection of the Living Master that He grants
the conscious contact of this Heavenly Melody, yet the
Satsangis do not pay proper heed to this most important
aspect of spiritual discipline. It may be added that the
dear ones who are engrossed in the pursuit of gross pleasures of flesh and matter seldom take to the Holy Path,
and if perchance some of them may happen to be led

to the Master and be granted Initiation, due to some past karmic evolution, they do not relish this spiritual discipline.

Human body is just like a radio set wherein these Divine Melodies are being received by all living. The Living Master is the One who can repair our damaged sets and grant us the knob and wave-length at which this Heavenly Song can be heard. Regularity and steadfastness coupled with untiring selfless service in a spirit of dedication are the chief helping factors for practicing this spiritual discipline.

Mind has a varying set of tricks to unloose on the initiate for evading this listening. Sometimes it poses as a friend to coax the disciple by putting forth family obligations, etc., and the dear one is caught in the noose of attachment. At other times it stands up in tough fight like a formidable foe. Besides, the temptations of worldly pleasures keep the mind constantly swinging and wavering. The only point where it can find rest is at the eye-center, the seat of the soul. The putting off of practicing Shabd is an age-old malady of the human mind for which divine grace of the Master is most essential.[143]

You are advised to hold fast to your meditations with religious regularity even if you feel confused on mundane affairs or overtaken by your mind. Please note that these are the tricks of the negative power which keep the dear ones snared in outer confusion and results in the wastage of precious time at your disposal. Catch time by the forelock and never relax your mind to be indulgent in gloom or sadness. It is during these moments of sheer bliss and harmony when your soul is charged with divine impulses and new vistas of right understanding open for your gratuitous joy.[144]

At present every soul has, on account of constant association with mind, acquired a tendency to flow downward and outward through the outgoing faculties. It is because of this, that she cannot catch the Sound Current (the Elixir of Life) within. A cup turned upside down may for ages remain in the rain but not a drop will fall into it. But if it is turned aright, it will get filled up in one or two showers. Exactly is it the case with the soul. As soon as the Master Soul gives her a contact with the life-giving Sound Current by turning it aright through the withdrawal of the sensory current, the lotus-like cup of the spirit gets more and more water of Immortality until she gets drenched through and through and is saved forever.

Mind, you know, is ever after pleasures of one kind or another. But the pleasures of this world are all transitory and have always some sting at the bottom. "Our sincerest laughter with some pain is fraught," says an English poet.

This renegade of the mind can only be subdued if some internal pleasure of rapturous strains of the Divine Music—the Word—is given to it in lieu of the external ones. When mind tastes the sweet Elixir, it is diverted from the worldly enjoyments and is subdued. The soul becomes free.[145]

You have mentioned regarding your introspection diaries—that when others are progressing on the Way, why should it not be so in your case. Meditation is a matter of love and devotion; it is meant to cleanse the vessel of all inner dirt and filth. Unkind thoughts, temptations for revenge, a pride of learning and knowledge, lurking doubts and skepticism, distrust of God and lack of faith in Him are some of the formidable barriers that stand in the way and prevent His grace and blessing from flowing in. Meditation done in an accurate way and with regularity, giving proper time with love and devotion, does bring good results and in abundance.[146]

What are the waves which oscillate in the ocean of the mind? This happens because the senses are boiling over. From the eyes alone, 83 per cent of all impressions enter our being, and 14 per cent through the ears. The remaining three per cent enters through other sense organs. These impressions through the senses are so severe that they are perpetually at boiling rate; so our first lesson is to learn how to control the senses. When the senses are in control, only then will the mind be tranquil. When the mind is stilled, the intellect also becomes still, and the soul can have connection with the Oversoul. If you make three holes in a container, fill the container with muddy water, and then force air through these three holes, you will see that the water will churn and bubble. But if you put a little alum in that water, it will become crystal clear and still. So the alum of Naam will cut through the dirt of birth upon birth.[147]

Under the influence of the senses it is very hard to reach the gaggan (the seat of the soul in the body) or rise above body consciousness. If a man has even one strong desire, say that of lust, outwardly people may consider him to be a great soul, yet inwardly, he is dancing to the tune of that desire. Outwardly he may be impressing people in many ways, but inwardly, he is digging deeper that very pit into which he has fallen. Directly or indirectly he is drifting away from the Truth, and whatever he has learned has become null and void. So I humbly repeat that to become a human being is very difficult, whereas it is not difficult to realize the Lord. But the attention must persuade the mind to leave the senses and become proficient in the science of rising above into the Beyond. When the senses are won the five enemies will not attack. The five enemies are lust, anger, greed, attachment and ego. Furthermore, if the ten senses are controlled, the Light is manifest in that soul. God's Light will fully manifest itself in that body wherein the five gross and five subtle senses are fully under control.[148]

Two very powerful forces are anger and lust. They rule over everything. If the attention dwells on lust, the soul falls very low; in anger the ego expands. The soul cannot be linked with Naam until it withdraws inwardly and rises above the senses. Our attention has instead become like an image of the mind. We want to enjoy all the low, worldly things, yet we say we want the highest thing of all, the Nectar of Life! It is all wrong—how far do we think we can go? Do one thing at a time; but do not remain under this false impression. One Saint says, "Where there is Naam, there is no kam (lust)— where there is kam there is no Naam. Two cannot remain at once—light and darkness.

Most of our precious time is wasted in indulgence of

jealousies, ego, scandal, criticizing, backbiting, possessive-ness, etc. There are other degrading pitfalls, but remember that lust and anger are the most powerful, and a soul under their influence can never go very far within, for there is no tranquility, serenity or oneness. He who has no lust and anger is the image of God. Just think, the merest glance from such a person can still the mind and the undesirable things leave their hold for a while. The words that come forth from this rare personality are charged with his inner tranquility, so much so that men who hear them will also enjoy a serene stillness. It follows that air which passes close to ice will bring a refreshing coolness and the air which passes near the fire will give warmth. So whatever the inner condition of a person, so his words will be charged with that atmosphere—be it anger, lust, or a sweet tranquility. Out of the abundance of his heart, a man speaks.

Everyone, literate and illiterate alike, is trapped in the powerful grip of these two most damaging traits. You have been asked to fully understand this, perhaps a thousand times, and you still do not understand the danger. Still, when the mind suggests something, you say: "Yes Sir, whatever you say." Guru and God are very easily and quickly pushed aside. Very few people want to admit their mistakes, and with such conditions, salvation is very far away. To become a human being is most difficult; to realize God is not at all difficult. If only the soul would leave the senses and the mind, and come up above the body consciousness, it would achieve something great.[149]

The obstruction caused by petty things during meditation might be attributed to your sensitive nature. The reservoir of the subconscious mind is filled with worldly thoughts, impulses and instincts inherited from past lives. This must be drained out completely before it can be filled with love and devotion to the Lord-Master. Reverential humility and self-abnegation are ennobling virtues. The spiritual aspirants grow in Divine wisdom giving no credit to themselves as they revel in the superb bliss of Divine intoxication.[150]

Oftentimes ill health will not permit proper meditations. Such periods intervene in the liquidation of past karma, yet their severity and duration is toned down considerably with the grace of the Master.

You need not be skeptical about your progress, and instead be cheerful. You are doing your job and giving regular time to meditation. Each bit laid for the spiritual edifice counts creditably and will stand to your side in the long run.

Karmic liquidation is indeed a chief factor, for which the loving initiates are stressed the importance of disciplined life full of loving humility and piety. You will be blessed with increasing grace from the Master-Power working overhead.[151]

It is a natural desire of an initiate to rise high in the inner planes and meet within the Radiant and charming Master and enjoy His grace and blessings as well as the perfect peace and bliss of those regions.

Difficulties often block the Way. They must be overcome. You have a Strong One over your head. Take refuge in Him!

Why should a child ever feel shy in writing to his Father? Everyone who has learned to ride has experienced many a fall. To fall in sin is manly, but to remain there is devilish.

Please do not be disheartened. Do avoid uncongenial society and be regular and earnest in your meditation. Do your best and leave the rest to the Power overhead and do not worry. No amount of worry will help you. Let Him worry for you. You do your small part in humility.[152]

In regard to your difficulty in concentration which you say has increased since your initiation, you will be able to understand this from a parable narrated for your calm consideration. Mind is just like a horse tied with the fetters of matter and normally it dominates the spirit. Mind being the agent of the Negative Power, is quite satisfied so long as one continues all efforts in its domain, and does not resent stillness and concentration. When the mind is attuned within with the holy Initiation from a Competent Master, the rope is cut asunder, and the soul is set free to travel back into the realms of peace and harmony, which are beyond the scope of the Negative Power. So the impeding forces make a futile attempt to harbor the efforts of the spiritual aspirant, lest the soul is completely dis-encloaked from the bondage of mind and matter. The factors with which you are confronted are the normal features of a spiritual aspirant. They work as a blessing in disguise when one's sincerity and integrity are tested at every step, and one becomes more firm and resolute with the grace of the Master.[153]

You complain that during meditation thoughts of business keep creeping into your mind. This is because you seem not to have developed a proper habit of doing meditation correctly. I find that you have certain debts to clear, and that you must discharge your duties as a husband and as a father, and this requires that you work hard in your business. You should do this earnestly. Work is worship. But after a day's hard work it is time to draw a curtain. At that hour, maybe 8, 9, 10 or 11 at night, you should forget your business entirely considering that you have handed it over to the charge of Someone else more competent and powerful. Then relax, and relax completely. And whatever time you have, devote it without a break to the spiritual practices with full faith and love and with as much earnestness as you put into your business in an accurate way. Do not have any clutchings. Let the Master Power that is constantly with you, working over your head, bless and grant what It considers best. You should have pleasure on your part and leave the results to the Master overhead.[154]

So what is meant by "not doing the practices properly" is simply another way of saying that the one-pointed concentration preluding complete withdrawal to the eye focus has not yet been achieved by the dear ones.

You are the indweller of your own body, but are not yet its Master. Your servants, the mind and five senses, have usurped the throne on which your soul should sit. Until they are dis-possessed and placed in their rightful place as servants, they will not allow you to withdraw and go in. The Master within, like any loving father, is eagerly awaiting the day when you shall have set your house in order. He only requires one opportunity to snatch you from the prisonhouse of the body, and like an expert angler, once He has successfully hooked His fish, He will not allow it to escape until He has it safely in His basket.[155]

How to Overcome Inaccuracies in Meditation

I FIND THAT despite your best efforts, you are unable to have any perceptible inner experience. For locating the discrepancy and its cause, you should please find out the following:

1. Do you repeat the sacred charged Names orally? If so, it is to be replaced, though gradually and slowly, to the mental repetition. It may further be explained thus— suppose you met somebody some days earlier, and had a talk with him and you want to recollect it now. You will neither use the tongue nor speak again, but mentally you will have all the conversation repeated. This is the true form of repetition or Simran. The five holy Words are to be repeated mentally during meditation.

2. Do you remain conscious of the breathing process going on in your body? If so, it is to be eliminated as the breathing process starts from the navel center and ends in the nasal center, and as such you remain in the body during your meditations. This can be done by looking sweetly and intently within, back and behind the two

eyebrows, altogether oblivious of the body below or of the breathing going on in the body. You will agree that normally while doing work all day, reading or writing, coming or going, sitting or walking, eating or drinking, or even while talking, we are never conscious of the breathing going on. Similarly, during meditations, you are not to be conscious of it.

3. Do you feel any numbness or stiffness in your body during Simran practice? If so, it is equally important to be eliminated as discussed above. The sensory currents from the body below are graciously withdrawn to the eye-focus, not by the single-handed efforts of the disciple only, but by the loving grace of the Master Power working overhead for proceeding within. You should not watch the withdrawal process in the body but keep your inner gaze constantly fixed into the middle of what you see within. The practice of Simran is indeed a slow process, but when established with the grace of the Master, one reaches the eye-focus without any special effort. You will agree that it is the loving devotion and the anguished cry of the soul which invokes mercy and one gets attuned.

4. Do you silence your thoughts during meditation? Naturally, you will say "no." The silencing of the intellect is the last nail in the coffin. How it may best be eliminated is explained below:

You should not have any clutching tendency to have one thing or the other. Simply sit at the door and wait. This sublime silence is best and easily achieved by lovingly and humbly reposing in the gracious Master Power, to grant and bless you with whatever It deems fit. That benign Power is incessantly with you and is quite aware of your earnest efforts. But so long as you are conscious of your actions, you stand in your own way, and when you lovingly eliminate yourself, He will manifest Himself to you in the celestial manifestation of Divine Light and holy Sound Current. It is something like inviting somebody to enter the room while blocking the doorway by standing in it.

From the above I hope you will be able to locate the fault and will be able to remove it, with the grace of the Master. I quite appreciate your yearnings, but the fact remains that He, the Great within, will surely bless you at the opportune moment when He considers fit.[156]

What the Master tells you to do is not really difficult if you could but comprehend the simplicity of it. He tells you to sit in a position most comfortable to you, one in which you can sit the longest without moving; that while sitting in this position you are to remain wide awake with your attention directed at the seat of the soul behind and between the two eyebrows; that you are to look sweetly and serenely into the middle of the darkness in front of you, repeating the Simran of five charged names slowly and at intervals.[157]

If the dear ones were to do their spiritual practices correctly, with due regard to self-introspection, they would, as sure as two and two make four, rise above body consciousness and transcend into the Beyond, where the Inner Master is patiently waiting to greet His children at the threshold of the astral plane. But because they are unable to do this, even for a short while, they erroneously believe their meditations to be barren of all concrete results.[158]

Dangers and Pitfalls on the Way

WHILE SITTING during meditation, one may forget the repetition of the five holy Names. In such a case mind and Kal (the Negative Power) can deceive us. So, to be on guard, do not leave off repetition when withdrawn or in a sitting. If the Form of the Master remains while doing Simran, the disciple should listen to and accept the words of the Master as true. Often if we fail to repeat the five charged Words, the mind comes up before us in the form of the Master to deceive or to mislead us. When the real Master appears to the disciple, He will answer all questions asked of Him. No deceptive form will remain while the disciple is doing Simran. If any reply is given by the Master in dreams, that cannot all be true. The Master's Radiant Form appears to the disciple while he is in a conscious state, and He stands during Simran. The Negative Power at times may tell us things, but does not stand before the Five Names. He may pretend to be our Master. Such words must not be relied upon.[159]

When the soul withdraws, it traverses with the astral body into higher regions and sees figures. At that time you should repeat the Five Names. The figures will disappear. Only such persons will stand before you as Those from the Fifth Plane, and from These you will derive some benefit. Soul traverses here and there and sees many events which are transpiring elsewhere. But we should not waste our time in engaging ourselves in such things, as that will retard our spiritual progress. If you are regular in putting time into the spiritual practices, you will go ahead and surely meet the Master within, face to face.[160]

As regards vision, when you rise above body-consciousness, you may see visions in the astral planes. Do not engage in looking at them, but repeat the Five Names. Sometimes you may see lions and snakes appear. These are not forms of the Master of Love. A snake at times represents the mind. So do not pay any heed to it; it will not harm you. Sometimes the five passions—lust, anger, greed, attachment and ego, leave us in the form of a lion or little children. These things cannot retard the progress of a soul who is doing Simran of the five holy Names.[161]

As regards voices coming to you, you should pay no heed to them. Please ask the one concerned to appear to you and talk. If he turns up, repeat the Five Names. If he stands before repetition, only then listen to his voice. Generally, these voices come from the negative and should not be given any attention.[162]

To cross the mental world is not so easy as it may seem to the untrained in the mysteries of the Beyond. It is the most delusive world where even the Mahatmas and the Rishis with all their learning and tapas, fail to hold on to their own ground. What is there in that vast universe (of the three worlds) which Brahman would not like to offer to these earnest souls who try to escape through his domains and reach the True Home of their

Father! At every step, be it in the physical world, the astral or the mental, he tries to block the way of the aspiring souls. The great Prophets and Messiahs and all others have given their experiences of the fierce encounters that they had with Satan, Mara, Ahriman, the evil spirits—Asuras, Demons and their agents in countless ways, fair or foul, whereby they try to obstruct the way, to win over the seekers after Truth by assurances of worldly kingdoms and principalities; and if they do not succumb to these temptations, then by threats of violence by fire, thunder, earthquakes, heaven splittings, cloud-bursts, lightnings and what have you. It is in predicaments like these that one can only stand these trials when one has by his side his Guru or Murshid, for the Guru Power then draws and absorbs the disciple's soul into Himself and takes him along the path of "Ringing Radiance." For each soul the Brahman stakes his all, and does not yield, unless he is convinced that the seeker clings to the protection of the Master Power (Akal or Timeless).[163]

Please do not bother about the negative powers and instead dwell more on the divine protection of the Master Power by keeping yourself immersed in the loving remembrance of the Master. Love coupled with inner humility and self-effacement surmounts all such impediments whatsoever.[164]

Dry Spells

I AM GLAD to find that you are devoting some time for your holy meditations with the grace of the Master. The casual spells of dryness or vague feelings do intervene as a result of reaction of past Karma, when the child disciple should muster more of courage and determination in sticking to the sacred schedule or regularity. It may be pointed out for your information that during such periods the loving protection of the Master becomes more strong as you have felt with His grace. The holy meditations when undertaken in a spirit of dedication to the Master become more fruitful with His grace. Your earnest prayer for having regularity is appreciated. You should stick to your resolution carefully irrespective of mind's protests. You will succeed with His grace. Please note that the mind relishes the grooves of habit having formed out of its indulgence in acts of repetitive nature through senses. You are to change its attitude from downward to upward, and all else will come of itself. You are to lay the line track carefully and the powerful engine will run on it with the same speed and velocity. Let your mind be attuned to the holy Feet of the Master —the Supreme Guide, and try your level best to abide by His Holy Commandments.[165]

The intervening dry spells in meditation which the spiritual aspirant finds sometimes are a blessing in disguise when the inner devotion is fostered for a higher step. You need not worry about it, but instead be earnestly devoted to your holy meditations with renewed zeal and vigor. The gracious Master Power will be extending all feasible help, grace and protection.[166] Man is so constituted that he cannot for long remain at one level. He either progresses or slips back. You may judge for yourselves which way you are going by seeing how far your minds and senses are coming under your conscious control.

This is achieved not only by ethical living, but also by the inner help and strength you get every time you sit for your meditations. So, if no apparent inner headway is achieved, know it for sure that the ground is being watered. Every time you sit, you are creating a habit which one day the mind will accept as in its best interest, as opposed to its present habit of seeking enjoyment in outside things. Habit strengthens into nature, and this is the reason for the present difficulties experienced by the dear ones in their routine meditations. The habit of the mind in running after outside enjoyments has become natural to it. Therefore, it resents sitting in the quiet. By creating a new habit, you will, in time, change the nature of the mind from one seeking pleasure in things external to one thirsting for the bliss and sweetness to be had from things internal.[167]

Retarding Factors

THE DIVULGING of inner experiences to others except the Master or more advanced disciples affects one adversely and retards the inner progress. It has a significance. A rich man would like to control his hard earned riches lest it be noticed by others, who would become jealous of him. Similarly, the spiritual treasures achieved by the devotee need extra care and vigilance to be hid from others so that the same may remain safe and well-guarded—just as a sapling is eaten away by a passing goat, but when it has grown into a stalwart tree, an elephant cannot uproot it. Again, the adverse thoughts of others do affect the disciple. Moreover, others growing jealous will not be able to give him or her proper guidance. The laws of the physical plane demand that each must behave soberly and must not exhibit his or her extraordinary qualities which relate to higher planes, and as such the disciplined devotee is required to cultivate tolerance and humility. You can see that one narrating his or her personal experiences many a time becomes elated, thus invites the ego to take the upper hand, and pride has its fall as a result. On these basic grounds, the Saints made a Law to be strictly observed by one and all that the inner experiences must not be divulged, except to the Master who is competent to give proper guidance on the Way.[168]

Moreover, one should be very cautious to avoid falling into carnal enjoyments as that darkens the inner vision.[169]

At the time of initiation, you would have been warned and clearly told about the things that tend to help the progress in meditation and the things that stand in the way and retard spiritual progress. They are recapitulated below for your guidance:

"Disclosing inner experiences to anyone other than the Master, neglect from abstaining from prohibited diet (i.e. all meat, fish, fowl, eggs or intoxicants), gaps and defaults in any part of meditation, retard the progress."

You could not keep within yourself the new joy and beauty that the Master had given you and erred gravely in speaking about the same to ——. The reaction of ——'s mind caused doubts to creep into your mind. Be rest assured. The Master is always with you from the time of initiation, seeing and reacting to everything that an initiate does. St. Luke said, *Take heed that the Light which is within you is not darkened*. So now again with love and devotion, pray to the Master Power within to open your way. He will listen. He is not away from you. Your meditations will again become sweet. Great opportunities will open up.[170]

Mind: Definition

MIND-STUFF is made of a highly rarefied matter of *Satva* substance in the elements. Gossamer-like it spreads in the body with its tentacles deeply rooted in the senses, working through sense organs. Its base also goes far above, rooted as it is in the universal or cosmic mind *chid-akash*. It serves as a link between the material body and the conscious spirit or soul in the body which is enlivening both the mind and the body. Like fire, it is a good servant but a bad master.[171]

So long as the soul is in the mind zone it is a prisoner. It is engulfed by the mind and is subject to it and has to obey the dictates of the mind. The mind and the soul combined in their turn are locked up in forms—causal, astral, and physical successively. The mind feels shy of going in and coming in touch with the Sound Current, for there it loses its identity and freedom. Instead, it is prepared to go to the extent of sitting in trenches in the face of bullets to win a bottom victory, or will gladly face the risks of crossing the Atlantic to gain a name or establish a record.[172]

What constitutes desire? All conceptions in the mind are desires.[173] At present the mind desires those things it cannot get. When it realizes the Truth, the whole of Nature will be at its beck and call.[174]

Mind is nothing but a storehouse of *karmic* impressions coming down from the beginning of time in an endless series of incarnations. The body cannot but perform karmas, and karmas fashion the body and all that is of

the body and bodily relations. The entire world is a play
of karmic impressions stored in the mind by the people
of the world. This is why the world is termed as *mano
mai shrishti* or creation of the mind.[175] The mind by itself is not conscious. It is the consciousness of the soul
that the mind reflects.[176] Anyone whose soul is under the
mind's influence and control becomes an image of the
mind, for he forgets his true self. We call this ego or I-
hood for one thinks "I am everything."[177] God plus mind
is man and man minus mind is God.[178]

Intellect

What are the attributes of mind?

MIND HAS four facets or attributes: to wit, (1) *Chit*:
It may be likened to a lake in which countless
streams of impressions are imperceptibly pouring in all
the time. (2) *Manas*: It is the thinking faculty of the
mind which cogitates over such impressions as rise on to
the surface of the lake in the form of ripples and waves
just as the breeze of consciousness blows over the waters
of the *chit-lake* and sets in motion an endless chain of
thoughts one after the other. (3) *Budhi* or intellect: It
is the faculty of reason, ratiocination, discrimination and
finally decision, after considering the pros and cons as
presented by the *manas*. It is the grand arbiter that tries
to solve the problems of life which come before it.
(4) *Ahankar* or ego: It is the self-assertive faculty of
the mind for it likes to assume credit for all the acts done,
and thus prepares a rich harvest of karmas that keep

one moving up and down in the giant Wheel of Life.[179]

All actions leave an impression behind which dull minds fail to decipher. Only when the mind develops, and this it does when we travel within and upwards, the memory revives and the record becomes intelligible.[180]

Q. We have been taught in our Satsang that all thoughts that enter the mind during meditation register on the astral and take the form of karma for us. Would you please comment on this?

A. The thoughts continue feeding the mind and register impressions in the Chita—the subconscious reservoir of the mind, and serve as seed karma to fructify at a later stage. However, the thoughts entering the mind during meditations become more potent to bear fruit at the earliest opportunity, and as such are considered more violently harmful than those entering the mind in the normal waking hours. It should be attributed to the inner concentration during meditations when the mind becomes comparatively more sharp and one-pointed. The listening to the holy Sound Current as coming from the right side with rapturous attention and absorption therein burns away these seeds of karmas and renders them infructious to bear fruit.[181]

Attributes of Mind

What part does intellect play on the path?

VERY LITTLE, where the practical side is concerned. But this does not mean that intellect is harmful to Spirituality. If an intellectual man comes on this Path and really gives himself up to the Master's Will, and does what he is told, then there is no better disciple for this Path than he, for there he has an advantage over an ordinary practical man. And that advantage is he will be able to give out the Truth to others in many ways in a language made with well thought-out words that will convince the intellectualists more easily than simple words uttered by a mere practical man.[182]

Q. *Does intellect play any part in Self and God realization?*

A. Yes, intellect plays an important part in understanding the theory of the problem of Self-realization. Once the theory is grasped, there is not much left for the intellect to do. Thereafter remains the practice, with heart and soul, to achieve the Goal by a process of Self-analysis, for the Science of the Self is essentially practical.[183]

Q. *Can we penetrate into the Beyond by intellect?*

A. No, intellect is just one of the faculties of mind, to wit, reasoning. The intellect is earth-bound and so is reasoning based on intellect. "How can the less the greater comprehend or finite reason reach infinity."[184]

Q. *Can we be ever sure of God-realization intellectually?*

A. No. God-realization is not a subject of intellect. It is a question of actual experience, beyond the pole of knowledge. All our talk of God is but inferential and at the most a matter of feelings and emotions all of which are subject to error. But seeing the inscape (with the inner eye opened) is believing, and admits of no uncertainty and skepticism.[185]

I would advise you not to dwell too much on ratiocination, for it tends to scatter the mind. This thinking-self continues to be with us for quite a long time, its range extending from the physical to causal states and until all these states which constitute the mind zone are successfully crossed, it does not drop off.[186]

For spiritual progress, stillness of mind and intellect is most essential. Any unnecessary wrestling with the intellect or free play of the mind retards spiritual progress. Concentration means the control of mental vibrations, and may be obtained by attuning within to the Sound Current which is the astral manifestation of the Master Power always present with you.[187]

Verbiage is simply a vehicle of expression when you try to put forth your inner-most feelings seeking solution for the confusion created by your mind. Each question carries a rational answer in its bosom. The human intelligence baffles at times at surface but if you endeavor to delve deep into the innermost recesses of silence of the heart, you will find ineffable divine bliss gushes forth from the fount of Godhead. Divinity dawns in deep silence—the seer becomes dumb and mute with overwhelming divine intoxication and relishes to absorb his little self in Him—the Light and Sound Principles.[188]

Philosophy deals with theory, but mysticism deals with contact with Reality, because philosophy works on the intellectual level whereas mysticism works on the level of the soul.[189] At the level of the intellect you may remember so many things about what the Master has said and given out. That has no life; you are talking only at the level of the intellect. So Life or Consciousness is something else than intellectual wrangling or wrestling.[190] You may, however, know that thought is an expression of soul being an abstract attribute granted to the humans for smooth working in this world. But you have to transcend this realm of intellect by stilling it, when the divine revelations of Light and Sound Current will recharge your soul with divinity and result in eventual mergence with the Absolute.[191]

It is beyond the ken of human comprehension to gauge the grandeur and limitlessness of divinity. Your questioning is within the domain of intellect, whereas spirituality dawns when the intellect is silenced by loving devotion and reverential humility. It is during the silent and sublime moments of holy meditation when the child disciple is nearer to the fountainhead of bliss and harmony, and the rare boon of right understanding is granted with the grace of the Master. Regular feeds of Holy Naam will manifest to you divine glory in its pristine beauty. The initiates are invariably advised to practice the divine virtues which are helpful for regular progress on the Holy Path. It is a slow but sure process.[192]

Obstacles of the Mind

BETWEEN GOD and spirit, there is no other obstacle but that of a veil of the mind. If this veil were to stop fluttering in the breeze of desires, as it does at present, the spirit can take in directly the Cosmic Energy from its very source.[193] The mind may stand in between, but the soul knows what Guru is and what God is.[194]

"In the temple of God, the mind drags us downward, away from the Truth." It is because of the mind that we cannot partake of that which is inside us. It drags us down like a weight of iron. In turn the senses are dragging the mind, and the pleasures of the world are dragging the senses. If the attention withdraws from outer environments, leaves the senses and calms the mind, then only does it realize that it is soul. Have you understood this? Our mind is the barrier between soul and God.[195]

Q. *Why does the mind forget the Bliss?*

A. Forgetfulness is the chief attribute of human mind. It is due to the gross *Maya*, or materialism, that we forget the inner Bliss and are overtaken by sensuous urges. When inner consciousness grows gradually, mind forgets its lower pulls and relishes inner Bliss perpetually with the grace of the Master.[196]

Those who are led by their mind impulses are known as *manmukhs*. Such persons cannot rise above the body consciousness. They do try from time to time but always keep their minds above the Master, with the result that time and again they fall helplessly. If they could pin their deep faith in the competence of the Master and rely less on their own intellectual reasoning, they could be blessed with this rare privilege of inner inversion to enjoy the supreme bliss.

Such dear ones cannot achieve inner stillness and silence. The Master tries to make them understand in one way or the other, but they are so much filled and intoxicated with their mental merchandise that they fail to comprehend the greatness and sublimity of the Holy Path. You will please understand that mind has its various grooves wherein it clings fast. Basically, when we try to sit silent, only then will we come to know where the shoe pinches. The alphabet of spirituality commences with inner silence, which necessarily requires solitude and seclusion. It is only during these sacred moments of silence that we can understand the basic principles of spirituality and imbibe their right import.[197]

The wiles of the mind are both very subtle and risky. It often lies in ambush and makes its inroads when least expected. The ingrained evil propensities though invisible are very strong, and time and again they come to the surface to deliver blows which often prove fatal. The coil strikes out like lightning, with such sharp and sudden twists and turns that man by himself is helpless in its clutches. Here comes the need for the long and strong arm of the Master, which stretches forth with equal agility to his rescue.[198]

Herein the Master once again reminds us that mind is very wicked and tricky, for it will not readily accept the gospel of the Guru, however reasonable it may be. Knowing full well that we cannot avoid the decrees of

Heaven by any amount of wishful thinking, the mind continues planning and maneuvering otherwise. Our intellect, finite and limited as it is, cannot possibly comprehend the subtle activities of the mind, which goes on thinking endlessly. The only remedy for taming the hydra-headed mind is that of the Holy Naam. By contacting the all-audible Sound Current within and the heaven's holy light, it becomes docile and forgets all else around it. This is the sovereign remedy for all the ills of the world, a panacea that cures all diseases of the body and mind. By administering to it regular doses of the celestial music emanating from the Throne of God, the mind gets rid of the lower propensities and begins to enjoy and take delight in the higher ravishing bliss of divine intoxication, which is the greatest gift of the Master. Never agree to the dictates of the mind as it has a hundred and one ways to keep you stuck fast in the physical body and the terrestrial plane.[199]

The hand of the Negative Power on your head will not allow the mind to obey you. He will go on increasing the duality to make it more and more difficult and confusing. The Negative will not help you to overcome this duality—only the Positive can do that. It is a marked difference between the Powers.[200]

The Negative Power puts two strong impediments which are encountered by the Initiates of the Master. Firstly, the mind will always be doubtful about the efficacy of Holy Meditations and one will start missing the meditations, and get devoted to alternative pursuits, substituting them with mere routine readings of the scrip-

tures and other sacred texts. Secondly, it will bring forth
an argument that there is no more need for him or her to
call on the Master, as Initiation per se is sufficient for
proceding on the Way back to the Home of the Father.
Complacency retards inner progress. We are living on a
plane which is governed by the Negative Power and
where the inexorable "Law of Karma" works supreme.
The mind is the agent of this Negative Power, and in
one way or the other, it will entangle you to be kept tied
to the many limitations of the body and worldly possessions. Such a skeptical mind will, instead of doing anything useful, find fault with the Master and His Path.[201]

Negative Power has a vast dominion engulfing the
first three planes and those who happen to fall prey to
the allurements of their mind—subtle and causal—are
caught in finer fetters or bondages. The Masters of the
Highest Order, who came in the past, have left behind
some useful treasures in the form of their precious experiences for our guidance so that we may safely tread
in their footsteps.[202]

"Through the illusion of the body you also become
attached to material objects, and the result is that where-
ever your attention is, so you become that. You are under
the influence of the mind and senses, are feeding the
senses through the outgoing faculties, and the more you
feed them the harder the mind will work and the more
strength it will get."[203]

Herein the Master conveys to us another sublime
truth by telling us that we have been caught in the spider's web, having prepared a vast net of attachments

for binding ourselves down in the mire of delusion and deception. You will appreciate that a spider weaves fine threads of its own secretions and gets entangled therein. Similarly, it is our own mind which has developed an unnecessary attachment with the physical body and its allied relations. Do you know what is the underlying basis of Maya or delusion? Its roots lie in the physical body from where it springs and spreads around like a gigantic Upas tree. We readily forget that we are ensouled bodies and not merely physical bodies. It is the soul currents which permeate through and through the physical plane whereby it is enlivened, and they in turn, get their sustenance from a higher life principle known as the Holy Naam or the Word. So long as that divine power is working in us, we are alive and as soon as that power is withdrawn, the whole structure collapses like a pack of cards, and it is then said: *Dust thou art and unto dust returneth.*[204]

It is better to guard the tendency of each other because the objective mind is very powerful in the physical plane and it is mutual Satsang only which checks out evil tendencies. Society of the people tends to scatter the mind. Mind is the most powerful, clever, and cunning enemy, and to release the spirit from its bondage it is necessary to break attachments from the alluring material objects, which are not ours and have been evolved by matter and Maya.

Human nature is the same everywhere. The Pindi Mind does not like to be subdued because it has been free since long and has become so much absorbed in this outer world that it has not only forgotten the worlds within but has forgotten its own source—the Brahmandi Mind. Instead of controlling the senses it is now subject to them and thus constantly wanders from one subject to another without anything to rest upon. If by good luck it is comparatively free from the anxieties of life and hears of the worlds within and occasionally has a point glimpse of the mere outskirts of these worlds, then instead of going in and bearing mastery over them, it is— alas!—held out by "fame, the last infirmity of noble minds," as Milton calls it. The fame and honor given by people keep it out just as much as ears are held by sweet music, and the eye is held by attractive objects. In the guise of doing good to others it deceives itself and in ignorance knows not that the valuable time is being lost. First know thyself and then preach. It is not proper to teach of a thing when one has not the first-hand knowledge of it.[205]

Step by step the Master is opening up new vistas of right understanding by telling us what the root cause of this misconception is. He says that it is foolish for the human mind to be attached to outer fancies, infatuated by the colorful shell, and caring little for the sweet kernel within. The mind may be likened to a parasitical plant which has no roots of its own, but draws its sustenance from the host tree to which it tenaciously holds. In exactly the same way, the mind in itself has no separate existence per se, but is a sheer projection of one's mental make-up and is inextricably mixed up with the sense objects, through the senses. It, at its lowest level, is bound to the body, while at its other end—the highest level—it is subtle enough to draw its sustenance from the soul.[206]

You must not feel disheartened and try to regain your inner happiness by doing your very best and leaving the rest to the gracious Master Power working overhead. Even the darkest cloud has a silver lining somewhere. He is fully aware of your distress and awaiting more eagerly to receive you within in faithful meditations. You are to be on the guard lest your subconscious mind is fed with thoughts of gloom and morbidity. It makes no distinction between constructive and destructive thought impulses. It works with the material you feed it with, through your thought impulses. The sub-conscious mind will translate into reality a thought driven by fear just as readily as a thought driven by courage or faith. Just as electricity will turn the wheels of industry and render useful service if used constructively or snuff out life if wrongly used. You are free to a great extent in this respect to be receptive to the thought impulses of faith, loving devotion, humility and self surrender, which will in turn bless you with peace and harmony. You must not dwell much on your confusion but meet every situation with courage. My love and blessings are with you.[207]

Befriend the Mind

IS THERE any good or helpful characteristic of mind? Yes, mind, like Janus, has another face as well. If it is trained properly by gentle persuasion and kindly words of advice, with a little patting now and then, it can be converted from a formidable foe into a valuable friend and a helping hand to the soul in its search to bring about this conversion, and when it is done, one can have no better help-mate than the mind. It has the capacity, chameleon-like, to take on the color of the ground where it squats and that indeed is a redeeming feature. When living on the circumference of life, it expands outwards, downward; but rooted as it is in the *Gaggan*, it is not impervious to the higher and holier influences of a Master-Soul to whom it responds and He channelizes it the other way about.[208]

The mind is undoubtedly our enemy and is too superior in strength to be annihilated. It is an innovation introduced by Swami Ji who tells us to make friends with the mind, which is an agent of the Negative Power and, in its present state, an enemy of the soul. Instead of fighting with it right and left and to no purpose, we may make the best use of the mind in a friendly way. You know that mind has a tendency to tread on much beaten tracks, that is, it creates grooves of habit and mechanically acts in a repetitive manner. Just see for yourself if you do something at a fixed time and continue doing so for a number of days at the same time, a habit is formed, and after some time it will become part and parcel of your daily routine.

So this is the easiest way of overpowering this powerful idiot, instead of fighting with it outright in an unequal struggle. We can turn to our advantage this weakness by devoting regular time to the holy meditations, at the fixed time with religious zeal and punctuality. It will be seen that after some time, the inner revelations will arm you with something far superior, and the mind itself, which used to resent inversion, will also start relishing the same and gradually give up its past pleasures. The Master gives us a positive approach for the solution of this riddle, which is so easy and interesting to solve by making a friendly alliance with the mind instead of making it an inveterate foe.[209] Nothing can be gained by cursing the mind, for the mind is no small thing; so the Master's advice is to befriend it.[210]

The mind's habit is to drag everything downward, yet as your friend, even if it wants to hurt you, it will not do so. Under such an arrangement he might even cooperate with you. If he desires food, then agree—"Yes, I will give you food, but first let us do a little meditation, then we will have food." If you immediately refuse the food, he will be tormented with the desire for it. He is like a stubborn donkey; the more you restrict him, the more stubborn he becomes. It is a very accurate definition of the mind. If you make a note in a book, "do not read page so-and-so," it will be the first page people will read; they won't be able to resist the temptation! So make your mind a companion; don't fight with him.[211]

The Satguru advises the soul to take the mind along if it wants to return home. He never says to ignore the mind, or leave it behind, but that the soul should understand and make it agreeable. As long as man does not kill the physical mind and withdraw from the sense level, he cannot proceed. One must leave all sense attractions and rise above body consciousness, otherwise it remains impossible to go higher and taste the Nectar of the Lord. Excessive eating and drinking, and frittering away the attention on worldly sights, sounds and sensations—all these are outer enjoyments which deny one the bliss of the inner enjoyments. Lord Buddha said we should be desireless, for desire is but sense enjoyment. Only by stepping aside from all this can one truly take a step ahead. If you can take the mind with you, it will be easier, but if you forget yourself and your aim in the mind's enjoyments you will lose all desire to progress. Make it your companion, and make it understand the situation, for the mind is unhappy—so much so that at times it cries out in torment.[212]

Make a friend of the mind. It is our cruel enemy which will go on tormenting our life, but by making friends with it we take the first step toward gaining the desired control. If one makes friends with an enemy, he may not immediately cease his enmity, but it will lessen the lengths of his cruelty. In this way there are chances of his becoming stilled, during which time you will be more awakened.[213]

So it is possible to gain control over the mind only in the company of a Satguru. He will help you to befrien it, and so make the path easier. Then it may start to listen to you, whereas it usually does not. Many find this difficulty in meditation, and say that their mind does not allow them to meditate. With love, make it your companion. Love is such a magnificent thing, that it can control even the worst charactered person. No matter how much you may hate your pitiful situation, yet hate will only serve to increase the problem. You may throw all the filth out of a dirty house, yet the smell of that will spread and permeate not only the interior of the house but the surroundings too. The true solution is to start washing with the water of Love and gradually the badness will be washed away forever. If you are good to your enemy, his enmity will be softened somewhat.[214]

Because of its vast area of rule, everyone is under the mind's control, so among those who practice meditation, very few rise above even the first region. Even fewer rise above the second, and to rise above the third is really something rare.[215]

Stilling the Mind

MIND IS ACCUSTOMED from ages to hop about and live on things of the outer world. The more it goes out the more it is scattered and the less peaceful it is. Peace comes from within and not from without. One must invert within to get it. You have been given the way for inversion and staying on within to enjoy peace and bliss in the Higher Planes. Outer life and inner progress go hand in hand. No spiritual progress can be made without ethical living—great stress is, therefore, laid on the latter. You need not be frustrated. Everything will come in due time by the Grace of the Master. Time factor is necessary. Please do not be impatient, but carry on your job steadfastly and lovingly with faith in the Master Power. The inner experiences will increase from day to day. Work is worship. During the day when you are busy in your worldly vocation, please be fully devoted to it with diligence so that your mind is fully absorbed in the work you do. Should, however, there be any moments when your mind is free, those moments should be utilised in repeating the five Holy Names or sweetly thinking of the Master or listening to the Sound Current, if that has developed. All this may seem difficult in the beginning, but slowly and slowly the mind gets into the habit and soon it begins to like and enjoy the meditations and this sort of truthful and straight life. The outer failings are to be viewed with a keen eye and the failures are to be removed from day to day.[216]

There is a sound of Truth vibrating within—a song which is sung in every being. There is a great attraction in hearing this Sound, through which all other attractions will fade away, and the stage of senses will be left behind: one becomes free of them. This mouse-mind has become heavy by drinking the weight of God's Name. The mind can be weighted down by the mercury-like quality of the Naam, rendering it impossible to run around loose or engage in its ever constant oscillation. There is no other means of controlling the mind. The accounts of Lord Krishna's life state that he jumped into

the River Jumna and controlled the hydra-headed serpent there with the sound of his flute. This many-headed
serpent is the mind, which has a thousand ways of inflict-
ing its poison, and without that Sound from the Beyond,
it cannot be controlled or overcome. Outer intellect and
knowledge have no power over it, for though it may remain quiet for a short time, it will then run away again.
If you cover a fire with ashes, it would seem there is no
fire at all, yet a strong breeze will revive it and reveal
the heat lying beneath. However, if you throw water
upon it, even a thousand tornadoes would fail to revive it.[217]

Brave is he who has control over his mind and senses,
for the inward progress is in proportion to this control.
It is the repetition that brings the mind in and the Sound
Current that pulls it up.[218] Please try to still the vibration
of the mind, and when it stands collected in the eyes you
will pass on to the regions of light.[219]

But they could benefit still further from mastery of
the mind if they could but learn the sacred technique
of self-analysis and withdrawal of the sensory currents
from the body. Herein you will certainly agree with
Swami Ji, who says that the human mind is gravely
foolish in having fallen prey to the outer sense enjoyments
and is endlessly entangled in worry and misery. You
know that the mind, at present, resents inner silence and
stillness, as it has a tendency to roam without for aeons
and aeons without end. You can keep it engaged in outer pursuits for hours at a time, but if you were to attempt
inner silence and stillness, it would cry out and run riot,

for then it behaves like a small babe who, when locked in a dark cell, shrieks, cries, and knocks to get out.

Now, if the baby were provided with some sweets to eat and toys to play with, it would stop crying. Exactly similar is the case with the human mind.

The Living Master holds the key into the Beyond; and when he provides the child disciple with inner links of divinity which carry him into higher regions, the latter gets a feeling of satisfaction. You know that the inner bliss is supreme and unrivaled. There is nothing similar to it on earth, but alas! the mind is so much intoxicated with the lust for woman, wine, and wealth that it fails to see and comprehend the greatness of the spiritual be-atitude within. But patient and persistent efforts to keep the mind still will gradually unlock the treasures of divin-ity within you with the Grace of the Master. Always be buoyant and fresh when you sit for meditation and wait patiently, like a loving baby looking up into the eyes of the nursing mother.[220]

Mind is enamoured of pleasures and runs after them whenever and wherever they can be found. It is stilled in the physical presence of the Master. It is by His Divine Radiation that the souls are attracted towards Him, and the mind which gets consciousness from the soul is stilled for the time being. Tulsi Sahib says:

> *The attention or the outer expression of soul*
> *is controlled in the company of a Sadh.*
> *It is only then that the mind attains some still-*
> *ness.*

But pleasures of the flesh are quite different from true

happiness born of inner peace in the soul. If the mind is provided with the appetency to relish something sublime, and gets an opportunity of doing so, it knows the value of real happiness, with the result that the sense pleasures lose all their charm, and thereafter seem insipid and valueless.[221]

All dedicated work is worship. Great is man and Providence has blessed everyone with untold energy and strength which if properly harnessed can bring in desired results. Just learn to do one thing at a time and that too with single-minded attention and devotion. Ordinarily the suns rays do not burn, but when the same are passed through a convex lens, these become so powerful that they burn anything placed in their range. Similar is the case with concentrated attention which will enable you to progress in every sphere of your life including meditation. Please be rest assured my love and blessings are always with you in all noble undertakings and enterprises.[222]

In proportion to the loosening of the union of mind with matter, the union of mind with soul strengthens. Carefully, therefore, examine the tendencies of the mind and study its weaknesses, and try to overcome them. So long as there is dirt in the mind it cannot stay within. Its attachments draw it out. Whichever pan of the balance is loaded, that pan goes downwards. Mind is our enemy and like an enemy its movements should be watched. The whole world—man, animal, bird, or insect—dances to the tune of the mind. Every creature is being tossed up and down by it. The only place when mind dances is when it is brought before the Current. Only then it becomes helpless. It cannot be controlled by the study of scriptures nor by the performance of austerities; neither the soldier nor the warrior nor the conqueror nor the moralist have succeeded against it. He who ever succeeded against it did so by catching the Sound Current.[223]

REFERENCES

References

The references to the books of Kirpal Singh can be found in the following editions:

The Jap Ji—second edition (1964)
The Crown of Life—third edition (1970)
Spiritual Elixir—first (one-volume) edition (1967)
Morning Talks—first edition (1970) or third edition (1974)
The Wheel of Life—first edition (1965)
Prayer—third edition (1970)
Baba Jaimal Singh—third edition (1971)
The Mystery of Death—first edition (1968)
Godman—second edition (1971)

BOOK ONE
SELF-INTROSPECTION

a. *Seven Paths to Perfection*, p. 4
1. *Sat Sandesh,* February 1971, p. 4
2. *Sat Sandesh,* October 1971, p. 4
3. *Sat Sandesh,* September 1971, p. 23
4. *Spiritual Elixir,* p. 121
5. *Spiritual Elixir,* p. 100
6. *Sat Sandesh,* October 1971, p. 18
7. *Morning Talks,* p. 118

8. *Morning Talks*, p. 122
9. Circular 66
10. Letter to an Initiate
11. *Excerpts from Letters to New York Satsangis*, p. 84
12. *Sat Sandesh*, March 1971, p. 14
13. *Sat Sandesh*, September 1971, p. 6
14. *The Way of Love* (Circular)
15. *Sat Sandesh*, April 1971, p. 29
16. Circular 17
17. *Sat Sandesh*, June 1970, p. 30
18. *Wheel of Life*, p. 50
19. *Excerpts from Letters to New York Satsangis*, p. 83
20. *Sat Sandesh*, April 1970, p. 25
21. *Sat Sandesh*, April 1971, p. 30
22. *Sat Sandesh*, March 1971, p. 30
23. *Sat Sandesh*, March 1972, pp. 3-4
24. *Morning Talks*, p. 154
25. *Sat Sandesh*, March 1972, p. 8
26. Circular 17, p. 4
27. *Sat Sandesh*, January 1968, p. 7
28. *Morning Talks*, p. 119
29. *Morning Talks*, p. 156
30. *Morning Talks*, p. 153
31. *Morning Talks*, p. 46
32. *Morning Talks*, p. 121
33. *Receptivity*, p. 10
34. *Excerpts from Letters to New York Satsangis*, p. 69
35. *Receptivity*, p. 9
36. *Sat Sandesh*, June 1971, p. 5
37. *Morning Talks*, p. 65
38. *Morning Talks*, p. 68

39. *Morning Talks,* p. 64
40. Circular 27, p. 10
41. *Excerpts from Letters to New York Satsangis,* p. 69
42. *Sat Sandesh,* March 1972, p. 31
43. *Excerpts from Letters to New York Satsangis,* p. 69
44. *Prayer,* p. 48
45. *Excerpts from Letters to New York Satsangis,* p. 78
46. *Sat Sandesh,* February 1971, p. 5
47. *Excerpts from Letters to New York Satsangis,* p. 53
48. Circular 22, p. 3
49. *Spiritual Elixir,* p. 106
50. *Excerpts from Letters to New York Satsangis,* p. 53
51. *Sat Sandesh,* February 1970, p. 28
52. *Wheel of Life,* p. 48
53. *Crown of Life,* p. 153
54. *Sat Sandesh,* October 1971, p. 7
55. Circular 17, p. 12
57. *Sat Sandesh,* September 1971, p. 24
58. Circular 29
59. *Spiritual Elixir,* p. 297
60. Letter to an Initiate
61. *Morning Talks,* p. 114
62. *Prayer,* pp. 17-18
63. *Spiritual Elixir,* p. 230
64. *Prayer,* p. 48
65. *Sat Sandesh,* July 1971, p. 3
66. *Excerpts from Letters to New York Satsangis,* p. 75
67. *Spiritual Elixir,* p. 248
68. *Prayer,* p. 81
69. *Prayer,* pp. 23-25
70. *Receptivity,* p. 16

71. *Excerpts from Letters to New York Satsangis,* p. 43

72. *Sat Sandesh,* September 1971, p. 22

73. Letter to an Initiate

74. *Sat Sandesh,* February 1971, p. 12

75. Circular 66

76. *Excerpts from Letters to New York Satsangis,* p. 42

77. *Receptivity,* p. 18

78. Circular 66

79. *Seven Paths to Perfection,* p. 19

80. *Seven Paths to Perfection,* p. 5

81. *Sat Sandesh,* December 1971, p. 10

82. *Seven Paths to Perfection,* p. 6

83. *Morning Talks,* p. 213

84. *Morning Talks,* p. 15

85. *Morning Talks,* p. 16

86. *Morning Talks,* p. 14

87. *Spiritual Elixir,* pp. 227-228

88. *Sat Sandesh,* December 1971, pp. 31-32

89. *Excerpts from Letters to New York Satsangis,* pp. 74-75

90. *Morning Talks,* p. 16

91. *Morning Talks,* p. 124

92. *Morning Talks,* p. 126

93. *Sat Sandesh,* July 1971, p. 6

94. *Spiritual Elixir,* p. 9

95. *Sat Sandesh,* April 1971, p. 28

96. *Spiritual Elixir,* p. 95

97. *Sat Sandesh,* February 1970, p. 28

98. *Spiritual Elixir,* p. 97

99. *Morning Talks,* p. 212

100. *Seven Paths to Perfection,* p. 6

101. *Excerpts from Letters to New York Satsangis,* pp. 79-80
102. *Sat Sandesh,* February 1970, p. 26
103. *Seven Paths to Perfection,* p. 5
104. *Sat Sandesh,* December 1971, p. 6
105. *Sat Sandesh,* January 1968, p. 27
106. *Wheel of Life,* p. 47
107. *Sat Sandesh,* November 1971, p. 10
108. *Wheel of Life,* p. 47
109. *Sat Sandesh,* Decembel 1971, pp. 5-6
110. *Sat Sandesh,* December 1971, p. 29
111. *Seven Paths to Perfection,* p. 8
112. Circular 2
113. *Sat Sandesh,* April 1968, p. 5
114. *Seven Paths to Perfection,* p. 9
115. Circular 2
116. *Excerpts from Letters to New York Satsangis,* p. 53
117. *Excerpts from Letters to New York Satsangis,* p. 21
118. *Sat Sandesh,* June 1971, p. 4
119. *Morning Talks,* p. 63
120. *Morning Talks,* p. 192
121. *Excerpts from Letters to New York Satsangis,* p. 19
122. *Seven Paths to Perfection,* pp. 12-13
123. *The Crown of Life,* p. 153
124. *The Crown of Life,* p. 138
125. *Seven Paths to Perfection,* p. 10
126. *Excerpts from Letters to New York Satsangis,* p. 19
127. *Excerpts from Letters to New York Satsangis,* p. 53
128. *Sat Sandesh,* July 1971, p. 27
129. *Sat Sandesh,* April 1968, p. 10
130. Letter to an Initiate

131. *Excerpts from Letters to New York Satsangis,* p. 61
132. *Excerpts from Letters to New York Satsangis,* p. 60
133. *Excerpts from Letters to New York Satsangis,* pp. 60-61
134. *Morning Talks,* p. 101
135. *Sat Sandesh,* April 1968, p. 10
136. *Spiritual Elixir,* p. 78
137. *Excerpts from Letters to New York Satsangis,* p. 59
138. *Sat Sandsh,* April 1968, pp. 11-12
139. *Sat Sandesh,* January 1968, p. 7
140. *Sat Sandesh,* January 1968, p. 13
141. *Sat Sandesh,* January 1968, p. 12
142. *Sat Sandesh,* January 1968, p. 28
143. *Sat Sandesh,* April 1968, p. 3
144. *Sat Sandesh,* January 1968, p. 12
145. *Sat Sandesh,* January 1968, p. 8
146. *Sat Sandesh,* January 1968, p. 9
147. *Sat Sandesh,* April 1968, p. 11
148. *Sat Sandesh,* January 1968, p. 11
149. *Sat Sandesh,* January 1968, p. 11
150. *Sat Sandesh,* January 1968, p. 10
151. *Sat Sandesh,* January 1968, p. 12
152. *Sat Sandesh,* August 1970, p. 26
153. *Spiritual Elixir,* p. 109
154. *Wheel of Life,* pp. 46-47
155. *Sat Sandesh,* February 1970, p. 25
156. *Sat Sandesh,* February 1970, p. 11
157. *Sat Sandesh,* April 1971, p. 30
158. *Seven Paths to Perfection,* p. 17
159. *Morning Talks,* p. 190
160. *Morning Talks,* p. 191

161. *Morning Talks*, p. 103
162. *Morning Talks*, p. 194
163. *Morning Talks*, p. 228
164. *Morning Talks*, p. 227
165. *Morning Talks*, p. 227
166. Letter to an Initiate
167. *Spiritual Elixir*, p. 112
168. *Spiritual Elixir*, p. 118
169. *Spiritual Elixir*, p. 112
170. *Spiritual Elixir*, p. 113
171. *Sat Sandesh*, February 1970, p. 32
172. Circular 2
173. *Spiritual Elixir*, p. 109
174. *Morning Talks*, p. 22
175. *Sat Sandesh*, February 1970, p. 9
176. *Morning Talks*, p. 20
177. *Sat Sandesh*, April 1971, p. 27
178. *Morning Talks*, p. 21
179. *Excerpts from Letters to New York Satsangis*, p. 70
180. Circular 3
181. *Excerpts from Letters to New York Satsangis*, p. 70
182. *Excerpts from Letters to New York Satsangis*, p. 14
183. *Spiritual Elixir*, p. 48
184. *Seven Paths to Perfection*, p. 19
185. Circular 3
186. *Sat Sandesh*, August 1970, p. 25
187. From a tape recorded by Bob Redeen, Sept. 1970
188. *Sat Sandesh*, August 1970, p. 25
189. *Excerpts from Letters to New York Satsangis*, p. 73
190. *Excerpts from Letters to New York Satsangis*, p. 73
191. Circular 2

192. *Spiritual Elixir,* p. 108
193. *Excerpts from Letters to New York Satsangis,* p. 74
194. *Spiritual Elixir,* p. 98
195. Circular 29
196. *Wheel of Life,* p. 46
197. *Spiritual Elixir,* p. 114
198. Letter to an Initiate
199. *Sat Sandesh,* December 1970, p. 11
200. *Morning Talks,* p. 2
201. *Seven Paths to Perfection,* p. 23
202. *Sat Sandesh,* July 1971, p. 8
203. *Sat Sandesh,* July 1971, p. 9
204. *Sat Sandesh,* July 1971, p. 9
205. *Wheel of Life,* p. 46
206. *Sat Sandesh,* June 1970, p. 32
207. *Sat Sandesh,* February 1972, p. 18
208. *Morning Talks,* p. 2
209. Christmas Circular, December 1967
210. *Morning Talks,* p. 11
211. *Morning Talks,* pp. 138-139
212. *Seven Paths to Perfection,* p. 24
213. *Spiritual Elixir,* p. 287
214. *Morning Talks,* p. 211
215. *Wheel of Life,* p. 49
216. *Morning Talks,* p. 11
217. *Seven Paths to Perfection,* pp. 26-27
218. *Sat Sandesh,* February 1972, p. 5
219. *Morning Talks,* p. 187
220. *Jap Ji,* p. 82
221. *Sat Sandesh,* March 1972, p. 8
222. *Morning Talks,* p. 171

223. *Morning Talks*, p. 169
224. *Morning Talks*, p. 169
225. *Morning Talks*, p. 52
226. *Jap Ji*, pp. 48-50
227. *Jap Ji*, p. 51
228. *Jap Ji*, p. 51
229. *Jap Ji*, p. 53
230. *Jap Ji*, p. 54

BOOK TWO
MEDITATION

1. *Sat Sandesh,* October 1971, p. 7
2. *Spiritual Elixir,* pp. 180-190
3. *Simran,* p. 18
4. *Spiritual Elixir,* p. 210
5. *Sat Sandesh,* April 1971, p. 32
6. *Sat Sandesh,* June 1971, p. 5
7. *Sat Sandesh,* June 1971, p. 2
8. *Sat Sandesh,* June 1971, p. 8
9. *Sat Sandesh,* June 1971, p. 8
10. *Sat Sandesh,* March 1971, p. 6
11. *Sat Sandesh,* September 1971, p. 23
12. *Sat Sandesh,* May 1971, p. 7
13. *Sat Sandesh,* June 1971, pp. 7-8
14. *Spiritual Elixir,* p. 142
15. *Sat Sandesh,* January 1972, p. 11
16. *Sat Sandesh,* March 1971, pp. 28-29
17. *Sat Sandesh,* March 1970, p. 7
18. *Sat Sandesh,* March 1970, p. 11

19. Letter to an Initiate
20. *Sat Sandesh*, September 1971, p. 19
21. Letter to an Initiate
22. *Sat Sandesh*, October 1971, p. 2
23. *Sat Sandesh*, September 1971, p. 15
24. *Spiritual Elixir*, p. 260
25. *Spiritual Elixir*, pp. 230-231
26. *Spiritual Elixir*, p. 204
27. *Sat Sandesh*, June 1971, p. 6
28. *Baba Jaimal Singh*, pp. 104-105
29. *Naam or Word*, pp. 148-149
30. *Naam or Word*, pp. 142-143
31. *Jap Ji*, pp. 30-31
32. *Jap Ji*, pp. 31-32
33. *The Crown of Life*, pp. 144-146
34. *Spiritual Elixir*, pp. 170-171
35. *Sat Sandesh*, June 1971, p. 4
36. *Sat Sandesh*, February 1972, p. 32
37. *Sat Sandesh*, September 1970, p. 8
38. *Sat Sandesh*, April 1970, p. 23
39. *Excerpts from Letters to New York Satsangis*, p. 54
40. *Spiritual Elixir*, p. 76
41. *Spiritual Elixir*, p. 259
42. *Sat Sandesh*, June 1971, p. 2
43. *Sat Sandesh*, July 1971, p. 31
44. *Spiritual Elixir*, pp. 155-156
45. *Jap Ji*, pp. 33-34
46. *Spiritual Elixir*, p. 259
47. *Spiritual Elixir*, p. 44
48. *Sat Sandesh*, August 1970, p. 26

49. *Excerpts from Letters to New York Satsangis,* p. 50
50. *Sat Sandesh,* February 1972, p. 11
51. *Sat Sandesh,* January 1972, p. 11
52. *Spiritual Elixir,* p. 134
53. *Spiritual Elixir,* pp. 148-149
54. *Spiritual Elixir,* p. 152
55. *Spiritual Elixir,* p. 264
56. Letter to an Initiate
57. *Sat Sandesh,* June 1970, p. 11
58. *Jap Ji,* p. 36
59. *Naam or Word,* pp. 152-153
60. *Jap Ji,* p. 95
61. *Jap Ji,* p. 96
62. *Jap Ji,* p. 96
63. *Jap Ji,* p. 96
64. *Jap Ji,* pp. 95-96
65. *Spiritual Elixir,* pp. 181-182
66. *Excerpts from Letters to New York Satsangis,* p. 44
67. *Spiritual Elixir,* p. 281
68. *Excerpts from Letters to New York Satsangis,* p. 57
69. *Excerpts from Letters to New York Satsangis,* p. 41
70. *Excerpts from Letters to New York Satsangis,* p. 25
71. *Excerpts from Letters to New York Satsangis,* p. 26
72. *Excerpts from Letters to New York Satsangis,* p. 27
73. *Spiritual Elixir,* p. 187
74. *Spiritual Elixir,* p. 173
75. Letter to an Initiate
76. Letter to an Initiate
77. *Spiritual Elixir,* pp. 157-158
78. Circular 4, p. 4

79. *Spiritual Elixir,* p. 145
80. *Sat Sandesh,* November 1971, p. 31
81. *Meditation and Spiritual Progress* (Circular)
82. *Excerpts from Letters to New York Satsangis,* p. 57
83. *Receptivity,* p. 8
84. *Spiritual Elixir,* p. 174
85. *Spiritual Elixir,* p. 163
86. *Baba Jaimal Singh,* p. 104
87. *Excerpts from Letters to New York Satsangis,* p. 23
88. *Spiritual Elixir,* p. 159
89. *Spiritual Elixir,* p. 153
90. *The Way of Love* (Circular)
91. *Spiritual Elixir,* p. 274
92. *Spiritual Elixir,* p. 188
93. *Sat Sandesh,* October 1970, p. 12
94. *Sat Sandesh,* June 1971, pp. 3-4
95. *Baba Jaimal Singh,* p. 125
96. *Sat Sandesh,* June 1971, p. 32
97. *Excerpts from Letters to New York Satsangis,* p. 72
98. *Sat Sandesh,* April 1971, p. 26
99. *Spiritual Elixir,* p. 144
100. *Sat Sandesh,* January 1972, p. 11
101. *Spiritual Elixir,* p. 183
102. *Spiritual Elixir,* p. 183
103. *Excerpts from Letters to New York Satsangis,* p. 45
104. *Sat Sandesh,* November 1970, p. 3
105. *Spiritual Elixir,* pp. 141-142
106. *Spiritual Elixir,* p. 226
107. *Spiritual Elixir,* p. 209
108. *Spiritual Elixir,* p. 63

109. *Spiritual Elixir*, p. 18
110. *Sat Sandesh,* September 1970, p. 14
111. *Baba Jaimal Singh,* p. 105
112. *Excerpts from Letters to New York Satsangis,* p. 49
113. Letter to an Initiate
114. Letter to an Initiate
115. *Spiritual Elixir*, p. 138
116. *Spiritual Elixir*, p. 222
117. *Spiritual Elixir*, p. 132
118. Letter to an Initiate
119. Circular 29, p. 9
120. *Meditation and Spiritual Progress* (Circular)
121. *Morning Talks*, p. 114
122. *Simran*, p. 16
123. *Excerpts from Letters to New York Satsangis,* p. 22
124. *Simran*, p. 15
125. *Spiritual Elixir*, p. 152
126. Letter to an Initiate
127. *Spiritual Elixir*, p. 176
128. *Morning Talks*, p. 82
129. *Spiritual Elixir*, p. 139
130. *Morning Talks*, pp. 80-81
131. *Sat Sandesh,* January 1972, p. 5
132. Christmas Message, December 9, 1969
133. *Baba Jaimal Singh,* pp. 106-107
134. *Godman*, pp. 104, 105, 107, 108, 112
135. *Spiritual Elixir*, p. 83
136. *Spiritual Elixir*, p. 156
137. *Baba Jaimal Singh,* p. 107
138. *Sat Sandesh,* May 1970, p. 13

139. *Spiritual Elixir,* p. 206

140. *Spiritual Elixir,* pp. 139-140

141. *Spiritual Elixir,* p. 13

142. *Spiritual Elixir,* pp. 77-78

143. *Spiritual Elixir,* p. 14

144. *Excerpts from Letters to New York Satsangis,* p. 63

145. *Simran,* p. 8

146. *Spiritual Elixir,* pp. 131-132

147. *Sat Sandesh,* November 1971, p. 19

148. *Sat Sandesh,* September 1971, p. 22

149. *Sat Sandesh,* September 1971, p. 20

150. *Spiritual Elixir,* pp. 252-253

151. *Spiritual Elixir,* p. 159

152. *Spiritual Elixir,* p. 90

153. *Spiritual Elixir,* p. 260

154. *Spiritual Elixir,* p. 193

155. *Meditation and Spiritual Progress* (Circular)

156. *Spiritual Elixir,* pp. 194-196

157. *Meditation and Spiritual Progress* (Circular)

158. *Meditation and Spiritual Progress* (Circular)

159. *Spiritual Elixir,* p. 174

160. *Spiritual Elixir,* p. 175

161. *Spiritual Elixir,* pp. 175-176

162. *Spiritual Elixir,* p. 166

163. *Mystery of Death*

164. Letter to an Initiate

165. *Excerpts from Letters to New York Satsangis,* p. 23

166. *Spiritual Elixir,* p. 165

167. *Meditation and Spiritual Progress,* p. 3

168. *Spiritual Elixir,* pp. 190-191

169. *Spiritual Elixir,* p. 148
170. *Excerpts from Letters to New York Satsangis,* pp. 50-51
171. *Spiritual Elixir,* p. 68
172. Letter to an Initiate
173. *Sat Sandesh,* April 1971, p. 30
174. *Sat Sandesh,* March 1971, p. 29
175. *Spiritual Elixir,* p. 75
176. *Spiritual Elixir,* p. 68
177. *Sat Sandesh,* September 1971, p. 14
178. *Sat Sandesh,* April 1971, p. 6
179. *Spiritual Elixir,* p. 69
180. Letter to an Initiate
181. *Spiritual Elixir,* p. 43
182. *Spiritual Elixir,* p. 80
183. *Spiritual Elixir,* p. 81
184. *Spiritual Elixir,* p. 81
185. *Spiritual Elixir,* p. 82
186. *Excerpts from Letters to New York Satsangis,* p. 44
187. *Spiritual Elixir,* p. 254
188. *Excerpts from Letters to New York Satsangis,* p. 44
189. *Sat Sandesh,* March 1971, p. 9
190. *Morning Talks,* p. 165
191. *Excerpts from Letters to New York Satsangis,* p. 56
192. *Excerpts from Letters to New York Satsangis,* p. 21
193. *Spiritual Elixir,* p. 251
194. *Sat Sandesh,* February 1971, p. 31
195. *Sat Sandesh,* March 1970, p. 14
196. *Spiritual Elixir,* p. 21
197. Circular 27, pp. 14-15

198. *Prayer,* p. 62

199. Circular 27, p. 10

200. *Sat Sandesh,* February 1971, p. 31

201. Circular 27, p. 5

202. Circular 27, p. 14

203. *Sat Sandesh,* January 1970, p. 12

204. Circular 27, p. 10

205. Letter to an Initiate

206. Circular 27, pp. 6-7

207. *Excerpts from Letters to New York Satsangis,* p. 45

208. *Sat Sandesh,* September 1971, p. 15

209. *Spiritual Elixir,* pp. 73-74

210. Circular 27, p. 16

211. *Sat Sandesh,* September 1971, p. 19

212. *Sat Sandesh,* September 1971, p. 20

213. *Sat Sandesh,* September 1972, p. 19

214. *Sat Sandesh,* September 1971, p. 16

215. *Sat Sandesh,* September 1971, p. 21

216. *Sat Sandesh,* September 1971, p. 18

217. *Excerpts from Letters to New York Satsangis,* p. 44

218. *Sat Sandesh,* September 1971, p. 25

219. Letter to an Initiate

220. *Sat Sandesh,* December 1973, p. 10

221. Circular 27, p. 7

222. *Spiritual Elixir,* pp. 74-75

223. *Excerpts from Letters to New York Satsangis,* p. 72

224. Letter to an Initiate

THE NEW LIFE

THE TEACHINGS OF KIRPAL SINGH
Volume III

THE NEW LIFE

*Compiled and selected from
the writings of Kirpal Singh*
by Ruth Seader

SAWAN KIRPAL PUBLICATIONS

Table of Contents

BOOK TWO
THE NEW LIFE IN GOD

BOOK ONE

THE NEW LIFE
IN THE WORLD

The New Life in the World

True Living

LIFE ON EARTH, as we have it, has a tremendous bearing in building the body and the mind. We must, therefore, strive to simplify life and learn to live truly. It is true living on which everything else depends, even the search for the self and the Over-self. The importance of true living cannot be over-emphasized. It is rightly said:

Truth is higher than everything,
But higher still is true living.

Simple living and high thinking has ever been an ideal with the ancients and they always strove for it. We in the modern age have seldom paid much thought to it, though we profess it at times and pay lip-homage to it. Though it may appear hard to achieve the highest type of life, yet it is worth our while to see what it connotes, the ways and means that may be conducive to attaining it and to adopting it for ourselves. In whatever we do, always place some objective before us, ascertain the principles involved therein, study the methods that may lead to the desired goal, and finally make a periodical survey, a thorough check-up, to find how much nearer we have come to the end in view. In this connection, one has, of course, to devote single-minded attention and make an

3

honest endeavor from day to day before one can note an appreciable improvement in his life and conduct, both toward himself and toward others around him.

"What constitutes the life of man?" one might naturally ask. The aged one with a lot of experience in life and fed up with what he has seen and experienced of the world, turns to self-analysis of life. Does life consist only in eating, drinking, sleeping, having children; fearing, fretting, and fighting; snatching, hoarding, and hating; in imprisoning and subordinating those that are inferior to us in strength, physical or mental; and in killing others and grabbing other people's possessions? Must we pass our days in enjoying the ill-gotten earthly gains with no other achievements in the end but to die a miserable death, with sorrow to self and those around us, the near and dear ones who helplessly stand by and mourn? Again, what about the worldly attractions—lands, buildings, money, pets and other countless possessions which, perforce, are to be left behind against our will? In the face of all these hard facts of experience, should the hoarding of worldly riches then be our sole aim—the be-all and end-all of our existence—or should we strive for something higher and nobler, permanent and lasting, that may abide with us here and hereafter? The reply is simple: the Almighty Power, the original source and fountainhead of all life, our home of happiness, peace eternal, and the means of our liberation from fearful bondage of births, deaths and karmas, should be the main objective and the only thing worth craving and achieving, for it is the *summum bonum* of life.[1]

Q. To what extent is outer behavior indicative of inner spiritual growth?

A. A keen sense of self-abnegation and self-naughting is the outward expression of one's spiritual progress. It is not exhibited to hide our weaknesses but to actually make one feel in the heart of hearts that one is nothing but a mere tiny cog in the vast machinery of Divine purposes. One who becomes a conscious co-worker of the Divine Plan never asserts but humbly describes in third person. He never despises anyone but always relishes to offer loving help and assistance to others. He does not criticize, but narrates the facts of life in a selfless manner for our spiritual benefit. He lives sincerely up to the Holy Commandments, irrespective of the results. He does not yield to the environments, but adjusts himself cheerfully, knowing it fully well that he is always under the Gracious Protection of the Master-Power. He is never gloomy and in his heart of hearts is always cheerful, even in the face of misfortunes. He does not blame others for their shortcomings but seeks to weed them out by careful living and adaptation. He does not attribute his spiritual progress to his own single-handed earnest endeavors but considers it as a Holy Gift from the Master. He is well-balanced in failure and success. He can forgive and forget easily. He is seldom provocative and is rather blessed with a keen sense of loving co-operation for the spiritual welfare of others.

He does not assert his authority nor claim any superiority over the less developed souls, but behaves like a friend or brother and inwardly prays for their redemption. He never feels burdened with the worries of others and can offer sublime solutions with much ease. He is ever compassionate in his heart and wishes the welfare of all men, animals, birds, or insects. He is always full of deep gratitude and seldom complains about his difficulties whatsoever. He is chaste and kind but hides his virtues under the cloak of studied science. He never boasts of his valor or intelligence but seeks to help others surreptitiously. He dislikes limelight. He shuns publicity and feels shy in large crowds. He does not like acting and posing, but is always unassuming and natural in his behavior.

He can silence his thoughts at will by attuning with the *Holy Naam* within and by turning his attention to the Holy Feet of the Master. He is ever protected by Him and is hourly fed—nay, rather, every moment is blessed with the loving life-impulses from the Master Power. He knows fully well that this physical life is but a passing phase of the soul from the lower categories of creation in the long drama of human existence, and nothing material will accompany it into the Beyond. He does not believe in hoarding but tries to live a frugal life full of contentment. He is not allured by the spell of high living but considers it as a strong fetter on the human soul. He does not vie with the so-called affluent and rich people, but inwardly prays for their spiritual liberation from the wheel of birth and death. He does not live for eating but eats for living a life full of Divine Bliss and Harmony. He is not fond of gaudy dress but is satisfied with the simple garments procured at reasonable prices.

He does not shirk hard work but undertakes mighty

jobs for the good of others at the cost of his physical endurance in a selfless manner. He does not demand reward for his labors but considers the sacred dedication as a boon in itself. He will seek to help others even at the cost of his own suffering. He is, in a nutshell, a righteous man of good thoughts, good words and good deeds.[2]

Today, it is becoming more and more difficult for an honest man to live in the world. Virtue is on the decrease and is to many the object of derision. Vice is on the increase, and its practice is even lauded as a virtue. The moral fabric of society, which is its warp and woof, is becoming threadbare, and if this process is allowed to continue, the fabric will tear apart. Even art, which in former years was a means used to educate people to a nobler way of life, has not escaped this destructive process. In the theatre, cinema and television media, the filth and dirt of perverted intellect is spawned forth without let or hindrance. Even the most respected of all educational institutions, the university, is becoming forgetful of its true function, which is to produce the highest type of citizen dedicated to the service of his fellow man.

It is to counteract this pernicious process that Ruhani Satsang has established, both in India and abroad, training centers or study circles where man can learn the true values of life, as taught from a spiritual standpoint. In these centers, the students are trained and guided by personal classes, through correspondence and submission of progress reports. The progress reports detail the success and failures that are experienced in the practical application of the principles of true living which are taught

to the students by such classes.³ Initiates should be guided by the Teachings of the Master only, in all phases
of life, whether material or spiritual. To allow other
concepts to creep in is to sully His Teachings and confuse the initiates.⁴

Worldly Attachment

ONE'S ATTENTION is his sole legacy and estate of
greatest price, and too much external expansion
is detrimental to one's spiritual interests, as well as worldly ones. One should therefore endeavor to make the best
use of all outer pursuits to achieve the ultimate goal of
knowing one's self by practical self-analysis and knowing
God.⁵

So love is innate in our soul and we are conscious
beings. If it is directed to all Consciousness, it is true love.
That will give you freedom, all bliss, and all joy. If it
is attached to the worldly things, the physical body, its
environments, the enjoyments of outward faculties, then
that is bondage and a sure way of coming again and
again to the world where you are attached.⁶

When God meets you and gives you initiation, something to start with, He guards you against reveling in
the outward enjoyments, in the low pursuits of lust, anger, and their effects. These impressions are received
through the outgoing faculties, which are open to the
outside world, and they are embedded into the astral

body. To give an example, if you take a glass and cover it with some wax, make some impressions on the wax and then pour some acid over it, all those impressions will be embedded into the glass. Similarly, all impressions from outside are impressed in our astral body through the physical body and outgoing faculties.[7]

The Master wants each of us to penetrate through the fleeting forms and patterns and pass on from the phenomena of Nature to Nature's God. He warns us not to be misled by alluring attractions and wild enchantments spread out by Dame Nature through her evanescent charms and fleeting beauties. We should take them merely as signposts pointing to the Lord, the Eternal God that resides within and pervades each of the ephemeral productions. He further wants us to summon up all our energies and press them into service, so as to make our bodies the living temples of the Divine Music—the Word—in our earthly sojourn.[8]

Attachment to the objects of the senses, the gorgeous display of riches and wealth, the luxuriant abundance and opulence, the licentious sensualism of ease and affluence: all these contribute to the imbalance of the unsophisticated mind. These are thorns and thistles that mar the beauty of the undisturbed state of mind, which is the soil best suited for the dawn of Divinity. Every day, every hour and every passing minute are leading us more and more into the bondage of sensuous worldly phenomena.[9]

Romantic life on the physical plane appears charming. It has its attraction, but it is debasing. It leaves behind horrible bitterness and a dislike for life. Life on the higher planes is more romantic and gives eternal peace and joy—so why lose a higher and purer thing for lower and debasing transitory things? One has, therefore, to stick to one's principles and not violate the rules of purity and ethics, and he who does this, receives all the necessary help in his efforts and is greatly benefited.[10]

Those eyes which are attracted to a beautiful woman or man are defective eyes, for that beauty is temporary and only for a few years. A thing which sweetens your tongue cannot sweeten it forever; the sweetness lasts only for a few moments. If we take Master to be all sweetness, then nothing will be sweeter to us. Instead of so many efforts to dig so many pits, put in all your efforts to dig a well so that you may be able to drink the Water of Life. We have got to accumulate wealth—what is this wealth? It is the wealth of Naam—that very Power which is giving life to the whole universe. Remember: God first and world second.

Like a flute, be all vacant within so that the Master may make sweet music of your life.[11]

Reading of books is a good thing. But their purpose is that one should mould his life so that the good about which one reads becomes a part of his life.[12] Mere book knowledge or intellectual development fails to awaken Spirituality. Through book learning the intellect is certainly stuffed, but the spirit receives no food. This is why each one of us can speak fluently of spiritual matters, but actual life gives no evidence of it.[13] Anything which is above the intellect cannot be explained—it can be contacted only.[14]

Photographs should be kept only for remembrance and not for visualizing. Dwelling on photographs will, after some time, bring the picture before you which will neither speak nor move to guide you inside. On the natural Path mind has to be stilled . Everything will come naturally and unasked.[15]

You ask about music. Music is not necessarily bad for spiritual meditations, as prayerful hymns sometimes prove beneficial in awakening the inner impulse. But outer music feeds the mind, whereas listening to the Holy Sound Current feeds the soul, with which it is surcharged, as it enables it to have regular flights to the regions of the Beyond.[16]

I note your inclination for golf and cards. The latter game is harmful and you have done right to discontinue it. Golf is a good game so far as its physical refreshing aspects are concerned. It is a good physical exercise, and if you can afford it, there is no objection to your continuing with it. You know gambling or the like is harmful. You will appreciate that the mind is already full of restless attributes—so feeding it with more of similar disturbing ideas will simply mean adding fuel to the fire.[17] Speculation or gambling is a great sin and as such, spiritual aspirants are warned not to indulge in it, in the larger interests of their spiritual progress.[18]

Most of our attachments and actions in life are to pay off the karmic debts. Your going to relatives again and again was one of them.[19]

One must not be led away by the world but look upon each object with discrimination. "The entire world is tied with the ropes of the love of parents, children, wife and earthly relations," and one must free oneself from this slavery. Running away to the jungles was no solution. It had to be an inner detachment, and this inner detachment could only come through the love of a true Master. Hence the great value of Satsang, for it was only through association with Him that one imbibed the true values of life, learnt of the delusions of Maya, and imbibed a love that displaced the love of the world. Peace and blessing radiate from the person of a Saint and whoever came under His spell was freed from worldly tensions, ambitions and jealousies. He saw all creatures as of His own essence and knew all worldly gains to be a passing shadow. Such a man alone could cut through the meshes of Maya and reach out towards the worlds beyond.[20]

O Lord, we are your ignorant children. The Guru teaches us and makes us open into awareness. Today you may do one thing, tomorrow something else; you are unstable and always wanting new things, from which you go on desiring other new things. The Master always gives permission for what you want, and remains with you in all you do, but gradually continues turning you toward the Truth: that your interest in It becomes more and more powerful. When He has your interest well established, He will make a new life for you and take you into a new world.[21]

Stay in the World; an Inner Detachment is Needed

THOSE PERSONALITIES who are Truth personified never advise the seekers to leave their hearths and homes to take up vigil in the jungles and lonely places. This is not at all necessary.

> *When you meet a complete Satguru,*
> *Competent is His method:*
> *Laughing, playing, eating, weaving,*
> *You will gain salvation by following Him.*

It is not a matter of leaving the condition wherein God has placed you; there is no need to change your location, but simply change your angle of vision. Bow down to the Satguru's words, not His body only, or you remain very far away from Him and from your aim.[22]

God is within you. The Guru or Master Power is within you. He is waiting for you, but you are attached outside. It does not mean that you should leave the world and go to the Himalayas. We have to learn swimming in water, not on dry land, and not only through intellectual wrestling. It is a training in which you are given something to start on within you. It is like the needle of a compass, which always points to the north. It is to be done while you are doing your work in the world. A true Master does not advise you to leave the world, but to remain in it and yet be not of it. A boat remains in the water and you may be rowing in the boat; otherwise, you will be drowned. If the outward impressions are overflowing within you, you will be drowned in the water of the world and will have to come back again and again.[23]

The seeker who had found a true Guide and who had begun to develop the right kind of love and faith in Him, would naturally attempt to fashion his life according to his Satguru's Will, and Baba Ji laid great emphasis on the need to transform our lives. It was not necessary, he maintained, to leave the world in order to pursue the inner path. What was needed for spiritual progress was inner detachment, and he who had surrendered himself completely to his Guru was free from all earthly ties. Some of his disciples would at times express the desire for complete renunciation, but he always kept such tendencies in check:

> "You say you wish to give up home and service and devote yourself exclusively to Bhajan. Home or service or wealth—are they really yours? Turn it over in your mind. It is all a magician's game and the world is a dream. Then wherefore worry about clutching and relinquishing.[24]

You are not the man-body, but are a conscious entity: you have got the intellect but are a conscious being. You have been given this man-body by the grace of God to enable you to go back to your Home. You are to remain here, pay off your debts, your give and take and find your way back to God.[25]

True Living: to World and to God

KABIR SAHIB says that all are human beings and this is the time to understand these noble things and awaken out of the slothfulness.

Awake beloved, why sleep?
The night has passed, why lose the day also?

This is the time to wake up—to become more conscious. Give unto Caesar that which is Caesar's and remember that your soul belongs to God.[25]

You can make your home a lonely forest. Is not the night a lonely forest? The disciples who spend their nights in sweet remembrance of the Lord become God themselves. If a man can control the dim hours from sunset to sunrise he becomes a true human being.

One Master has said that in the night, the Lord's fragrance is given out—he who remains awake receives this precious gift. Do the worldly duties in the daytime, and at night consider that you are all alone, deep in the country. One's duties and social obligations with family and friends should be performed with pleasure, because God has joined you together, for the sake of give and take. But in the night you can feel free from all this and repose in His lap. It is not at all necessary to leave your home and family for meditation when you have the long lonely nights. When you are wholly absorbed in some object, it is a true sanyas, cutting off from all other things; and if we start from today, most definitely our lives will change.[27]

We should cultivate true humility, which is neither servile nor assertive. These are the things that will please the Master and make us receptive to the gracious Master Power working overhead. If you live a life of humility and simplicity, you will have peace of mind. After all, what is there on earth that belongs to you? Why be attached to the vanities of the world when the treasures of divinity lie within you. If you live for God, all things shall work out in your best interests, not only spiritually but also materially. This is the fundamental law of God and can be realized by all who practice true living.

Another important aspect of the "good life" concerns outer behavior, which should be natural to the society into which one is born; no acting or posing is required. There are some dear ones who believe that they should adopt the outer symbols of dress and name that characterize the society into which the Master was born, in the belief that this is pleasing to Him. The life of the spirit does not call for conversion to outer modes of living in name, appearance or apparel. The Masters do not come to make or unmake social orders. Their mission is just to fulfill the law of God, which is to redeem His lost children. They simply ask us to convert ourselves inwardly, to be poor in spirit and pure at heart.[28]

You need not worry about the opinions of others. Views based upon one's own testimony are the best. Every person receives help according to his individual -receptivity. All are on the way to Perfection. All that each dear one has to do is carry on with meditations regularly, with love, faith and devotion, and to develop from day to day. All necessary help is extended from the Master Power within and without.[29]

Just learn to live in the living present, making best use of time at your disposal. The precious moments of earth life spent in meditations and honest work count much for inner spiritual progress.[30]

With continued spiritual progress toward inner development, outer things become less disturbing. Remember, events come and go. Inner development, as it progresses, will gradually eclipse the physical temptations. One begins to do things in order to carry on with the higher ideal always before him or her, the fulfillment of which becomes an all-absorbing vocation in one's life. Such things as are conducive to higher progress become joyful.[31]

Everyday and every hour convey thanks to the Master —the God in Him, Who has put you on the Way—and for all other gifts you enjoy. In this way you will be aware of the Master all the time. Without Him you can do nothing and with Him you can do all things. The more time you will spend with the Master, the smoother your everyday life will become.[32]

Try to develop within, and you will see for yourself how the karmic circle works. The why and the wherefore of all things will become as broad daylight when you rise into the causal plane.[33] The possibility of future incarnations can be ruled out by gradual development of loving devotion to the Master Power and aversion for worldly possessions.[34]

If you sleep in remembrance of God, the very thought

will be circulating in your bloodstream, and when you awaken, you will arise in His sweet remembrance. They say that if one's early morning hours are wasted in sleep, one dies before living.[35]

So whatever labels are stuck on your physical form, allow them to remain, and keep your own faith, language, symbols and customs. The soul, however, is of the same essence as God, and we are all His children. The soul therefore belongs to God—give it to Him.[36]

If you will run Godward, all else will follow of its own acccord.[37] The greatest purpose of human life is that one should know one's self and know God, and all the rest is mere dissipation.[38]

Master is "Word made flesh." *He is Light, Life* and *Love*. If you live and move in Him, He will be your very *Life* and give you more *Light* and *Love*.

Word is the "Bread of Life" and "Water of Life." When you are hungry and thirsty, enter into the inner stillness and receive amply of the same, which gives Life Eternal. This is within you; none is barred from it.

Forget the past, forget the future—relax fully. Be still; be alone to your own self, giving yourself wholly to the Master. *Light* and *Love* will be generated through you to all the world over.[39]

Right Thoughts, Right Actions

EVERY THOUGHT, every word, and every deed, good or bad, leaves an indelible imprint on the mind and has to be accounted for. Hence the necessity for right thoughts, right aspirations and right conduct, all of which constitute the hedge around the tender sapling of spirituality.[40]

I wish you to "simplify, simplify, and simplify." To be simple in all aspects of life is to accept Life.

Try to help all others with a spirit of self denial. Your self will expand to cover all humanity and other creation. Such an enterprise will lead your soul on to God.

Be pure in thought, word, and deed and love all. Love is the panacea for all ills of life. Be good and do good. These five words contain in them the essence of all religions of the world. My work shall be amply repaid if you live up to them.[41]

Man is what he thinks about all day long. One can only live one moment at a time. Emerson said, "There is no moment in eternity more important than this moment." All real good or evil that may befall a man is from himself. If a man lives in a good or bad way in the real present, he will ensure the same in the future. If you have bad thoughts for others, you will harm not them only but yourself as well, as thoughts are very potent.[42] Nothing is good or bad in the world, but our thinking makes it so. We, like the one or the other of the seeds, draw upon impulses from the atmosphere as suits our own mental make-up.[43]

The road to perfection lies in walking rather than in talking, and such a thing as judging others or the Master from one's own viewpoint or understanding gained so far, is hardly justified or proper for anyone. All are on the road to Perfection and it is not wise for anyone to find fault with others.[44]

Talking is easy. Doing is difficult. Nothing is gained by talking, but by doing one may progress on the Path.[45]

Too much talking dissipates spiritual energy. You should try to control your speech by resorting to Simran of the Names silently. You will be able to tide over the difficulty and improve in due course. Think twice before you speak. Think out as to whether what you speak is true, kind and necessary.[46]

The Master's strong and protective arms and His loving vigilant eyes are always on His fold. He is for their progress. When outer difficulties seem hard, His inner grace increases. If someone says something unpleasant about you, consider it calmly. If what has been said is correct, partly or in the main, try to remove those defects and thank the person for his kindness in pointing out those truths. If, on the other hand, those things are incorrect, accept the fact that the person is not fully informed and has spoken through a misconception. Excuse him for it and *forget* it. Should an opportunity occur to remove this misunderstanding, remove it lovingly and with an open heart. This will hasten spiritual progress and help to clean the vessel which is destined to be filled with the ever-ready and over-flowing grace of the Master.[47]

So long as one has not attained universal consciousness, differences of opinion are bound to exist. But if
one has understood their cause, one will not allow them
to disturb one's peace of mind. Whatever the outer opposition, whatever the opinions of others, if one has surrendered oneself completely to one's love, then nothing
can ever disturb one's equanimity or obstruct one's spiritual course. He who is upset by what others have to say
is without question one who is still controlled by the ego
and has yet to conquer his self. He has yet to learn the
rudiments of spirituality.[48]

So whenever anybody hurts your feelings in word or
deed, forgive. Forgiveness is the only sweet water that
will wash away all dirt. Justice won't do it, mind that!
If you want justice, then that will react. Forgiveness only
washes away all dirt. Forgive and forget, this is the way
to spirituality.[49]

Good books are helpful but too much dwelling on
such like books results in bewilderment.[50] An unbiased
and careful study of the sacred books published from here
will bless you with more of right understanding. These
do not require further interpretation. Howsoever, if you
will attempt to elaborate the subtle points discussed in
them, you shall have to be more receptive by eliminating
yourself totally and let the gracious Master Power work
through you. Smooth channels do get moist with the in-
flow of divine grace and for deriving maximum spiritual
benefit you should be more self-abnegating and humble.[51]

The ethical and clean life is most essential, but without
some degree of inner conviction, one would generally

run the risk of a lapse, under some severe stress and strenuous strain. This conviction and growth, in fullness of bloom, is necessary and the Master, through His sheer grace and kindness, helps to obtain it. Your welfare is as dear to me as a loving Father has for His child.[52]

Try to live by the precept of the Master and then alone your words can have weight with your friends. You cannot preach of chastity with lust in your heart and a leer in your eyes.[53]

If there are those who do not understand or who do not wish to understand the Truth, we must not feel irritated with them. They are all God's children as we are and must be won over by love and persuasion.[54]

All initiates are on the Way. Some have developed more than others. So some may have more faults and failings than the others. We have to hate the sin and love the sinner.[55]

We should be happy in the happiness of others and suffer in the sufferings of others.[56] If we have helped even one person by removing a little misery from his day, we have done a great service. With sweet words, with kind sympathy, share the unhappy burden resting upon our poor fellow-beings, or it spreads and grows as the days go by.[57]

It is indeed a great service to make a dreary child find its way to the Father, and contrarily it is the height of sin and stupidity to prevent one going the right way and to misguide him.[58]

You are beginning to learn that things in life happen according to plan. That plan is a direct result of reactions of one's own actions. It is therefore stressed that one should act lovingly and sweetly so that further reaction is properly channelized, side by side with the liquidation of *Pralabdh* (destiny) karmas.[59]

You are advised to be more calm, patient and tolerant in face of harshness. Such like passing phases of trials and tribulations come up as a reaction of past karma and as such should be treated in the like manner.[60]

It is sure that laws of Nature are very rigid and any transgression must be paid, though their severity is, to a great extent, toned down at the feet of a Great Master. Each one has to earn and cleanse one's own vessel before it is filled with blessings of the Master. There are no windfalls, although the labor bears more fruit in the house of the Master.[61]

Yes, the philosophy of karma has a specific place in the Science of the Soul. But it should not induce morbidity nor create a sense of frustration among the initiates and non-initiates. Man is the maker of his own destiny. Though one cannot alter the past, he may forge the future.[62]

The past is dead and buried, and repentance, though good in itself, cannot cure or undo it, while the future is chiefly based on the reactions of the past karmas, and is affected to a great extent by what we are doing in the living present. So, if we care for living a nice, honorable, and honest life in the living present, abiding by the Holy Commandments of the sages and seers, there should be little to worry for the past and nothing to become anxious about for the future.[63]

We must, therefore, pay proper heed to the sowing and not to the harvesting, for the harvest will come of its own from the seeds sown. Guru Nanak has beautifully said: It may be very well to worry about events and happenings contrary to the divine plan (which, of course, can never be): and what is destined will, of course, happen in spite of us. Learn the sacred technique of doing one thing at a time and that, too, with one-pointed, wholehearted, and undivided attention. In this way you will accomplish much more in less time and with far less effort. So the Master tells us that all we need to care for is our spiritual perfection and take the routine round of the fated karmas as superbly beneficial for soul emancipation. In this way we will cultivate a state of perpetual resignation which will be helpful in holy meditations.[64]

It is a happy thing to note that you have a dominant desire to better the world in which you live, and that you worry about the human race and let your salvation take care of itself through good works and clean living. It is a very noble idea. But the practical way of effectively carrying it out is to first grow into a beautiful flower yourself and then to emit fragrance and sweetness to all, as a matter of course.[65]

"Service before self" is a very good thing. But very often one does not even know the true significance of service and with all his well-meaning intentions actually does disservice, instead of the much wanted service of which we so glibly talk. Until we discover the true "Self" within us, we cannot visualize, much less actually realize in others the self-same Life-Impulse vibrating in the universe. This is why emphasis is laid in the first instance on Self-Knowledge, for it paves the way to God-knowledge, and when it dawns, one sees nothing but the Spirit of God working in all harmony, in each creature. "Service to others" now assumes quite a different aspect, becoming a dedication to the Spirit of the universe pervading in and around you, because when one grasps the Human in himself, he understands all mankind.[66]

Every initiate has to be put on the Way and will one day reach his True Home in *Sach Khand*. Those who work earnestly and live according to the commandments of the Master will progress quickly, while others will take more time to reach their goal.

The journey home is a long one, but a pleasant one, and when one reaches the True Home, he may be selected as a Master. This is, of course, a commission from God. Anybody who after a little progress, considers that he has become a master, just harms his or her own interest. This is ego and should be avoided.[67]

It is most difficult to please a Guru: he is above offerings of money, property and worldly goods. You cannot have his pleasure by demand, either. His pleasure may be gained through respectful attention, obedience to his wishes, devotion, and selfless service to humanity.[68]

Gratitude is a very rare virtue. Because of friends and relatives, we even risk our Guru's displeasure; and this is due to lack of gratitude and faith.[69]

If the child comes up one step, He comes down a million steps to pick up the child. We are all laborers in the vineyard of the Lord. We should learn to appreciate the good in others. It helps us all around.[70]

These three things will help you: to eat less, sleep less, and have mercy, forgiveness and love.[71]

Do not dwell upon past happenings or try to recapture their past pleasures, for in that way the mind is fed surreptitiously.[72]

Procrastination is the thief of time.[73]

Abortion is unnatural action and amounts to the taking of a life. It should not be encouraged for obvious reasons of karmic debts.[74]

So we are:

To be just and friendly to everyone.

To be sincere and to be true to one's self.

To be good and to do good to others.

To make others happy.

To comfort the sick and the afflicted.

To serve the poor and the needy.

To love God and all His creation: man, animals, birds, reptiles, and also the least conscious.

They are all members of the One family of God.

There is one caste, one religion, and one God.

There is only one caste—the caste of humanity.

There is only one religion—the religion of love.

There is only one Dharma—the Dharma of Truth.

There is only one God—the Omnipresent.

                           the Omniscient.

                           the Omnipotent.

There is one language—the language of the heart.

Family

LET YOUR HOME be peaceful, as a peaceful home contributes much toward success in the spiritual practices. Even the bees will fly around in a noisy home to disturb the equilibrium of the mind. I am glad you are progressing. I have love for you. Any father will do all in his power to see that his children are at ease.[76]

If you have children, or father, mother, wife, husband, see the Light of God in them. He has united you in this relationship, not merely for an outer bond but to see and serve God in them. If you do so, there will be no bondage in your relationships. Bondage occurs only when the I-hood steps in and the Lord is forgotten. So you can do all the world's work, but live like a compass whose needle always points in one direction. Keep your attention on the Lord, for if the direction changes, then? *The Giver is forgotten, the gifts become loved, and miserable Man forgets the approaching death.* Man is fully enwrapped in the world—he is all "me and mine," and wherever "me and mine" are, there rules Illusion. "Me and mine" have some bearing on one's life, but the Lord Himself has arranged it, and when everything is seen in the correct perspective there will be no binding effects.[77]

I have led a householder's life. You also should live in the world, but there is no need to add to its degradation, and to your own. Women in the home should maintain it properly with cleanliness and tidy habits, look after the children with interest, and serve their husbands wholeheartedly. This is also a dharma (principle of righteous living). To him whose home is heaven, the whole world is heaven. How can anyone hope to realize the Lord if they declare they serve Him and ignore the needs of others? Does it mean that we dislike God in some forms?[78]

I told the people in the West also, that every home should have a church—a temple, a gurudwara, or mosque—call it what you will; then morning and evening the whole family, big and small, should sit down in remembrance of God. The children's lives will change, and yours also. Example is always better than precept, and seeing you doing what is right, the children will copy you. We are in fact responsible for the coming generation's character, and if we will not change, how can we expect that character to be decent and upright? Stop for a while wherever you are, and review your situation. Search for true meanings hidden behind all things, and make sure you have got the right understanding.[79]

Please realize that it is your inner craving and fondness that keeps you bound hand and foot, as it were, to your dear ones, and this attachment or infatuation makes you worried and miserable at all times. You see, the very ties of affection which should be a source of happiness become fetters of bondage, as you are always in the grip of fears which to say the least, are imaginary and baseless. The heart, as you know, is the seat of the Lord God. It is an asset entrusted to us for a higher purpose of life: viz., self-knowledge and God-knowledge.

Where the heart goes, everything follows on its own. So herein the Master warns us against our attention being directed always towards our worldly relationships, which always cause distraction and disturbance.

You know very well that the impediments which stand in the way of the child disciple and recklessly intrude upon him in the precious moments of holy meditations, are the family ties that drag us down, again and again, from the seat of the soul, the eye focus. We have, of course, to live in the world, yet in a completely detached manner, just as a lotus flower, which grows out of mire and yet holds its head aloft and above the muddy pond, retains its pristine purity.

Similarly, we are to attend to the mundane duties entrusted to our care without being concerned with the worries and cares of our relations, who, apart from us, are sufficiently protected by the Gracious Master Power.

You can very well understand it by a simple example. A man traveling in a train has a box beside him on the berth. Now both the man and his box are being carried by the train. If a person were to put the box on his head, he would surely be a fool, for he would break his neck for nothing. This is exactly the state of affairs with the worldly wise. We generally lack faith in the gracious Master Power and unnecessarily create problems for our bondage, as, otherwise, everything would progress smoothly in the well-established divine plan. You might well have noticed that disturbed waters do not reflect. Always try to resign your precious little self in favor of the Gracious Master Power, while sitting in your Holy Meditations, and thereby prepare a receptive ground for the inner divine grace to descend within you and fill you in abundance.[80]

I am sorry for the family disruption caused by a misunderstanding on the part of your dear mother and dear husband. Such things do happen sometimes for testing the integrity of spiritual aspirants. I appreciate your calm attitude in the face of provocation which will have a salutary effect on their strained nerves. The golden principle to be applied in such a situation is to leave the place and allow the atmosphere to become more favorable for weighing the sequences and consequences. A tumbler full of cold water when taken very often helps to bring down the temper and should be resorted to and astute silence be observed. This is a tried medicine for your guidance, which may be communicated to both of them.[81]

As regards your attitude towards your dear parents, you may please note that your duty is to be humble, polite and sweet outwardly and at heart. Everybody is free to choose his or her course of faith and action, which is chiefly determined by past karmic evolution. You should try to exhibit and inculcate more of loving humility which will be more effective to prove your greatness and that of the Holy Path on which you have been put. You do owe them some parental debt which can best be repaid by service and loving devotion. Please convey my love to them.[82]

The grown up children should deem it a rare fortune to serve their aged parents in all sincerity and humility, when they need much of care.[83]

Q. If one has great love for relatives and wishes them the highest good in the world, can one pray to the Master that that person will get Initiation, or is it a destiny fixed before death which nothing can change?

A. It is always beneficial spiritually for the initiates to radiate compassionate feelings for guiding the footsteps of their beloved ones to the Master for holy Initiation. The destiny of every person changes every moment by virtuous or wicked deeds. The holy Path of the Masters is open to one and all. It may, however, be understood that it is due to the evolution of some rare noble karma of past lives that the inner yearning of the soul gets strong for spiritual enlightenment and those dear ones who benefit from such chances by putting in extra effort are put on the holy Path, whereas others simply drift and have to wait for some better future chance. There are instances, though rare, when the sincere aspirants have seen, and received Initiation from the Master even without meeting him physically.[84]

God has united you, some as brothers, some as sisters, mothers or fathers. It is God who has united you, and you should behave in the proper way as a matter of devotion to Him. Because God has done this and because you love God, then pay off fully, as best you can. But all the same, you should be detached while doing this, just like a nurse who looks after somebody else's child. She nurses it, of course, but with all that, she knows at the heart of hearts that it is not her child. She does it for the sake of earning a living. Similarly, we should be in the world, pay off our debts, love those with whom our debts lie because God has united us, but all the same remain in air-conditioned rooms. They will only be air-conditioned if we become self-centered.[85]

So you should please be a loving and patient wife and mother to your dear husband and children. Do nothing that will upset them. Participate with them in your family life, which should include sitting down to eat with them at the dinner table. Be outwardly devoted to your mundane obligations in every way, but be inwardly and silently attached to God.[86]

Marriage

MARRIAGE MEANS to take a companion in life who will keep one another together in weal or woe during the earthly sojourn, and both of them meet the Lord. One duty may be of begetting children, for which the scriptures lay down that this power should be used for begetting the children and rest from any such communion during the conception period and also thereafter the child is taking milk of the mother. In this way, the child, the mother and the father will all be healthy. Most of the diseases the people are suffering will be eliminated. The Saints say that if the children are to be given birth, let them become either Saints, a donor to all the poor and the server of the needy or be valiant ones who can protect the forlorn and the weak.

The Saints do lead an ideal married life and when they take up such a role, they stop such a course. So, married life is no bar to spirituality if led in accordance with the scriptures. The partners in life are advised in their best spiritual interests to observe chastity by leading a moderate life by mutual cooperation. The check marks on the diary forms are essential for the people seeking improvement gradually. One learns by self-introspection and careful living. The dear ones are not forbidden to marry or have homes. But they should have ideal family life flavored with the divine grace of the Master Power. The young ones before marriage should be asked to lead chaste lives, as chastity is life and sexuality is death. A lamp burns splendidly when it has oil within, but if all the oil is leaked away, how can there be light? A life of self-restraint goes to make body and brain strong.

An impersonal deviated approach or slight relaxation in the observance of ethical code of morality in accordance with the sacred tenets of the holy Path is likely to cause harm. Normal association and company breeds attachment. But when this is flavored with divine fragrance and relished in the Name of the Master, this is bound to have much deeper impact. Opposite sex has much strong hold amongst one another when the charm results in gradual infatuation and bondage. A slight slip and attraction involved is too much to be resisted. This can cause much havoc when the dear ones are hurled down in the abyss of sensual gratification.

Divine Love and sex are quite opposing poles. Sex is not only sinful, but a serious impediment on the holy Path. It is by long cultivation when one can expect some degree of success in living a clean, chaste life. This aspect of life should please be kept in view by the senior members of Satsang when they can guide the "young buds" in their larger interests of spiritual progress.[87]

The serene love between the partners of life starts from flesh and dissolves in the souls. It is an attachment for the achievement of some higher goal of life and ultimate liberation from the Wheel. It is rather a life full of spiritual beatitude and dedication, serving as a sure sheet anchor against the injustices of society.[88]

Both of you should serve as the two wheels of a carriage thereby traveling on the way back to God. My love and best wishes are with you.[89]

Q. Please tell us something of the help which marriage partners might give one another when both are initiates in the matter of helping balance and harmonize the physical, mental and emotional fields of energy of individuals so as to increase their receptivity towards Shabd. This could be very inspiring for students yet to come as well as for those already begun.

A. Marriage is a sacrament and a companion for life in weal or woe, during this earthly sojourn. It is a rare boon of the Master when both the partners in life happen to be initiates. Both of them should exhibit and inculcate a deep sense of loving cooperation and tolerance for the rights of each other. The physical, mental and emotional fields of activity should be kept under check and control lest these degrade the soul in pursuit of carnal satisfaction.

To fall in sin is manly but to remain therein is devilish. The vital sex energy should be rationally transmuted and sublimated by exercising self-restraint and chastity. The procreation of children is one of the legitimate functions of married life. The scriptures prescribe this sacred purpose as and when such a necessity arises. The couple having such disciplined lives will be an asset for spiritual progress.[90]

It is due to the evolution of past karma that persons with varying temperaments are brought together in the sacred bonds of holy matrimony for the liquidation of their give and take. All efforts should be made for cementing the relationship. You should try and be more obedient and serviceable to your husband. Loving devotion and respect for each other's sentiments will bring in more of right understanding and harmony. You are both dear to me and I wish for you both to be happy together and help each other to know God and to fulfill the highest aim of man's life. My blessings are with you.[91]

It is incorrect to think that you have married a wrong person, as it is strictly in accordance with the Divine Plan that only destined people are married to each other for the karmic reasons.[92] Two people are brought together by the unseen Hand of God. Whom God unites, let no earthly power disunite. You are one soul in two bodies.[93] St. Paul said, "It is the unseen hand of God which has joined wife and husband, and given the former to the latter and the latter to the former." Therefore, you should be careful that you love each other and have a pure and spiritual life. Let no earthly power separate one from the other who are united by the unseen hand of God. We should not dream of divorce. I note that you still have love for each other. Love knows only of sacrifice and of giving—cannot your love for each other make you tolerant of each other's views to the maximum extent and work jointly for your higher aim and ideal of life?[94]

As regards your wife, please treat her with love and toleration; when she will slowly understand the true worth of higher life, she will begin to appreciate your action on this side. Until such time there is no occasion to feel bad-tempered. She speaks from her present level; when it is raised, she will become more understanding; so she needs your love and indulgence to bring her around. Hate does not make amends for a bad thing. It is love that corrects, so give increasingly your love to her.[95]

It is due to the evolution of some past karma that persons of varying temperaments are blended together in the bonds of matrimony for the liquidation of their give and take.[96] The karmic debt of many an intricate nature is to be paid and it is proper that it should be paid while in physical frame so that there is no stop on the Way within.

Sympathetic waves often draw the effects of the karma of one's partner in life. Moreover, wife's and husband's right and wrong love goes a long way to help or retard each other's progress in the spiritual uplift. This you witness in daily life.[97]

You should be more obedient and serviceable to your husband which will enable you to win him. Love and humility surmounts all troubles whatsoever. Please convey my love to him.[98]

I have noted your remarks in regard to your dear husband. He is so dear to me and I wish him all spiritual success. Your attitude toward him should be one of service and kindness. You must not lose your temper, but be patient and considerate. All spiritual aspirants should inculcate and exhibit rare tolerance and humility in their behavior, so that others may know that you belong to the Living Master. The balanced mind never becomes irritated or annoyed at the slightest provocation. One learns swimming in water and our daily living should be fashioned in such a manner that we make it a point to learn something new every day. Patience, humility and a sense of self-abnegation are the ennobling virtues which should figure prominently in the lives of the initiates. You will progress in this field in due course.[99]

On Raising Children

I HAVE NOTED about your lovely children . . . The raising of children is a virtuous duty. The young ones imitate their parents, who should reflect peace, harmony and sobriety by leading a disciplined life full of spiritual beatitude. The assertive attitude of dear —— shows the greatness of his soul. Self assertion is the innate attribute of soul which is all divine in miniature scale. This kind sentiment is mostly predominant in promising personalities who inherit congenial environments most helpful for their spiritual progress. You need not worry over his learning late about dressing or talking. So far as his demands are concerned, these should be met with lovingly as far as possible, so far as these are legitimate and within the scope of his raising. The young sentiments should not in any way be injured. It is the unbounded love of the parents for the children which makes them bold, brave and adventurous in their lives. You must be an affectionate and bravely stern mother so far as your love and discipline is concerned toward your children. Your good action of sitting with them regularly for listening to the Sound Current is appreciated, and will be helpful for their spiritual growth. Please convey my love to them.[100a]

You may please try to lavish the things for her which she is prone to steal. You will find that when everything is procured for her, the tendency to obtain them by stealing will be overcome in due course. Simultaneously, you can ingrain in her mind that anything and everything she is desirous of having will be provided for her.[100b]

Mother's affection for the child is innate and should not be misconstrued as unchaste. Your recurring desire to hug him is a natural human instinct. You should know that mother's love is an inner impulse and goes a long way in the healthy breeding of the child. Every soul coming to this world relishes such loving care and affection which create an inner sense of bravery and boldness. Your sacred instincts are injected in the child, which will enable him to grow gradually, and the child will come out a healthy stalwart with the grace of the Master.[100c]

If the children make mistakes, appeal to their finer instincts, with love and careful understanding. Losing one's temper, shouting, and taking violent action will only confuse them; they will not know what they have done wrong. Take time to explain, even three or four times, and it will eventually have effect.[101]

If you wish to have one or two children, well and good, but look after them properly and help them to become something good. Set a worthy example for them, and remain aware of the responsibilities of parenthood. Furthermore, the whole family should sit together and sing the praises of the Lord.[102]

Protection to Family and Friends

TRY TO REALIZE that God has concern for all His children and that He is Himself looking after all the dear ones in your family. Try not to worry about them, and the more you are devoted to your meditations, the more help you will be to all of them.[103]

Master takes care of and extends protection for all who are dear and near to the disciple and looks after their best interests.[104] The relatives of initiated persons do get help from the Master Power in proportion to the love that the initiates have for the Master and their relatives have for the initiates. Even the souls that have left the physical plane get feasible help in the manner indicated above.[105]

The near and dear relations of the sincere initiates are granted feasible protection in the Beyond, even if they had left much earlier before they took Initiation.[106]

Diet

OUR FIRST and foremost problem, then, is food, for food conditions body as well as mind.

Right Type of Food
Rightly Earned
Rightly Taken

helps a lot in this direction.

One must, therefore, earn his daily bread by the sweat of his brow, as the saying goes, and should not depend on others' earnings. We must for our livelihood engage in some honest and useful pursuit, maybe physical or mental, but it must be free from all guile, hypocrisy, ill will and animosity, for Karmic Law is inexorable in its working. Every action leads to reaction and thus the endless series rolls on interminably. Hence, the need for an honest living, howsoever poor it may be. You cannot have riches by honest avocation. Riches grow by the groans of the poor and the downtrodden, the hewers of wood and the drawers of water, and thrive on the lifeblood of our fellow beings. We ought not, therefore, run after rich foods and dainty dishes, for these bring in their train much blood-sucking and are tainted with the untold miseries of the lowly and in the long run make us miserable as well.[107]

Now, foods are of three kinds:

1. SATVIK: Pure foods: milk, butter, cheese, rice, lentils, pulses, grains, vegetables, fruits and nuts.
2. RAJSIK: Energizing foods: peppers, spices, condiments, sour and bitter things.

3. TAMSIK: Enervating foods: stale foods, eggs, meat, fish, fowl and wine, etc.

Out of the above, we should always prefer satvik or pure foods. These do a lot of good. Again, even of these, we must partake a little below the saturation point of the appetite. When we get delicious foods, we are tempted to eat more than what is actually needed and the extra food taken, instead of giving extra health and energy, proves baneful. The food which is not digested properly and assimilated in the system causes colic pains and aches and in some cases even cholera, and one has to pay with one's life itself. "Do not overload the motor of your stomach," else you fall an easy prey to nausea. A surfeit of even what is good does prove harmful at times. A moderation in victuals and viands helps in the growth of vital powers in man.[108]

Fresh air is the most essential part in our food. One must intake long breaths, retain them a while and then exhale them out fully so as to cast out all the impurities of the body. Besides, one must drink a lot of pure water and take fruit juices to flush the system through and through to make one clean. But avoid all types of hot and soft drinks, spiritous liquors, and intoxicants, for they render the mind and intellect morbid. Grains and fruits should form our normal and staple foods.[109]

The satvik food keeps the head and heart free from all types of impurities.[110] The prohibited food flares up carnal desires.[111]

Q. Alcohol is not allowed to the initiates. Does it apply to such cases where it has to be administered under medical advice for the restoration of health?

A. A certain percentage is generally there in most of the medicinal preparations for their maintenance, and there is no bar to the use of such medicines. All homeopathic medicines are prepared in alcohol. In both cases they have no intoxicating effect. But to take alcohol as such for the so-called reasons of health, even when prescribed by medical men as medicine, is prohibited, for every action has a reaction, and no amount of alcohol can prolong life even by a jot or tittle when the sands of time are running out. Do you think that alcohol can stop the process, and if not, why prolong the agony by administering deleterious substances?[112]

Food, as you know, is made for man and not man for food. We have to make the best use of food like all other things of life. One who is a slave of the palate, cannot do anything useful. By a righteous control of the palate, we can control our entire physical and mental systems. A simple diet is more nourishing and wholesome and conducive to spiritual advancement than all the so-called delicacies which the modern culinary art provides. It will always give a comfoltable feeling and serenity of mind, help you to live within your means, however limited they may be, without extending your hand before others.[113]

Sheikh Saadi, a great mystic poet of Shiraz in Persia, always preached to divide the stomach into four compartments: two for filling with a limited quantity of simple diet; one for pure and clear water while reserving one for the Light of God.[114]

Light evening meals are very essential for a spiritual

aspirant. As regards sleeping, six hours rest is more than sufficient for a normal and healthy person.[115]

The more we live a regulated life, the better our health will be. All phases of life are touched upon by the Master to help people. If you have a simple diet and eat only that much which can be digested, you will be healthy. If you eat more than can be digested, the result is that you cannot sit, you cannot think clearly, you cannot devote time, you feel lazy. So simple living, simple diet and high thinking is what is wanted. You should eat only what is really a necessity. Do not overfeed. Overfeeding will make you lazy and slothful. You will always be procrastinating. You will say, "No, I will do it later; let me rest." This is because the stomach is not well.[116]

It is the moral duty of the housewife to cook the satvik food with heart engrossed in sweet remembrance of the Lord. A food cooked like this, with the mind entrenched in the Beloved and the hands engaged in the work, becomes a manna from heaven and proves a blessing to those who partake of it. The great Master, Hazur Baba Sawan Singh Ji Maharaj, often used to give us an instance of an Indian peasant with his hands on the plough but singing paeans of soul-enthralling songs to his lady love. Such indeed should be our attitude in these things.[117]

Sickness

THE PHYSICAL ailments come up as a result of reaction of past karma and have to be born willy nilly, yet much of the severity and duration is toned down with the loving grace of the gracious Master Power working overhead. The barest minimum which cannot be dispensed is to be passed through the gracious protection of the Master.[118]

When Baba Sawan Singh Ji's leg was fractured, Baba Ji revealed that it was the result of no mere accident but of past karmas whose fruit could not be avoided. But his suffering, if not wholly cancelled, had been mitigated through his Satguru's intercession. "Whatever suffering has come to you," Baba Ji wrote, "is only a fifth part; four parts have been condoned," and went on to add:

Suffering and troubles are blessings in disguise
for they are ordained by the Lord. If our benefit lies in pain, He sends pain; if in pleasure,
He sends pleasure. Pleasures and pains are tests
of our strength, and if one does not waver or
deflect, then the Almighty blesses such souls
with Naam.

Whatever troubles befell his disciples, Baba Ji told them to be of good cheer. The sooner their accounts were cleared the better, and special grace was theirs in the hour of trial:

Sickness and pleasures are the fruits of past actions. All those who are sick are extended spe-

cial grace. Let them, therefore, have no worry,
but bear it with equanimity. During suffering,
the mind wanders not and turns to Bhajan
readily in sorrow. So blessed are the periods of
sickness when the mind is turned towards Bhajan. This is a special gift to Satsangis. So whenever sickness and pain afflict you, accept them
as the Lord's Will and devote yourself to your
spiritual exercises. So long as the surat is absorbed in the Shabd Dhun, pain will not be
felt . . . Has it not been said: "Pleasure is the
disease and pain the remedy."[119]

Saints, when seemingly ill, are generally seen taking
medicinal doses as may be prescribed by the physicians,
but actually They do not need such treatment. This They
do just to keep up the worldly order of things. In this
way, They set an example to man to continue his worldly
routine wisely and resort to proper treatment whenever
necessary. It is, of course, expected of the disciples to resort to such medicines as do not contain products of or
substances from animal sources; but some of the disciples
who have an unshakeable faith in the benign power of
the Master-healer within, usually avoid the so-called re-
medial measures, and allow nature to work on its own,
for the healing power within is a part and parcel of the
human system. The bodily disorders as they come should
be accepted and borne cheerfully, for they are generally
the result of our own dietetic errors and can be set right
by resort to proper hygienic measures and selective foods.
Hippocrates, the father of the medical system, emphasized

that food should be taken as medicine. Even serious illness, resulting from karmic reactions, has to be tolerated with patience without grumbling or bitterness, because all karmic debts are to be paid and their accounts squared here and now, and the speedier it is done, the better, instead of keeping any outstanding balances to be paid hereafter. In the time of Hazrat Mian Mir, a great Muslim devout and mystic, it is said that one of his disciples, Abdullah, when down with an ailment, withdrew his sensory currents to the eye-focus and closed himself safely in the citadel of peace. His Master, Mian Mir, when He visited him, pulled Abdullah down to the body consciousness and ordered him to pay what was due from him, for he could not indefinitely evade the payment by such tactics.[120]

Adversity

THE LIFE-PLAN of each of us has already been drawn by the Great Planner, and what actually we see and come by is nothing but an unfoldment of the Divine Plan, which if rightly adjudged is being executed with fine exactitude. But it should be taken as certain, that all things work to the good for them who love God; and since you are all directly linked with the God-into-Expression Power within, you are under His Grace and not the Law, to the minutest detail, and so severity, intensity and duration of the trials and tribulations of life, whatever they be, are suitably and gracefully mitigated, softened, and toned down by the Master Power. Just have more of deep

faith in the Supreme Power within you, for undoubtedly
It will come to your aid, guide you aright, and eventually
take you out of the seemingly impossible situations, in
such a sublime manner which you cannot possibly
imagine.[121]

The physical bodies of all are apt to undergo change
and are liable to be influenced by diet, climactic conditions, seasons, age and the like. The laws of Nature affect everyone to some degree according to the extent of
one's knowledge of them, or whether he neglects or follows them. A devoted disciple living simply and cautious-
ly and reposing all trust in the Master Power need not
feel concerned with karmic situations even if they appear
to be intolerable at the time. A loving devotion to the
Master has always cushioned the hardest of conditions.
Meditation is the most important thing and must not be
neglected. Procrastination is the thief of time. Mind also
is ease-loving by nature and should not be let loose to allow any neglect in one's program of life. As much time as
possible should be devoted to this side.[122]

Divine Will works for the spiritual benefit of the dear
ones, and fortunate are they who resign in His favor
and accept the weals and woes of earth life cheerfully,
considering them as helpful for their spiritual progress.
Every day brings in untold chances of goodness and progress for a wise person to mold him or her in the cast
of divinity. Reasoning is the help but reasoning the bar.
Human intellect is prone to error and doubt which assail
weak minds. Holy Naam is the bread and water of life
given to you. These should be eaten and drunk lovingly

and regularly for having strength of soul. Any time you happen to be obsessed with negative thinking, just give out five charged names and think sweetly of the Master, and you will be blessed with instantaneous protection.[123]

Sometimes it so happens that something comes in our way which we think not good, but that very thing which appears before us is a remedy to set us right, so that we may have something higher. Man learns swimming in water, not on dry land. When you develop that angle of vision, you will have opened your eye to see things in the proper light.[124]

Physical troubles do crop up at times due to the reactions of past karmas, when the child disciple is obliged to undergo a purification process for eventual spiritual progress.[125] Many good and necessary lessons are derived from adversities.[126]

The storms of life, no matter how severe, must be faced, but with complete trust in the Master Power working overhead, and by trying to be regular in meditation and placing all hope in Him. This lessens the severity of the storm and brings hope and cheer. The storms are passing phases; they come and go.[127] It is the essence of right understanding to be contented with whatever comes, as it is invariably flavored with divine mercy and is for our spiritual benefit.[128]

Silent suffering strengthens character and has much compensation.[129]

I am sorry for your troubled affairs which dominate you and cause mental agony and disturbance. The inexorable law of karma operates and much of the severity and duration of the strain is toned down by the intervention of the gracious Master Power. That is all that you can do, and doing so, you will be finding a new approach to your problems and will be accepting the results with cheer, knowing it to be a passing phase.[130]

When the Lord wants to make a great poem of a man's life, He sends him or her to the school of privations, worries and difficulties, and all the time He keeps extending His protective hand over him or her to pass through unscathed.[131]

Man would do little for God if the devil were dead. A man living under the shadow of an impending calamity lives at his best for he strives the hardest.[132]

Fear is not good and should be discarded by giving your worries over to the ever-present gracious Master Power working overhead. Fear is always based on some unknown apprehension, and one should look at it squarely and then it will flee in no time, as it is a result of your self-created frustration.[133]

We should be constantly on the watch not to stumble and fall when obstacles come on the way. Even if you fall, never allow such fall to throw you off balance in any way—pick yourself up and continue on your way with patience and perseverance with full trust in the Master working over your head.[134]

Even if prayer may seem to fail to avert calamity, yet it has the power to take the sting out of it. With an inner transformation there comes a change in the angle of vision, which greatly affects the outlook on life. Everything puts on a new mantle of color superbly Divine.[135]

As soon as a person collects himself and focuses his attention at the seat of the mind, he strips up the mercy of God which, in turn, fills him with a strength and fortitude never experienced before. These enable him to find a way out of the difficulty whatever it may be.[136]

Morbidity

YOU NEED NOT dwell much on your personal character or impurities of mind. It amounts to self pity. Although it is a very happy augury to be conscious of one's shortcomings, undue apprehension sometimes breeds morbidity which hampers inner progress.[137]

Any moment you feel depressed you should resort to the counting of manifold blessings granted to you by the gracious Master Power.[138]

Depression and despair breed in egoistic hearts. Ego is a human element. It is annihilated very slowly by meditating on sound current and light principles. Gradually it will dawn upon you that you are a doll in the hands of divine power dancing to His bid.[139]

Prayer

THE GRACIOUS Master Power working overhead sets in motion all forces of nature to save the child disciple under all circumstances. An intense yearning, an imploring and fervent prayer coupled with sincere effort will never fail you.[140]

The trouble with us is that we do not know how to pray. We may in a case like this simply ask, "O Lord! teach us how to pray."[141]

Since all souls are of the same essence as of God and are correlated with each other, one may as well pray for the benefit of others. High souls always pray for the good of the entire humanity. They are not content with the greatest good for the greatest number as is commonly sought by the leaders of society. Their prayers generally end with the words: "O God, do good unto all."[142]

It is a common experience that most of our prayers get no response. The reason for this is not hard to find. We have not yet learned the Will of God and how that Will works entirely for our benefit. In our ignorance we very often pray for things that in the long run are likely to do more harm than good, and no wonder that the loving Father in His boundless compassion for us does not accept such prayers and they bear no fruit, or else we would never be able to escape from sensual enjoyments.[143]

Spontaneity. A prayer being the cry of the soul in agony is most beautiful and most natural when it gushes forth spontaneously like a spring of cool water from the bowels of the Earth. It needs no embellishments of particular words and peculiar phrases. On the contrary, such adornments mar the true beauty of free expression, and very frequently the man of prayer is imperceptibly drawn in and imprisoned in the net of verbiage. All this makes a prayer artificial—a product of deliberate art divorced from feelings. Such prayers make us false to ourselves

and are not at all beneficial. God is concerned with genuine emotions expressed in howsoever simple words and
not with set speeches, vain repetitions, ostentatious phras-
eology and learned expostulations.[144]

A Disciplined Life

APPRECIABLE INNER PROGRESS cannot be made until
you learn to lead a well-regulated and disciplined
life. A regular schedule of devoted meditations, morning
and evening, coupled with weeding out of all lower desires and sensual impulses, will bless you with inner
strength and fortitude to carry out your daily obligations
and also ensure inner spiritual progress.[145]

The way to salvation lies not outside; it is within. Outer rituals are of no avail and, though it is desirable to
honor the memory of past Masters, to be lost in the worship of their samadhs, statues or pictures cannot be of
any substantial use. One must hold up their lives as a
model and, like them, concentrate upon the world within.
Baba Ji himself would spend weeks in Bhajan and Simran with only short breaks for food. He always encouraged his disciples to give as much time as possible to the
sadhans he had taught. Constant remembrance of the
Lord was the best protection against attachment and
Maya; and one should maintain the five-fold Simran all
the hours of the day.[146]

It is a path of love, discipline and self-control. After
the initial spiritual experience given at the time of Initi-

ation, the rest depends on relentless regular practice as enjoined by the Master. Daily practice with loving faith, in all sincerity and humility, is the cornerstone round which each disciple must turn, so as to make progress on the Path. Love for the Master means implicit obedience to His commandments.[147]

If, after all these means are applied, the disciple still does not understand and progress, he uses yet other means to keep him on the straight path. Forgive me, but when he pulls the rope, the soul writhes in torment. When the child does not obey and wastes his life, the Master shakes him hard, and though he might be a hopeless case, the unceasing love of the Master will infuse a breeze of enthusiasm into his heart eventually.[148]

After initiation by a Competent Master, the disciple is assured of going on to his True Home. Those who after initiation fall back to sin and to an evil life and remain attached to the world, will have to be incarnated again as a man or as a woman and then continue their progress on the Path. Those who have a deep love for and faith in the Master and are progressing and have given up all attachment for the world, will not be incarnated as a man or woman. They are placed in the lower planes inside where, with the help of the Master, they may progress on and eventually reach their True Home. Usually an ordinary initiate would take four births to complete his course, but it can be shortened even to one birth according to the disciple's love and faith and obedience to the Master.[149]

Association with People

QUESTION: *Should I avoid if possible those who, because of their worldly ways and negative vibrations, cause me to suffer—especially prolonged contacts?*

A. A man is known by the company he keeps. It is the association which molds our character, and the spiritual aspirants should be careful in keeping a keen vigil. The worldly-minded people are usually engrossed in physical and sensual pleasures and their activities affect the spiritual aspirant adversely. You should know that yours is the Way into the Beyond, whereas the worldly wise have their own ambitions of sense gratification. You should carefully avoid uncongenial society in the larger interests of your spiritual progress. Even the reading of obscene literature affects adversely, and as such, should be avoided scrupulously.[150]

It is always better to avoid company of those who have a tendency to pull down one's genuine spiritual desire.[151] Those who are far away from God are like cotton full of tangles. Without thread there is no cloth, so beware of those people in whom He has not manifested Himself, for they will fill you with further doubts. Though one may be already seeing a little truth, through association with such people, doubt will come and one will begin to wonder about it. Kabir Sahib says, "Run away from these people." If you desire some company, find a good and truthful person—otherwise keep aloof and lead a lone life. Each person's company has a very big influence, and in the company of him whose attention is wandering, one will be further adrift. The company of him who is the controller of his attention will bring an exceptional stillness.[152]

The man whose astral body is quite clear of outward impressions, with no lust, attachment or hatred, but who is imbued with the love of God, such a man, when you come into His company, will radiate those qualities to you. In the causal body are the impressions of the past births. When these are also cleared, that man is called a Saint, in the true sense of the word. The Masters always deprecate the love of the physical body and outward attachments. If you have the company of or think of someone whose astral body is not cleansed, who is not imbued with the love of God or is imbued with the outer attachments of loves and hatreds, the company of such a man will give you a like radiation.[153]

So to develop this love, we must first obey His commandments; second, weed out all imperfections; and third, devote time to the spiritual practices. You should also have the company of somebody who just reminds you of your ideal. Avoid the company of all others in whose society you are attached to the world or forget Him. If you cannot have the company of those who can help you to remember Him, then it is better to live alone. Live with the Masters speaking through the books, through the scriptures. You will be better off.[154]

Q. *Are all initiates related spiritually?*

A. Yes, more than blood relatives, as they are destined to reach their True Home to meet there in due course, where all will become one with the primordial

Source. This is a true relationship which never breaks.[155] The souls treading the same Path naturally develop affinity for one another. Those who love one another are very dear to the Master. This mutual love should enable you to develop love for the Master and will in no way intervene between you.[156]

Work

CLOSELY ASSOCIATED with diet are the means of livelihood. There are no short-cuts in spirituality. The end here does not justify the means, as it may be construed to do anywhere else. Ignoble means to earn one's living do contaminate one's diet, the very source of life itself. So an honest living by the sweat of one's brow is essential in this line. The life plant has therefore to be nurtured with pure water to make it sound and healthy, a fit instrument for the efflorescence of spirituality.[157]

The Master's teachings do not touch the social structure of life, and therefore the thousand little duties of every day life that one may have to do are not interfered with. Work should be done as a part of the duty is all that is stressed and that one should not be fully submerged and attached in such work to the detriment of one's spiritual uplift. Work one must and work one should. Work is worship, but one should dedicate all to the Master and not be grossly attached to it. A nurse would do the work of rearing up a child efficiently and with joy in return for the remuneration she gets without any attachment. So should we do all the work. In this way the performance of physical duties will liquidate the give and take smoothly. So you may do any honest work that may bring you more financial gain subject to the condition that you are able thereby not to forget and ignore your meditations. While you do your physical duties, let not your spiritual duties suffer.[158]

You must work earnestly for your livelihood. Work is the grand cure for all maladies and miseries that ever beset mankind. Work is worship, and as such, all honest work should be honored and undertaken in a spirit of dedication.[159]

All honest work is good and it should not bore you. You may consider that you are simply doing your duty to your Master when you are doing work, for duty is worship. Until such time therefore that you can find some other suitable work, you will carry on with your present work in the most cheerful way and not consider it boredom. You must support yourself and your family by honest means. It is just a way of thinking. Consider it to be Master's work and do it as your duty.[160]

It is good to work, and one should work wholeheartedly; and then forget it. To continue concerning oneself with countless petty matters will fritter away the attention. This only causes further enmeshing attachments, and wherever your thoughts are, there will you reside.[161]

Devotion to God does not mean procrastination. The lover of God works harder than other people because love knows no burden. Out of love he serves everybody.[162]

So please develop the habit of putting your heart and soul in the work before you; be it worldly affairs or meditation. The habit of doing one thing at a time will help you to progress inwardly from day to day.[163]

"Work is worship" and as such, all honest work should be honored and accepted in this sense. The usual fatigue and exhaustion are the routine functions of the physical body, yet you can relax completely by fixing your inner gaze at the eye-center, releasing the pent-up tensions by rolling down all your worries and cares on to the holy Feet of the Master within. You will find a radical change in your thought pattern and will be greatly relieved with the grace of the Master.[164]

If somebody else is looking after you and serving you, that will be debited against you. You will become bankrupt. If you have got money in your bank, that's all right; otherwise, it will go against you.[165]

If some sincere seeker after truth who was living on the earnings of others came up to our Master, he was told to put in three hours meditation for himself and three hours more for those who served him. Nobody serves you without wanting something in return. So our Master asked those who were served by others to put in double time for their meditations to be successful in the way to reach God.[166]

Riches, Responsibility

RICHES *per se* are no obstacle in the way of "spirituality," for it is the common heritage of all, the rich and the poor alike, and neither of them can claim it as a special gift for himself. All that is required for success on the Path is genuine desire, honesty of purpose, a pure living, and a steadfast devotion to the cause. A rich man has, of course, to see that he does not use unfair means in amassing his wealth and that he uses his honestly acquired treasures in fruitful pursuits and not on wasteful and ephemeral gains. He should always look upon his riches as a sacred trust from God, wherewith to help the needy and the poor, the hungry and thirsty, the sick and the ailing, for all such people have a claim on him as human beings and children of the same Father.[167]

Gifts

IT IS DIFFICULT to go through life without going through the motions of give and take. It is this very give and take which has to be worked out by the pilgrim soul that brings us back to this world. There is no harm in accepting small gifts from those with whom you come into contact in your business or family connections, provided that you have been or are in a position to do them some service in a direct form. Likewise, small gifts may be exchanged during this season of goodwill among a family. However, it is not wise to accept gifts from acquaintances, business or otherwise, who are outside your areas of immediate contact with whom you have no give or take.[168]

The Law of Karma is immutable and inexorable. The exchange of gifts amongst the satsangis will result in mutual balancing and adjustment. It should be understood carefully that the karmic binding lies in the fact that any gift is given or taken with the inner intention of doing so, whereas if the giver gives in a spirit of selflessness as a dedication to the Master Power, and the other receiving the same receives in a spirit of gratitude as a token of grace from the Master Power, both are relieved of the burden involved.[169]

Death

EACH MAN has to cast off the mortal raiment in a manner predestined and pre-ordained by past karmas, viz., by disease or accident. Death cannot befall anyone before it is due. Then why worry? We may not know as to how we will meet death, by disease or by accident, but one thing is certain, if the sweet remembrance of the Lord exists at the time, we will have a peaceful death, as the Master's presence will be overhead.[170]

Wherever our desire is, we shall go there. That is why a person's thought should be on God at the time of death.[171]

The initiates of the Living Master have a rare privilege for they are granted divine protection at the time of their final exit from the world. Such disciplined souls are at the last moment greeted by the Radiant Form of the Master, who escorts them graciously into the realms of unalloyed harmony and bliss for further progress on the Path as may be necessary for each individual. There are living instances of such events when those leaving the earth plane for good bore testimony to the presence of the Master and made a happy transition, with the kindly grace of the Master.

Death is no bugbear; it is the name given to a change which comes when one leaves the coarse atmosphere of the earth and enters a finer one of Light. Something like the sun setting in one place and rising in another. We have to leave the body one day, and at the very first sitting, the Master raises the consciousness above the body and gives an experience of the Light and Sound Principle. Then, through daily practice, this is increased. The fear of death will leave. *He who is afraid of birth and death should sit at the feet of a Perfect Master.*[172]

This is another indication of the value of Naam. So we should now begin to earn it: become the controller of who we are and what we are, and with this all fear of death will go. A child cries at birth, and when he leaves he should have good reason to rejoice.[174]

There is no court of trial after death for a love-hearted disciple. The Master is ALL![175]

The major events of life are predestined. Your deep agony over the great loss your entire family has suffered is natural. You should please be rest assured that the blood and near relations of the initiates are granted feasible protection and help in the Beyond. You need not nourish any feelings of sadness in this behalf, as such an attitude will not only affect your spiritual progress, but will cause disturbance to the departed soul.[176]

Yam Raj, the Lord of Death, is so strong that no one can overpower him; but the Guru's Shabd is all-powerful and so those who are connected to the Guru have full protection, and he cannot approach them. This shows something of the greatness of the Shabd. And yet Yam Raj was made by the same God Power. Why did the Lord make him? For His own work. But it has been seen that if a Satsangi who has the real connection with Naam, in whom the Naam has manifested (has appeared), sits at the deathbed of any person, even a non-initiate, while he remains there, the Lord of Death will not come to claim that soul.[177]

Q. Can an ascended Master help His initiates who are still on the physical plane?

A. Yes, a Competent Master is a Master to His initiates for all time, and does not rest till He takes the souls to the highest pinnacle of blissful glory in *Sach Khand.* He is not a physical being only, but Word personified, and on the higher planes acts as a *Gurudev* and *Satguru,* which terms would become meaningless if His activities were to be confined to the physical plane. If it were so, how could He take charge of the souls of the initiates on death after His passing away? A Master, in essence, never dies for the initiates. It is His troth to take them up to the True Home of His Father, and inwardly His Light and Sound forms are permanently implanted though He may have left the earth plane.[178]

Religion and Ritual

THE OBSERVANCE of religious practices, rites and rituals, keeping fasts and vigils, going on pilgrimages, etc., and doing breathing exercises are the elementary steps only which go to create in you a desire for turning to or meeting God. You have made the best use of them when you are put on the way back to God, which is the science of the Word or the Sound Current and is one for all humanity. A devotee of this science need not indulge in the elementary steps. In short, all acts involving physical labor belong to the realm of the physical world, while we have to rise above the body and bodily consciousness to get contact with the primal manifestations of the Godhead: Light and Sound. You cannot pray God with hands. "God is Spirit and can only be worshiped in spirit."[179]

I have no rituals, no forms, nothing of the sort here. No temple, no church, no mosque. Why? Because what I am telling you is the highest thing. Remain where you are; you are not to leave your religions but to make the best use of them and see how far you have proceeded, advanced, progressed on the Way. So that is one of the reasons why I have got no church, temple, or anything. I take them as elementary steps. People are stuck fast to them. They don't bear the fruits of performing the rituals or methods of outward performances. Here we have got no forms; we do not care what label you are wearing or what school of thought you have belonged to. We never care for it; we want just to enjoy that you are a man, you are a soul. The same God is within you. You must rise in that God-consciousness. This is the main purpose of Ruhani Satsang, what we are after here. This is what the world needs today.[180]

Miracles and Yogic Powers

THE SCIENCE of the living Masters is the most ancient and the most perfect science the world has ever seen. It is the most natural and the easiest to follow, and can be followed by men of all ages. Married life, avocation, caste and creed, social and religious beliefs, poverty or illiteracy, etc., are no bars. It is an inner science of the soul and consists in contacting the soul with the Oversoul, with the help and guidance of the spiritual adept, well-versed in the theory and the practice of *Para Vidya* or the Science of the Beyond and capable of granting some first-hand spiritual experience at the very first sitting. Nothing is to be taken on trust or make-believe. Miracles, spiritual healings, psychic phenomena, fortune-telling, akashic records and worldly desires are all to be left aside, for these are positive hindrances on the Path. The entire energy is to be conserved for internal progress.   •

> *Seek ye first the Kingdom of God, and all things shall be added unto you.*

This is the highest Truth that has been taught from hoary antiquity by sages and seers since the day of creation. It is unalterable and shall remain so. God, Godway, and Godman can never suffer any change and shall ever remain eternal.[181]

Master Saints never show any miracles to a disciple except in rare cases due to special circumstances. Miracles are in accordance with the laws of Nature but are nevertheless terribly entangling webs detrimental to the highest ideals of man in his approach to Almighty God. It is a subject that an ordinary man would not care to study, for the simple reason that it requires immense self-control and training of the mind, with restrictions that he would not like to tolerate or pursue. The miraculous powers achieved after a lengthy period of time are instrumental in doing both good and harm, and as they are utilized more for harm than anything else, they are termed as a disease by all truly spiritual persons. The Masters are in possession of Supreme Power but their mission is sacred. A disciple whose inner vision has been opened sees any number of miracles at each step. To hesitate to believe in a Master without seeing miracles is as foolish as our refusal to believe that a certain person is a multi-millionaire unless he shows us his money. He may have all his money deposited in a bank and like to spend it in the way that he chooses, without caring for public applause or approval. Out of an audience of several thousands watching a magician perform his tricks, only a very small number would thereby be induced to learn the art. Those who are anxious to see miracles are not true seekers.[182]

Saints do not display miracles nor do they allow any of their disciples to indulge in such vainglorious and empty baubles.[183] Making prophesies and performing miracles are simply collections of mind.[184]

Yogic Powers: The duty of a superintendent in a jail is to keep the prisoners in prison, to chasten, and to reform them. Similarly, the aim of the deities and divine incarnates (Avtaras) has always been to keep men tied to themselves by showering the gifts of various *ridhis* and *sidhis* on them. (This refers to the granting of gifts, boons, favors, wealth, ease, and comfort in worldly vocations and giving super-human powers for doing good or ill.) These limited salvations and comforts they grant to their devotees are only up to the stage which they themselves have attained and they may even permit nearness of sojourn in the various regions wherein they preside. They cannot help in the bringing about of union with the Almighty because these subordinate powers are themselves deprived of this highest privilege.

The *sidhis,* or extraordinary powers referred to above, are yogic powers which of themselves come to aspirants after Truth with a little *sadhan* (practice) but these are positive hindrances in the way to God-realization, for one is generally tempted to indulge in miracles like thought-reading, foretelling, transvision, transpenetrations, wish-fulfilling, spiritual healing, hypnotic trances, magnetic influences and the like. These *sidhis* are of eight kinds:

Anima: To become invisible to all external eyes.

Mahima: To extend body to any size.

Garima: To make body as heavy as one wishes.

Laghima: To make body as light as one may like.

Prapti: To get anything one likes by mere wishing.

Ishtwa: To attain all glories for the self.

Prakayma: To be able to fulfill the wishes of others.
Vashitwa: To bring others under influence and control.[185]

Spiritual Healing

S PIRITUAL HEALING is prohibited by the Masters. It has reasons and deeper significance behind it, which ordinarily people ignore, considering the face value of the profits accrued and attributing it as service to the suffering humanity. The inexorable Law of Karma is supreme and demands adjustment of each farthing. The human body is the highest rung in creation granted by Providence for the spiritual perfection of the soul during this incarnation. The soul in man being of the essence of God Himself has the same attributes as those of God, but having been environed by mind and matter has lost its true heritage. Soul in its present state is gravely enmeshed by body and bodily attachments, which are more or less the reaction of past karma, which it has been contracting all through up to the present incarnation. The present earth life is a passing phase in the long journey of the soul from the lower categories of creation on to the True Home of the Father. Physical body is material but the soul is spiritual, but when reaction of karma occurs, the man is bound to suffer pain and pleasure.

Now the sufferings demanding spiritual healing fall mainly in the domain of physical troubles, which may include even mental agonies such as nervous breakdown, etc. These being the reactions of past karma must demand adjustment and as such are to be borne by the victim. The healer, whosoever he may be, conducting this service, takes the karma on his head, to be borne by him at a later stage. Besides, the bit of spiritual attainment he has attained in silencing his mind is dissipated in such gestures of a miracle healing. Moreover, this process of healing is administered on weaker minds which usually fall a prey to their sentiments. What can ordinarily be cured by undergoing a bit of suffering and medicine, is exchanged for spiritual dissipation, and the debt remains standing, awaiting adjustment at a later stage. Again, this sort of healing becomes professional and at times encourages corruption and misery. It not only invites malpractices, but brings in more of mental agony and wretchedness in multiplied form added with interest. This is a causal postponement of payment for a future date, and adds strong fetters over the soul.

Contrarily, the Masters advocate right living and right thinking. A disciplined devotee of the Master is advised to lead a pure, clean, chaste life, thereby pursuing a spiritual goal under the protective guidance. The implicit obedience for the dietary regulations and leading a simple truthful life leads to happiness and joy. If, however, some suffering due to the evolutions of past karma comes, its severity and duration is much toned down by the intervention of gracious Master Power, like a penny for a pound, or a needle prick for the gallows, and the disciplined child disciple comes out unscathed with the grace of the Master.

The healing which is said to have been administered

by Jesus or others, was of a higher quality, as when you merge in the cosmic awareness, and lose your identity, you become so spiritual that even thinking of a person or those touching the hem of your garment will get healed, as termed colloquially in the Bible. You have not to exert on your part to heal others. Yet above all, it is the faith which cures, and the sincere initiates do not indulge in these things and rather aspire incessantly for the attainment of their spiritual perfection, which is the highest goal of earth life. The soul which has to go far higher to merge into the Oversoul is retarded by engaging herself to lower pursuits. The initiates are, therefore, warned not to administer this spiritual healing in their own larger interests, which would result in spiritual dissipation and bankruptcy. It will add strong fetters over the soul and karmic debt will be very heavy to be repaid.[186]

Other Yogic Powers

Q. Can I teach Yoga?

TEACHING YOGA is all right; you may earn your money in any way you like, but don't be your own subject of yoga. If you do, then you will go the longer way. Our way can be done very quickly. That way would take at least hundreds of years to come inside; you would have to take the longer way. If you want to take the longer way, all right, do it. You may want to teach it, that's all right, but don't do it your own self, that's all. If you want to go the longer way, very good, you may choose it if you like. That is the longer way; it was introduced in the past ages. In the Golden Age man lived for one *lac* of years. People could put in 70,000 years, 80,000 years in that practice. Then came the Silver Age. In the Silver Age the age came down one tenth to 10,000 years. People could put in two or three thousand years in that way. Then came the Copper Age. Life was cut down to one-third. Even then you could put in two or three hundred years. Nowadays man does not live 70 years. How can you follow those methods that were introduced in those years? We cannot live up to that age. So Kabir and Guru Nanak introduced this simple way that we do —even a child can do it. It is the quicker way, you see. Have you read *Crown of Life?* I wrote this book about the comparative study of all yoga. There is one part that explains what you do, what you are teaching. There are other forms of yoga in it too. But our method is the quickest way through all the ages, for any man of any age. Now, is it clear to you?[187]

Q. *Hatha Yoga groups have grown in popularity in this country. Could we have your comments on the value of such groups?*

A. So far as the physical aspect of Hatha Yoga exercises is concerned, it is all right to have a few simple and light exercises for maintaining good health; but it does not seem advisable to go in for strenuous exercises involving several other hazards of breathing, etc., which are rather diagonally opposite to Surat Shabd Yoga. You will please note that there is a world of difference between soul and physical body, and these are separate entities. Besides, chanting or too much outer singing scatters the attention, which on the contrary requires introversion and inner silence.[188]

Baba Ji maintained that "religious wranglings and disputes, the pride of caste (the Varnashram), of worship, pilgrimages, mere reciting of scriptures, worshiping those who were past and gone, and such other actions and disciplines" were all "a great deception" and a trap set by Kal to keep the soul within the bondage of the realms of relativity. In like manner, the outer kriyas or practices of traditional yoga—pranayam and various mudras and asanas—were ineffective for taking us to our real goal.[189]

He had at a very early age experimented with many a yogic method and whenever he pronounced on the subject, he spoke not as one who bases himself on academic learning, but as one who has himself practically experienced what he says. His words carried conviction, for there was not a trace of prejudice in what he said. He simply explained that he himself had explored all avenues and found the path of Sant Mat or Surat Shabd Yoga to be the highest. He had a great deal to say about the wonderful miraculous powers that could be acquired through yogic sadhans; but his one criterion was: did they make one the master of one's mind, freeing one from the tyranny of desire? If so, then there was nothing to be said against them, but if not (as was usually the case), then they were hardly of any use. While in Murree in 1894, he, in response to many questions addressed to him by Baba Sawan Singh Ji, dwelt at length on the subject of comparative yoga and concluded by demonstrating how Kabir and Nanak had assimilated the best from their predecessors; how they had penetrated far higher into the Mystic Path; and how they had succeeded in developing a method for mergence with the Formless Absolute that was within the reach of all.[190]

What was this Science of the Surat Shabd Yoga that represented the crown of mystic achievement? It was, said Baba Ji, the path most economical in effort and the one most rewarding for reaching back to the Primal Source of all life and light. Its secret lay in the insight that if the soul was to merge back into the point from where it had descended, the way of ascent must be identical with that of descent. The Nameless One when he had assumed Name and Form had projected himself into Shabd, Naam, Kalma, or the Word. It was this spiritual current, whose primary attributes were melody and effulgence, that was responsible for all creation.[191]

As regards the Kundalini, you should not pay any attention to that as it is fraught with danger. You have been put on the Path, the Natural Way.[192]

Astrology, Reincarnation Investigations, I Ching

Astrology is a regular science, but few there are who are really conversant with it. This requires a clear mind vision. Moreover, it affects those who are under the influence of the Stars; but those who transcend the starry sky, or are taken under the care of Masters who transcend the starry sky, the predictions in their cases do not stand correct.[193]

Q. Is group investigation of reincarnation and karmic relationships advisable among initiates?

A. You are kindly advised to leave all such studies well alone and devote your precious time in holy meditations and the study of the sacred books of the Master. The holy Path of the Masters offers a direct conscious contact with the divinity within after rising above body consciousness. This sublime principle differentiates the holy Path from all other schools of thought.[194]

The book *I Ching* has been seen. Stop altogether asking questions of this book, as these are not only misleading but fraught with dire dangers. It is incorrect to understand that Master speaks through the book.[195]

On Military Service

EVERY CITIZEN has an obligation to the country in which he resides. If that country is threatened by an invader, then it is the duty of every man and woman, in accordance with his or her mental and physical capacity, to protect the innocent people of the country. For example, one could render service in a non-combatant branch of the army such as the Medical Corps whose primary duty is to relieve the suffering of the wounded and the like.

If a government, for any cause, orders a general conscription of all able-bodied men to the armed forces, there is little that can be done. If one can honestly be excused from military service because of physical disability or any other valid reason, then by all means this may be done.

All Saints and Masters have greatly deprecated not only wars, but all forms of violence that bring suffering to mankind. These conditions are brought about by man himself, who, in his ignorance of the fact that God resides in every heart, will not allow his fellow men to live in freedom and peace.

All the dear ones who are obliged to fulfill their duty to their country should have full faith and courage in the gracious protection and guidance being extended to them by the Master Power working overhead.[196]

Baba Jaimal Singh (the Master of Hazur Baba Sawan Singh) served in the army for 34 years, and saw active service. I have written a biography entitled *Baba Jaimal Singh—His Life and Teachings* which may be referred to by the dear ones for an account of His life during and after His active army career.

Similarly, both Hazur Baba Sawan Singh Ji and myself served the military in connection with the construction and accounts work in the field under fire.[197]

The Master

THE MASTER is always with His children who are all dear to Him. Where more than one meet in His loving remembrance, His grace takes a practical shape and happy and fortunate are those who are able to benefit from this grace.[198]

There will be moments in the course of developing love for the Master when one, judging from one's own limited understanding, doubts the validity of the Master's instructions, but such moments are only tests to make our self-surrender more complete and more secure, and he who passes through these tests successfully, will one day radiate with the glory of God.[199]

The Master-soul's vision is correct: he does not dance to *anyone's* tune. He can never see anything inaccurately, so naturally he will never do anything wrong, like the depraved man with his smoky spectacles.[200] Though the Masters know everything, they do not disclose what they know, but allow things to come out openly of their own accord on the material level.[201]

We sometimes consider the Guru to be less able than an ordinary man. With this type of outlook, what can we hope to achieve in progress? The worldly things are more beloved; Guru and God are accepted casually for whatever can be derived through them materially. The attitude is one of tolerant duty, with respects paid in a condescending manner. Man always thinks he is the greatest of all, but if he really *became* great he would not be in this blind egoistic state.[202]

Correspondence

ALL MAIL is dealt with confidentially and but for my personal correspondent who receives instructions for drafting replies, nobody else reads the letters received from the dear ones.[203]

Hearing Shabd Before Initiation

THERE ARE those who see the Light, even before initiation. This is good and is a reaction from the good karmas of past lives—but to progress farther into the Beyond, correct guidance and protection is necessary.[204]

Hearing of inner music at its lower links by a person is not something unusual. It gives some pleasure and joy to the hearer, but he does not know how to develop the process from stage to stage to reach one's True Eternal Home of everlasting Peace, Joy and Bliss. This is not at all possible by one's own unaided efforts.[205]

Dreams

QUESTION: *What is the significance of an initiate having terrifying and vivid dreams?*

A. Dreams are the outcome of past recollections based on hearings, seeings, readings or dreadful thinking. The terrifying dreams generally are attributed to some digestive disorder; a bad stomach which can be cured by simple medication. The vivid dreams denote clarity of inner vision when some people can recollect their dreams very clearly whereas others cannot recall them.[206]

Pets

THE PRESENCE of pets like cats or dogs in the room during meditations is no harm provided these do not disturb you to be there during meditations.[207]

Your dog should not be fed on meat as it will contract karmic debt for you. It can live on vegetarian diet all right, just as you have switched over.[208]

It is better to avoid looking in the eyes of others and this includes animals.[209]

In caging birds and keeping pets collared, chained and imprisoned, one wrongly takes it for granted that these poor, dumb creatures have no court of law where they can lodge their complaint.[209a]

It is a Noble Search

To FIND OUR true self—does it mean that we are lost? If you ask me for the truth, I would say we are *completely* lost.[210]

The whole play of Spirituality is with the attention. *Where the attention is, there you are.* Through putting your attention wholeheartedly on physical exercises, with a little training you can be a wrestler of powerful strength. With your attention directed on scholastic subjects, you can become an intellectual giant. If you put all your attention on the Greater Attention (God), you will grow in spiritual stature. On the spiritual health depends the health of mind and body both. This teaching is for all, but most of us are still playing with toys. *We are disinterested with this doll's play when we see the true form of our Beloved.* How beautiful must the real thing be, if the imitation is so attractive! But, unfortunately, while the blind lead the blind, both continue to fall into the ditch. This is a very frank talk.[211]

This pure subject—the study of the attention, which you can call Spirituality—is ever in existence, but sad to state, we are not interested in this higher knowledge. Our attention is on the body, on sensual pleasures, and on intellectual deliberations. Bookish knowledge is all wilderness; there is no way out. By reading the stories and anecdotes of the Masters, we can enter a state of pseudo-intoxication, but first we should see something of the Truth and then sing the Lord's praises.[212] If the soul is a conscious entity, then its food must be something conscious, and the expression of the Lord, which is Light and Sound, is the bread and water of life. And he who has it, can give to others. *My Beloved is everywhere, no place is without Him; Glorify that body in which He is manifested.*[213]

The Master has the same physical form as other men, but although he lives in the world, he remains aloof from its effects. He is in perfect control of all his faculties, and can rise above the body at will. Or he can work in the bodily senses, at his own choice. We see his body on this earth, but his soul travels in all the spheres. Contrary to this, we are tied to the body and cannot rise above it. Therefore only in his company and with his assistance can we have true realization. Yet while I utter these words you will not have true conviction unless you see for yourselves.[214]

The Naam has an indescribable intoxication. *Delightfully sweet is the beloved Naam. Also, Nanak is perpetually intoxicated with the Holy Naam—day and night.* Who gets it? *Those who have merit from the distant past will get the gift of Naam to bring them near to God.* Those children who God has decided are to return to Him are connected to the Naam by the Satguru, and the Naam takes them back to whence it emanates. A Muslim fakir says, *You have sacrificed the true mosque for the outer one.* The outer mosques and temples are for those whose inner eye is not open to see the true Light of God. He cannot be known through senses, mind and intellect, or through pranic practices (i.e., practices involving the motor current in the body)—but only by self-analysis. When we achieve self-knowledge, then the Life Sustainer will be met. *The attachments will break, salvation will be given, and you will go home.* You will be released from all ties, and living in this world, yet you will be free.[215]

Dear friends, this world is a sea which we must swim across with the aid and support of God's inner Light. It is really very clear and simple when one sees everything from the right angle of vision. And the definite indication that a Master is true, is when he lights that flame within another.[216]

Most of the world's population is in the dark; not knowing whence they came, to where they are going, or what their purpose is on earth. Basically, all religions indicate that there is Light and Sound; I have mentioned that Lord Krishna spoke of it. The Muslim fakirs also referred to it. It has been termed the Music of the Spheres, Truth clothed in Light, and the Unstruck Fire; Buddha called it Intrinsic Hearing. The teaching remains the same, though man forgets it; but the Masters come to revive the Truth again and again, and give the right understanding of true integration. Some people want to know, "What do we get out of this?" Apart from the benefit of becoming detached while living in the world, we are told: *Unhappiness will not touch us; The illusion will be revealed as mind and matter.* What a wonderful blessing! He who becomes one with the Unchangeable Permanence, life and death are the same to him. Someone is born, someone dies—he feels neither happiness nor misery. Such elevated existence comes through development of the inner being. You cannot start to dig a well on becoming thirsty, for you will die of thirst before reaching the water. The spring of the everlasting nectar of life comes through the inner contact, and to drink from this spring daily will render ineffective all the pinching consequences of worldly experiences.[217]

It is said, *After meeting the Satguru, one knows.* When is this? *When attachments and outer effects are finished.* Is it possible to be free from attachments while living in the body? If one is in full control of one's attention, and can direct it at will, then it is possible. If one daily rises above the body and journeys into upper regions, how will one remain attached to the world and its environments? Also, one will work in the world with a double zeal without that clinging nature to hinder.[218] There are three kinds of heat which burn within man. One is *adhibhutak*, connected with the physical body. Another is *adhidevik*, through the outer, untoward happenings. The third is *adhiatmik*, and that is when one gets a higher contact within and one is then no longer dragged around by the mind and senses. When death comes, one merely says, "Let's go." A true disciple is thus ready for the change. When your condition has become like this, then you will know that you have met the Satguru.[219]

Be grateful that you have got something at last—even if it is after a long search. Only the power of the Naam can overcome the difficulties of this age.[220]

The clue lies in the Guru's teachings through which you will develop true love for God, wherever He has manifested Himself. A small spark of fire can burn to ashes a huge pile of logs, and similarly life upon life's sins can be burned away through a small spark of Light from the Satguru. On the very first day of Initiation, he manifests the radiance of Naam within the seeker, who then should take great care of it and value it. *By repeating the Naam, the Light of millions of suns will be seen.* Also, *In the darkness, He came and lighted the Lamp.* You receive the very thing that the true Master teaches, for the Light is manifested in him, and he gives a spark of that Light. *The Master placed a small share in my safekeeping*. Guard that small share carefully. In the ages past, the Master would keep the disciple at his feet until he had become ready to receive the precious gift. These days, which disciple has the patience and will to learn? So, on the very first day, the connection is given, and then it is up to the disciple what he makes of it. The value of Naam can never be estimated—always remember this. Keep a watch over your whole life—each action—day by day, and through meditation increase your inner progress.[221]

Out of the abundance of the heart, a man speaks. Whatever is the state of mind at the time, so the speech will have similar effects on others. If the mind is filled with anger, lust, greed, etc., even though these thoughts be hidden behind sweet words, yet the effect produced will be drastic. The breeze which passes through fire will bring heat, and on the other hand, that which passes through ice will bring coolness.[222]

There is great charging in the Master's words. Due to His elevated condition, there is a sweet fragrance radiating from Him. If you visit a perfumery, though you may buy nothing, yet you will freely enjoy the delightful perfume permeating the atmosphere. A Saint's name is glorified throughout the four corners of the earth. He may or may not declare Himself, but His radiation is spread everywhere. *O Nanak, the Gurumukh is a rarity.* It is seldom one meets such a personality, but the world is not without them. He is our true friend, meeting whom all doubts are erased and right understanding established in our hearts. He who can do this is a friend indeed.

Such people have always been hard to find, but when they do come, through radiation a flood of Spirituality pervades the world.[223]

Today there is a great awakening beginning. Some have got the answer, some have not, but the search to solve the mystery of life has been born all over the world. The day that question arises in the mind is the greatest day of one's life, for once it is born it does not succumb until it is satisfied.[224]

Whoever approaches a Master with full devotion and humility will get the rareness of the gift. After getting the human form it is our hereditary right to realize God. Of course, if we do not make the best use of our life, then who is to blame?[225]

It matters not to which religion you belong—if the Light is burning within you, all is well. *A true Master is one who brings everyone together.* With right understanding, man and man become one, for each has a soul and that soul is of the same essence as that of God, the Life Sustainer of all things. If all men truly realized this, then who would hate his fellow, and who would cheat or take another's goods? The police and military forces would become superfluous, for man's very neighbor would be his protector.[226]

My friends, no matter in which town or country you live, you should live as true brothers and sisters of the one Father. The morals of all daughters and daughters-in-law, their protection and welfare, should be your concern, for in this will be your own family's protection. Live in love for one another. If husband and wife are

happy, loving, and loyal together, then no one and nothing can come between them. Similarly if the people
of any country are one in each other, then no power or
politics can disturb their peaceful living. All laws are
for the lawless; if you are good, nothing touches you.
Each one of you should make your life a model, and you
will see that the whole world will have peace and happiness. Lack of this simple existence is bringing unhappiness
everywhere.[227]

As long as the higher contact is not made, the world's
misery will not be resolved. As it stands, whatever a man
sows, so shall he reap.[228]

Just see, only by talking about these things so much
peace enters our hearts. How much more happiness will
we gain through true realization—received through the
radiation from a perfect Master. So, make your life an
example of the teachings you follow—live up to them. If
you have already got the connection, take the utmost
care of it, and value it. If you have a strong desire to
get it, then God Himself will make the arrangements
for you. When you get the contact with the Holy Naam,
remember it is the soul's very food. Furthermore, intro-
spect your daily thoughts and actions and see where you
have reached. Many ages have passed by since you were
first given a human form, and many years have passed
since you joined some religion; now consider, where have
you got to?

As long as inner contact is not established and practiced daily, and you don't avoid all that may lead you
away from it—through self-introspection—then where-

ever you have reached up to now will be hidden by a dark curtain and your path of progress will be obstructed.[229]

BOOK TWO

THE NEW LIFE
IN GOD

The New Life in God

Love

WHAT IS THIS LOVE of which all mystics, Eastern and Western, have spoken so insistently? Is it like the love of the earth that we know? If you study the bonds of earthly love, you will find that at some point or another a trace of self-assertion is present in every case. Parent and child, friend and friend, man and wife; each is involved in a more or less strong drive for possession. It is a love that can often rise to great heights of self-sacrifice and yet it is a love that is not wholly selfless.

But the "Love" of which the mystics speak is a love that must be completely purified of the self. If one has not attained complete purification in this respect, one's love is still not perfect and not truly acceptable in the eyes of the Lord. And so the love of mystics is one in which one completely and unreservedly surrenders one's self to one's love. The seeker who, having found a true Master, has developed such absolute love for him, steadily purifies himself of all imperfections and makes himself a fit recipient of Divine Grace. You may well ask why there is this insistent stress on complete self-surrender on the mystic path. The answer is simple: without this absolute surrender of the last vestiges of ego and selfhood and without such complete absorption in the object of one's love, one cannot attain that unwavering concentration of all one's faculties which is the prerequisite of all inner progress. Absolute love and self-surrender are only other aspects of complete and flawless concentration. The moment the "self" enters into the picture and the question of "I-ness" arises, the single-pointedness of concentration is dissipated and inner advancement is made impossible. Besides, the goal of the spiritual aspirant lies far beyond the limits of individuality. His goal is union with the Absolute and such union must necessarily be a denial of the limits that separate us from each other. He who cannot rise above the ego, the faculty which creates these very limits, cannot hope to attain to that station which is the denial of all individuality and a realization of the oneness of all life.[1]

Love is innate in our souls. God is love and our souls are the drops of the Ocean of all love, which is also love personified. But love knows attachment. The love of the soul which should be attached to the Oversoul, or God, has been attached to the physical things and outward enjoyments. That very love has been turned into attachment. You go where? Where you are attached. That thing within your mind is where you are attached, the love of which you have got in your heart. If you have got love for worldly things, naturally you will come again and again to the world. If you have got love for God or the God-in-man, then where will you go? Where He will go. If He is not going round and round on the Wheel of Transmigration, how will you go! He comes from the

Father and goes back to the Father. He comes with a commission to take souls back to God.[2]

Love for the world, outer attachments, to meet with your own wishes or purposes is lust or attachment, not love. One prophet said that love is like a bridge to cross over the river underneath. It is only for the purpose of crossing, not to remain on the bridge. So your love for the God-in-man is for crossing the bridge, to be attuned by His company, where naturally the love of God is radiated. If you are attached to the physical body and outward attachments, that is no love.[3]

It is said that love can be found by just giving the heart away to somebody and then to go around heartless. If your heart is taken away by somebody, then what is left to you? Only such a man can really realize what love is. The outer sign of a man who loves is that he gives implicit obedience, complete self-surrender. He cherishes what the Beloved or the Master wants. He always wants to please the Master, not to please himself. Love is no business. It is not grown in the fields, nor bought from any shop. It is already innate in your soul, but can be flared up when you come across somebody who is overflowing with love. We have got the man-body, in which this love can be developed. As I told you, love is already innate in your soul. It just requires attachment to somebody. Instead of attaching our soul to the Overself or God, who is all Consciousness, we have attached it to the body, to the outgoing faculties and the world outside. This has been the reason of our coming back again and again to the world. If we have love for God, who is already controlling us in the body, then naturally where will we go? We will go to where God is, we are not to return to the world. Love is flared up only in the company of somebody who is already overflowing with love. In His society, we will have the infection of love, the radiation of love. So who can follow this way? He who can completely surrender his body, mind, and soul and also his very faith. The Beloved is everything to him. He will be ready to sacrifice everything for the Beloved.[4]

Through getting attached by love to the Guru, the darkness is dispelled; thousands of suns shine forth with the repetition of Naam. Due to the difficulties of Kal Yuga, this blessing is being given freely. In the past, restrictions were imposed before connection to Naam was given. After many years of service, the Master would then give the first part of the theory, and so on. But the darker the age, the more mercy does the Master extend, and today everyone receives an experience from the very beginning. This special concession is due to the bad condition of the world, which is drifting speedily into negativity. A Master would use any means to save the souls from such a terrible fate, but if the soul receives the gift and then wastes it—well, that is a tragic misfortune.[5]

"What is love? Where is it? What does it want? How can it be developed?" If you love somebody, he is always in your mind. If you keep somebody always in your mind, naturally you will feel attracted to him; when somebody comes to you and speaks of the Master, you take him as your true relative. So this is a feat of love. The most practical and competent way in which you can develop it is just to sit in the radiation of somebody who is over-flowing with the love and intoxication of God. This is the quickest and most natural way of being, what you say, infected. You will get infected by the society of the Master, who is overflowing with the love of God. And what does it cost? It costs nothing. The Beloved wants that the lover should not look to anybody, not to hear anybody, not to think of anybody, except the Beloved. This is the feat of love. The man who has got such a love, why should he return to the world? He may return as a Teacher, as a Master, to bring back the children of God to His Home. But He will never come as a prisoner, as the reaction of the past, being attached to the world. So this is the feat of love and what it gives us.[6]

Renunciation truly lies in the fact that we are not tied to the world, to anything outside. A man who has got love within him, love of God, is attached to God so much that all other things leave his mind, he is not attracted by anything else. For instance, if such a man is sitting here, there may be hundreds of others sitting around him, but he will be wholly and solely absorbed in the Master. This is a feat of love. Love also knows sacrifice. The Masters say that those who would like to play the game of love, should come with their heads cut off and placed in their palms as an offering. Even then, they would not mention what they have done. God knows the very trend of our mind, what lies in our mind. This is one fact that I show.[7] So the main thing is to have love of God. The criterion of love for God is sweet remembrance of God. You never forget Him, even while eating, sleeping, coming or going.

If that is developed, then naturally you will go to God.[8]

We must constantly remember that our aim is God. And we must not be concerned with anything that makes us forget Him.[9] Your attention is divided in so many ways. It is just like a pipe that has so many holes. When the water flows through the pipe, it will ooze out from each hole drop by drop. If you close all the holes except one, the water will shoot forth. So if our love, which is now divided into so many things, is withdrawn from the outside and only one avenue is left, to God or the God-in-man, naturally it will shoot forth. Love is already innate in our souls, it is simply divided in so many things. In the body, in enjoyments, in children, for the name and fame of the world. If we just keep one hole open and direct our love there, naturally it will be detached from the others. That will work wonders.[10]

If you direct your attention, which is the outward expression of your soul, wholly and solely to God or to the God-in-man, then you won't see His face, but you will see the Light emitting out of it. That is the criterion. Such a man is asleep from outside and awakened from within. So we are attention or surat, you see. Our attention is the cause of all this machinery going on in the body. The *premi* or the lover is really awake within and asleep outside. He is in the world yet out of it. This is the ultimate feat of love, which is called charity. It is not lust, but love or charity and is innate in our own self. God is love and love is God, and that is part and parcel of our own selves. When that is withdrawn from outside by the concentration of the attention, then wherever it is di-

rected, you wholly and solely are there. If you direct your
attention to the Master, you will become what He is.
Whatever is in Him will be transmitted to you, reflected
in you. One Master said that the Master who has become
a Master was once a sikh, or a follower. When a sikh or
follower is fully absorbed into the Master, he becomes
the Master, but first he has to become a true sikh, a true
follower. When he is absorbed in Him, he becomes the
Master. When he speaks, it is the Master speaking in
him.[11]

Now the question arises, how can the Master be
pleased? There are two ways and the first one is, whatever attributes He has got in His life should be adopted
in our own life. We should copy, live according to those
qualifications which we see in Him. The qualifications
in Him are the qualifications of God on a miniature
scale. God gives to everybody whom He created, because
naturally the Creator will love His Creation. So the Guru
will love His disciples, because it is He who has given
birth to them in the inner way. As He loves us, so should
we love all. He won't let anybody suffer and you should
not let anybody suffer. You must share with others. These
are some of the qualifications that the Master has and
are the attributes of God reflected in Him. The second
way is to just live up to strictly, literally, what He says.[12]
If the Master or anyone whom you love says "stop," then
stop there, don't take a further step. But do we keep His
commandments? We don't; then where is our love?[13] So
to obey the Guru's commands is the first and the last
lesson on the path of Spirituality. Those who do not obey,

who show one thing on the face and feel something different in the heart, will never gain the Guru's pleasure.[14] He says, "All right, devote regular time to your meditations. Weed out all imperfections within you from day to day." We say that we have got no time to keep the diaries. We have not even started as yet, what to speak of love. Further, if we wish to have thoughts of somebody, love of somebody, we shall always be thinking of him.[15]

Having found a genuine Master after resolving all doubts, one must live up to the ideal of a perfect disciple. And what is it to be such a perfect disciple? It is to have full faith in the Satguru, never questioning his wisdom and authority. It is to be lost in his love while at work or at play, for such love alone can purify the heart of the imperfect loves of the world. Further, given such faith and love, one is to follow to the best of one's ability his injunctions: *If you love me, follow my commandments.* If a disciple develops those qualities and surrenders himself completely to the Satguru's Will, he shall be freed from worldly desires, become an apt receptacle for the Shabd Dhun, and the Master's grace and generosity shall descend upon him like a flood that breaks open all inner gates and obstructions.[16]

So love is God and God is love. Whom should we love? We should love God. We are conscious entities and we should love the human body where God is manifested. It is not for the human body that we love him, but for the God manifest in the human body. That is blessed, because He is manifested there.[17] If every day our love for God grows more and more and becomes more dear as compared to anything else in the world, that is love for God.[18]

To speak of love is one thing; to have that love in your heart is something else.[19]

Love is the shortest cut to spiritual beatitude. Love is the kind sentiment of the Master which when properly nurtured by the dear ones by gradual assimilation weeds out all imperfections and shortcomings.[20]

It is very clear and simple: if you love God, you become what God is.[21] Love is the giving of your heart once and for all. It cannot be retaken and given to somebody else.[22] Where our love is, there we have to go.[23] You should know that to love God, we must live for God and die for God.[24]

Have you understood what is love? It is a subject of heart, not of head. A very learned man may be devoid of heart. Love overrules head, but sometimes head stands in the way of love, of the heart.[25] Those who yearn for it, get it.[26]

God is Love and Master is Love Personified. He emits rays of love to be attuned to by those on the way as well as to others who are struggling to find God. Happy and fortunate are those whose vessel is cleansed and are ready to receive the sweet Nectar of Master's Grace.[27]

The dear ones often ask, "How can we develop love for you?" You have all been given the proof of this path, so remain linked with it; for the more you are joined to that, the more will the love flow out of that union. This is the only thing lacking.[28]

The first criterion to show whether you have got real

love for the Master is: even if he calls you names, you will be attracted to him. The second is to have those qualifications which are reflected in him from God in your own life. These are simplicity and kind words imbued with humility. The third is to live strictly up to what He says, not even caring for your own life. If you leave everything to the Master, the Master has to take care of the child.[29]

Ego is really a big enemy on the Path against spiritual progress. The love for the Master is like fire in the brick kiln. If the fire is blown out rather than conserved, the bricks do not gain their proper maturity, and so it is with all spiritual matters. The initiates should conserve and keep veiled their love for their Master so that they may progress quietly.[30]

If we love somebody for the Master's sake, or for the sake of God, this is a sign that you are growing in love for your Beloved, for your Master. These are the foundation stones, not love as yet, mind that! Love is giving away of your heart. The heart is one and when it is given away to somebody, then what remains?[31]

Love one and all for the sake of the Master. If you love for the sake of the man concerned, this will stand in the way of your love for the Master. If you love the Master, then keep his commandments.[32] If you love somebody, then you will also love those who go to him. We criticize, we sometimes fight, even with those who are on the same Way as us. Then where is our love for the Master?[33]

The love of God-in-man is the love of God. He is overflowing with the love and intoxication of God. He is not bound to earth, but is sent here to guide the child humanity to go back to His Home. If you love him, where will you go? You will go where he goes. If he is not to return to the world, why should you return, how can you return?[34]

What is Love? Everybody says that—"I love God, I love the Master"—but what is love? Love is the fruit of a tree. It is the ultimate goal, which develops and comes up within us. We should love God with all our heart, with all our soul, with all our strength. Is the heart one or two? The heart is only one, and you can only give it to somebody whom you love. If you give away your heart to somebody, then what remains with you? You will think in the same way that He thinks, not in your own way. This is the ultimate goal. If your heart has already been given to the God-in-man, then nothing remains to be given separately to God. So first, our heart should be whole, not broken into pieces. When it is complete, only then can you give it.

Our Master was once giving a talk, and He said, "All right, if any of you can give your heart, you can go straight to heaven." One man stood and said, "Well, I give my heart." The Master asked him, "Have you controlled your heart?" "No," replied the man. "Then how can you give it?" said the Master. You can only give something which is under your control, that is in your possession. The heart is led astray by the outgoing faculties here, there and everywhere. Unless it is concentrated, how can you give it? We have no control over our heart. It is dragged away in so many ways.[35] The heart is given only when you withdraw it from all outside things, and it is under your control.[36]

So there are steps leading to this and the first step is, *If you love me, keep my commandments.* What are these commandments? *Love thy God with all thy heart, with all thy soul, with all thy strength.* The word "heart" is there. With all thy heart, not a heart that is cut into pieces, here, there, and everywhere. So let it be complete.[37]

What does one who loves want? He always wants to see the Master. He loves everything of the Master.[38] If you have got real love for God in your heart, God will come to you, He will manifest to you. But generally, we want only worldly things, here and hereafter. Those who care for the love of God don't hanker after the worldly things, nor the wealth of the other worlds. They don't even want emancipation. They would like to have only one thing. No heaven, no earthly things, no emancipation, only to be with God, that's all. If we have really got that hankering in our heart, then naturally we must meet God. God will come to us. If we take one step that way, He will proceed one hundred steps to receive us. We have to decide what we want at our heart of hearts. Are we here only for the worldly things? Are we here only for the name and fame of the world? Are we here only to have things of the other world, or heaven? Are we really after emancipation from birth and death? A real lover wants none of these things. He wants God and God alone. This is the highest ideal that we can achieve in the man-body, and in no other. So you have to decide by an honest searching of your heart, what you want. If you want God, then God will meet you, sure and certain. If you want something else, you will have it, that's all. You will get nothing short of whatever you want. But why, when you go to a King, do you want ordinary pebbles and stones?[39]

When Baba Sawan Singh Ji once wrote that he did not even yearn for Sach Khand but only prayed that he had "Love and faith at the Satguru's holy feet," Baba Ji was extremely pleased and replied that such self-surrender was "indeed the highest *karni* (discipline)" and assured him that "he who had such a love for the Master would certainly reach Sach Khand, and passing through the Alakh, Agam, Anami-Radhasoami, get merged in the Wonder Region."[40]

Love is developed in the direct company of the Master or indirectly when you become receptive, even from thousands of miles. The time will come when you will say, "Who is living in this body? Am I?" You will forget yourself; you will see the Master in there. When you fold your hands, they will be the Master's hands, not yours. So love is the ultimate fruit of the goal.[41]

When you grow in love for God or the God-in-man (they are one and the same), naturally you will hanker after Him. You cannot forget Him. You would like to have the company of somebody who has first-hand experience of Him, or who has been with Him. Further, you would like to be near Him, as near as possible. If you are not there, but you hear someone who speaks of Him, your heart becomes full and overflows through your eyes.

This is a symptom that you are growing in love for Him. These are the blossoms which herald the appearance of the fruit. If rain is expected, first you will have clouds. If there are no clouds, there will be no rain. If there are no blossoms, there will be no fruit.[42] Ultimately, when the fruit comes, you are for the Master and the Master is for you. These are the steps and we have now to judge where we stand.[43]

The spontaneous flow of trickling tears goes a long way in washing off the dross of the mind and fortunate is the eye that sheds these, for they leave unending trails of ravishing bliss and harmony.[44] As flowers precede the fruits on a tree, similarly yearning and anguish of heart precede the coming of the Master within. Each tear shed in sweet remembrance of the Master brings you closer to Him. If you keep Him in your mind, naturally you are in His mind.[45]

One cannot expect fruit on the tree when even the flowers have not yet formed. *Whosoever got Him, did so with tears; Could He be got with laughter and joy, none would be without Him.* Through sobs which rack the body, one receives the Lord. The water from the eyes washes away the sins of many lives; the accounts are washed clean.

*Without seeing the Beloved, sleep does not
     come;
This separation has now become unbearable.*

When the seeker goes through this, he is often advised by others to cease the searching and desiring for God, but Guru Amardas replied, "Do not utter such words, for even in pain there is a sweetness." Then after crying in vain for so long, the soul becomes both desparate and helpless, and she appeals to the Masters: "O Masters, you go to God daily, my voice cannot reach so far; take this message and tell Him, 'O Lord, she is pining with the separation from You. She does not know the road which leads to You, and her voice does not reach You, so she is sending this message.' Please tell Him that 'Night and day she is crying with flowing tears, and cannot exist anymore without the Beloved—she cannot fly for she has no wings and does not know the Way. How can she reach You?' Please tell Him my condition." A true seeker reaches this condition.[46]

Those who love God, love the Master, the God in Him of course. It is no matter of show. That very Power is within you and knows every act of yours, what you are doing and why. He knows the very trend of your thoughts. Love knows no show. Love knows service and sacrifice. The outward symbol of love is a sweet tongue, imbued with humility. When you have developed that love, what should you do? You must have patience, perseverance and go on with it. Just like a moth which burns itself on the flame of a candle but never makes any sound. So those who want to love God should not care for their name or fame, honor, this or that thing. They should leave every greatness they have got physically outside, and lay down at His feet. If they lose their life in sacrifice, even then they won't mention it. So this is a very delicate question, I would say. Those who have love for God, or the God-in-man, well, this is a relation between you and the God in Him and nobody else. You have to develop it. For that you must have perseverance. It takes time. The work of the servant is to do work, that's all. It is for the Master to see what He has to give to Him.[47]

The tongue of love is very sweet, and full of humility. The sweet tongue of remembrance, imbued with humility, is the very basis of all virtues. The tongue of a realized soul is filled with sweetness; his heart is brimming over with the nectar of love. Out of the abundance of his heart, a man speaks, for the words are charged with whatever lies in the heart. Masters have love for everyone, and their words are filled with love, and so have a particularly attractive quality. If the parrot talks in a cage of love, he eats and drinks the Naam; his soul leaves the body without effort, at will. If you sit in the Guru's company with single-pointed attention, and listen to the Inner Sound regularly, your soul will also withdraw without effort. When people complain that their mind is not stilled, it is due to lack of love. The True Lord can be realized through the Guru's bhakti, and with ease He will manifest[48]

The body is like a cage; but if the cage becomes one of love, the soul will live on the Truth, the Elixir of Life, by connection with the Naam. The world is a two-edged sword, cutting in two whatever it falls upon, but when the sword of love descends, it binds the two in one. The very criterion of love is to absorb oneself into someone or something, so a lover is a true renouncer, renouncing all other thought, save of that which he loves. He may be surrounded by thousands, but he is alone with his love.

A man without love will never realize the Lord, so make this body a cage of love, and then talk. If no love is developed through outer practice, what is the use of it? Such practice is a mere performance of gymnastics. Unless we remember Him with tears, it is a dry remembrance; the remembrance that comes from a heart overflowing with love will bear fruit. The tenth Guru says, "Hear ye all, I tell you the Truth: God is realized by those who love." God is love, and the soul is a drop of that very Essence, and is therefore also the image of love. What kind of love has he who boasts of loving the Lord but hates his brothers? Sheikh Farid says, "If you desire to meet the Beloved, injure not any heart." A true devotee of God will have no enmity toward any other being. Shamas Tabrez says, "Hundreds of years in prayer will not make you a *namazi*" (true worshiper). He in whom there is no love awakened cannot fathom the secrets of the Lord. So live in a cage of love if you want to realize God, and that love will drag you toward Him. Life will become an agony, a yearning, a restless, lonely misery without Him, for love is a sea without a shore: there is no end to it, save in the all-encompassing absorption in Him when you give your whole life to Him.

How can this love be developed? It is not grown in fields or sold in shops. There are only two ways to develop love. One way is to sit beside one who is love, from whom you will catch an infection of that love. From life, so is life created. A glimpse of love can be seen only in a true lover's eye. These things are mentioned in books, but words cannot really express what love is. The other way to develop love is through remembrance. If one loves someone, one cannot forget that person; his face is always before the vision, in the heart, in the mind, even vibrating in one's blood as it runs through the veins. One should remember Him so much that one can never forget Him, and that constant remembrance will drag one to Him. The overpowering yearning to meet the Lord grows into a oneness, a blending with Him.[49]

Simran

EVERYONE OF US is constantly dwelling on one thing or another. This close association leaves an imprint in the human mind which in course of time becomes indelible enough and leads to complete identification of the subject with the object; and hence it is said, "As you think so you become," or "where the mind is there you are also," no matter where the physical self is. This being the case Saints take hold of a person from the line of least resistance. As no one can do without Simran, the Saints try to set one type of Simran for another type. They substitute for Simran of the world and worldly relations and objects, a Simran of God's name, or "Word." As the former leads to distraction of the mind, the latter pulls heavenward, leading to peace of mind and liberation of the soul. Three to four hours in a day has been enjoined as the minimum for Simran, and it may be gradually increased. The Mahatmas are never without Simran even for a single moment. As it is altogether a mental process (for it is to be done by the tongue of thought), no amount of physical and manual labor can interfere with it. In course of time, like the tick of a clock, it becomes automatic and ceaseless for all the twenty-four hours. While the hands are engaged in work, the mind rests in the Lord.[50]

When anybody would complain to Hazur about inability to still the mind, he would reply, "Your Simran is not constant enough." And for the complaint of not being able to sit for long in meditation, the same reply was given. Our real difficulty is that the world's color has drowned us! If it could be bleached out then we would become clean and ready for a new fresh color to enliven us. A dirty cloth must first be washed clean before attempting to dye it. Our heart and intellect are stained with that color coming from the level of mind and senses. We are stained with the actions of life, and added to this are the stains of the past—birth upon birth. Even if you put aside past lives and consider this life alone . . . how many years have passed already? It might be that through the mercy of some Master you were fortunate to be in His company and enjoy the benefit of a little of that Naam color, but even so it is said that we must *do Simran and serve the Satguru*. We are dyed in the worldly color through doing the world's simran, and it can only be washed out by doing the simran (remembrance) and *dhyan* (contemplation) of the Lord.

So you can say that the first step is simran—controlled thought—and it should be constant, without a break. This is the washing process, before the soul is ready to be drenched in the color of God. With true service of mind and body, in love and devotion, one should increase one's remembrance of the Lord until there is nothing but constant sighing for Him. Then there is indication of awakening. We sigh for worldly things, but it is rare to find someone who sighs in remembrance of the Lord.

Simran is the first step. Logically, one will be drenched in the color of the one in whose name the simran is done. If you keep someone in your heart, you will reside in his. If the disciple remembers the Guru, the Guru will remember the disciple. And if there is remembrance on both sides, that creates receptivity, and the Guru and disciple become one. Satguru protects the disciple with His life. In such conditions, the disciple becomes suffused in the Guru's color. In the clear heart, the true knowledge becomes apparent. Naturally, those who do not do simran will not be dyed in that color. When Masters feel so inclined, they reveal themselves somewhat and great wisdom comes forth— for *our* benefit, in whom the color of the Lord is not yet fast.[51]

The practice of Simran begins with the repetition of the Master's objective Names *slowly* with a mental poise. At first the practice is objective, but in time it becomes subjective. Then the constant thought of the Lord continues without cessation. Once this starts, the remembrance becomes automatic, continuous and constant and one never forgets the Lord.[52]

Master souls always do and recommend Simran of the highest type, to wit, of the Original or Basic Names of

God, for these open up charmed casements and bring to view vistas leading to spiritual realms within the body. Such names are charged with and electrified by the thought transference that usually accompanies them when communicated to an aspirant by a Master Soul. As these are magnetized, they have the power to attract and pull the spirit up to the planes to which they relate. The engrafted "words" charged with the Divine Spirit of the Master very soon bear fruit.[53]

By doing Simran of the world and its environments, they have so much taken possession of us that we have become the world and its environments. We have to use the same methods so as to eliminate all worldly thoughts from within by remembering sweetly of the Lord in so many words devised by the Saints so far. So there are two uses of Simran: one use is to withdraw from the body by Simran of the electrified words given by a competent Master, and the second is to drive out the world and its thoughts from within us by the constant remembrance of the Lord in so many ways as prescribed, the description of which has been given above.[54]

Simran makes man introspective and concentrative. Extraordinary powers inevitably follow as a result of the concentration of mind in the inner planes.[55] The repetition of the charged Names is given to the disciple as a weapon against all dangers. It acts also as a password to all spiritual planes, gives strength and sustenance to the body and mind during trouble and affliction, and brings the soul near the Master. It is instrumental in achieving concentration and imparts many other diverse powers.

The five charged Names given by a true Master are electrified words.[56]

Again, these charmed words of the Master—Basic Names of God—have the power to dispel the forces of darkness that may meet and assail a Spirit on its onward journey. Simran of these names helps the soul both in the physical plane and supra-physical planes, one after another. Hence it is imperative that Simran be done of such Names as the Master Soul enjoins, for they are charged with a tremendous spiritual power which negative powers can hardly put up with and from which they flee as from an enchanter driven. Immortal and everlasting as these words of the Master are, they bestow life everlasting to the soul in which they sink and take root.[57]

You will please appreciate that the sacred charged Words are highly efficacious and carry the thought transference of the Master. And when one repeats them lovingly and mentally, the sensory currents from the body below are automatically withdrawn towards the eye-focus.[58] In Simran lies the seed that helps in the development of the soul.[59]

Saints give a very simple definition of sin as "forgetting one's origin" (or God-head). Every thought, word or deed that keeps a man away from God is a veritable sin, and on the other hand whatever brings man nearer to Him, is pious and holy. A Persian divine while commenting on the nature of the world said, "World comes into play only when one forgets the Lord. By constant remembrance of God, one while living in the world among friends and relations is yet not of the world."[60]

By concentration at the blessed feet of the Master, by implicit faith in His instructions, and by putting them into actual practice, we can attain a stage of perfect bliss. There is no short cut but that of Simran as enjoined by the Master.[61] To forget the Master is to lose His protection thereby giving an opportunity to the negative power to pin you down.[62]

We remember God only when we are hard pressed from every side. It is affliction and not affluence that turns us Godward. If one were not to forget God in prosperity, adversity would never come near him. Hard times only come as a result of sins committed when forgetful of the Lord. Simran (or constant remembrance of God) is a tonic for the soul. It makes the will grow stronger from day to day. Troubles and trials however severe cannot cow him down. With a smiling face he pulls through the storms of fate or destiny unscathed. Simran is a panacea for all the ills of the world. It is a potent remedy and works wonders to remove worry where all human efforts fail. A man of Simran never has any worry or anxiety. Simran to be very effective must be constant and ceaseless.[63]

A pauper collects his money by begging coppers and keeps counting the same day and night. Whether sleeping or waking, he is dreaming all the time of his little hoarding. We, too, should like a pauper always keep an account of the Simran that we do and try to accumulate bit by bit the wealth of Naam—not forgetting it for a moment.[64]

It is very good that you commence and end the day

with repetition of the sacred Names. These sacred Names are charged with the life impulse of the Master and their Simran (repetition) invokes His mercy. To the best of your efforts you should resort to the repetition of charged Names all along your vacant moments and keep yourself immersed in the loving remembrance of the Master.[65]

If you do Simran for some time and have sweet remembrance of the Master as the last thing in the night before going to sleep, the dreams will, in due course, cease to afflict you.[66]

Prayer should be ceaseless, overflowing as a lover's passions are, forgetting not his love even for the twinkling of an eye. When a man falls in love with a woman, he carries her image in his mind at all times whether sleeping or awake, sitting or standing. *If one could carry with him the love of God like this, it would be grand indeed.*

Kabir goes on to explain how the sweet remembrance of God should be done. He gives another example of the same type. He says, "Attend to the prayer as do the village maids, who move talking with the attention always fixed on pitchers overhead." The daily routine of life, says Kabir, does not interfere with Simran. The village maids as they go to fetch water carry pitchers of water one above the other on their heads; in spite of an unseen path, they keep jesting and talking among themselves while the pitchers remain steady on their heads, as their attention is pertinently fixed on them. Similarly one need not forget Simran even in the midst of the hustle and bustle of life and worldly obligations.[67]

Another example he gives: "Love the prayer as the

moth loves the light. In its flame doth burn itself, never
turns aside." Light is the very life of the moth. He loves
it so passionately that he does not hesitate to singe himself to death, rather than avoid it. Kabir Sahib therefore
says that we must love Simran as the very breath of our
life; whether rich or poor, healthy or sick, awake or
asleep, like a moth be ever ready to sacrifice our very
self in our devotion to our ideal. Again He says: "Lose
yourself in the sweet remembrance as the keet doth
bhirangi who for sooth loses itself to rise bhirangi-like."
Bhirangi (an insect) after almost killing a keet (another
insect) revivifies the latter to life by bestowing its powerful attention to it. The keet when charmed back to life
is no longer a keet but becomes a bhirangi-being saturated with the life impulse of the latter. In just the same
way Kabir says that one who does Simran and gets firmly
engrafted therein will have new birth and a new life
quite distinct from the old sensual life he has been living
hitherto.[68]

The more you direct your attention and absorb yourself in the sweet remembrance of the Master, you will
develop receptivity and feel that Master is within you
and you are in the Master, as St. Paul said: "It is I, not
now I, but Christ lives within me." The lover becomes
the Beloved and the Beloved becomes the lover. All differences of mind, body and soul are swept away.[69]

Ordinarily mind should be fully devoted in the work
one does, as work is worship. But when mind is vacant, it
should not remain vacant as a vacant mind is the home
of the devil. It should be kept busy either in repeating

the five Holy Names or in sweet remembrance of the Master or listening to the Sound Current if it has developed so much as to be audible and reverberating all the time.[70]

While doing any manual or mechanical work or in idle moments, you can continue repeating the five Holy Names or recite some prayer lovingly all the time and you will feel new strength is entering within you and that Someone is working with you, sharing much of your labor. Any interval, however short, during the day, may also be devoted to meditation and that will give you freshness and real energy for your work.[71]

Thoughts are more potent than deeds. You can eschew negative thoughts of worldliness and entertain godly thoughts by cultivating a keen sense of continued loving remembrance of the Master. You will please appreciate that it is like an armor with the initiate against the onslaughts of mind and matter when you are mercilessly exposed to their attacks. It is the inborn ego which distracts the mind from the receptivity of positive thoughts of goodness. The watch of thoughts comprises a vigilant attitude of the mind against the several vices known to you. It is a gradual process of replacement of vices with ennobling virtues.[72]

Mind has a vast sphere of activity. It resents inner silence and absorption with the result that instead of quietness, more of confusion intrudes. You are requested to avoid all thoughts whatsoever all along your daily chores, and try to keep your mind enchained whether with the Simran of charged names, or loving remembrance of the

Master, or listening to the holy sound current as coming
from the right side. This is the sublime solution for all the
troubles caused by the mind. You will find that such a
sacred schedule will have salutory effect on your regular
holy meditations, which will become more fruitful with
ravishing bliss and harmony.[73]

God is with those who love Him each and every moment; they are aware of Him. If one truly loves someone,
does not that person reside in one's heart? In that case,
can one love any other? This constant loving remembrance of a loved one comes after getting to know him,
enjoying some happiness together, or living together in
harmony; but what real love can one have for someone
one has never seen, known, or lived with? We cannot
develop love by just saying we love.

So the Gurumukh's life is lived in constant remembrance. The new life starts from initiation, and then
he lives on remembrance, remembrance, remembrance
which increases that new life—it begins to *surge* within.
As a person thinks, so does he become. It starts as a remembrance, but eventually the remembrance occurs by
itself—that means he has become that very remembrance.
Only a person who has given his heart to another can
know what it means to give the heart. It is a practical
matter, for in true love there is incessant remembrance
of the loved one—perpetual. *Gurumukh's remembrance
is only one—continuous.* It continues without pause or
end, unlike us; we remember many times with breaks in
between. What kind of love is here today and gone tomorrow—with this person one day and another the next?

Love is only one. That is not love which changes. And the truest love is that which the soul receives through experience; that never changes.[74]

If you accept the Simran of Charged Names as the basic Names of God in the Master, then you will be able to repeat them with affection, love and devotion.[75]

If you forget the Lord, then you are attached. You will go where you are attached.[76]

A child leaves the shelter of homestead to visit a fair for a day with his parents. There is such a huge crowd of people there, but as long as the child is holding his mother's hand he cannot be separated from her. Masters have said, "I do not ask you to renounce the world; I only ask you to remember the Lord in all you do." By quoting this, I am not saying that you should leave life in the world and take the road to the lonely forests. I mean that no matter where you are or what you are doing, you should not forget God. It is possible that the child might be inclined to leave his mother's hand if he could, but if the mother is holding him firmly, how is it possible? You should dedicate your hand—surrender it. If you have not seen God, then you can surrender yourself to one in whom God is manifested—a God-in-man. With such surrender to the God in him, his hand will always be holding you. You understand what I am saying?[77]

God's Grace

HOW CAN a puny child of clay, powerless as he is, constantly ridden by mind and matter, entangled in the meshes of blind infatuation and beset with desires, anger, greed, attachment and egoism, escape unscathed by himself and become a successful pilgrim on the Path?

In such a weird setting, all baffling and bewildering, with no way out, God takes mercy on His creatures; He Himself comes down in vile man's attire, to suffer woe so that His children may be blessed. But again the same trouble confronts us. To understand the teachings of the Master and strictly follow them from day to day, to confide in him and to completely surrender one's self, body and soul, to his will, is not an easy thing to do. Unless God and Satguru both take pity on a *jiva*, he cannot possibly see through to Reality and escape from bondage.

We with our limited understanding cannot even listen comprehendingly to the Master's words.

But in the fullness of time when it so pleases God, He brings about a meeting between a jiva and a Sant Satguru, who establishes his contact with Naam—the power of God or God in action—the Primal Sound Current, wherewith a jiva is gradually led on and on until he reaches the source and the fountainhead of Shabd or the Sound Current.[78] It is through the grace of God alone that one is initiated.[79]

Those who serve not Truth wither away like
a broken reed,

O Nanak! Whom the Master blesses gets linked
with Naam.
With a special merit alone one meets a Satguru;
and he brings about a union between Surat
and Shabd.
Meeting with a Master is a pure gift of God,
and so is the union with Hari Nam (God).

The Master is in the likeness of God, though in physical
raiments. He, too, is endowed with the same attributes
as God Himself. He, too, comes to save the sinners and
administer His Saving Grace among the rest.[80] The saving grace comes through contact with Naam, and continuous cherishing of His love and saving grace in turn helps
the other way. Both grace and Naam work in reciprocity
and help in developing each other.[81]

The blessings of the Supreme Lord are limitless and
do not at any time suffer from scarcity, but one partakes
of them only by extraordinary merit. A particle of grace
is enough to save a jiva from the ceaseless cycle of transmigration.[82]

His grace descends by acceptance of His *bhana* (will)
and recognition of His *Hukam* (commandment).[83] Who
understands the will of the Master and follows it scrupulously? One in whom the grace of the Lord works.[84] The
panacea for all ills and the only way to win God's grace
is perfect surrender in all humility at the feet of the Master Soul.[85] It is only the Gurumukhs who get this grace
and not the manmukhs.[86] The grace of the Master is as
limitless as his greatness, so much so that he forgives even

those who talk ill of him and accepts them as his very own.[87] The Master's grace is boundless.[83]

The Kali Yuga is at its height and in full force, and therefore so is the Master's grace and mercy.[89]

We cannot win God either by flattery or by vain repetitions, nor does He stand to gain or lose anything whether we offer prayers or not. Compassionate as He is, His grace is always at work in each and all alike for we cannot live without It. We can, however, attract that Grace to our advantage by becoming a fit receptacle for It. Humility and faith purify the mind and make it a fit instrument for God's Grace. These two aids help in inverting the lotus of the mind which at present is attuned with the senses. Unless we are able to turn its direction upward, God's Grace cannot flow directly into it. Prayers, humble and sincere, help in establishing a harmony between man's mind and God's Grace. He needs no forensic arguments and legal acumen in defense of our deeds and needs. All that is required is a pure and loving heart attuned to His Grace and the latter is automatically attracted to it.[90]

God is all Love, and we cannot ask Him to be more loving. He is omniscient, and we cannot by loud and strong prayers make Him any wiser. Perfection cannot be made more perfect by our protestations and prayers. We must learn to "stand and wait" as the classic poet Milton puts it, and His Grace shall of its own be attracted and flood our very being.[91]

Divine Grace is never slow. A good mother says not, "Will you?" but gives. From among the aspirants, they

are given the lion's share of Divine Faith in the Master
who come with downcast heads, heavy hearts and the
shuddering anguish of a lost soul, speechless with anxieties, to unburden their worries. Meekness is no weakness.
It is a strong, cemented road of humility which leads to
the Benign Reality.[92]

Purity

A PERFECT MASTER, capable of imparting the experience of inner Light, is hard to find. Even if you
find one, you cannot reach the Goal without purity of
life and forgiveness. If you follow and act on what I have
just said, you will be liberated from the bondage of matter and mind. These virtues will bring to you higher consciousness and you will develop faith in the existence of
God. After all, what is the purpose of worship? It is
to develop firm faith in the existence of God. By self-
introspection, you can see what your condition is.[93]

So purity of thought, purity of diet and purity of conduct are most essential. If our inner self is free from all
blemishes, the divine Light and celestial Sound will
emerge in the silence of the heart. The very silence will
become vocal. Our meditation is not successful because
we have yet to come up to the necessary standard. Kabir
says: "If our heart is polluted, we shall be pushed out of
the Kingdom of God."[94]

He is ever with us and is showering his abundant grace.
However, to realize Him, it is essential to have a pure

heart. Can you ever expect the Lord to manifest Himself till our heart is spotlessly clean? The Lord cannot be realized so long as our heart remains littered with lust, anger, jealousy, recrimination, etc. Our soul lies dormant and defiled by these vices. Just as a magnet will not attract a dust-covered iron, God within us will also not pull the soul up till it is free from all blemishes. In such a hopeless state only a competent Master can come to our rescue. This, in fact, is the greatness of a Master-soul. For example, if a loaded donkey is stuck up in mud, it cannot come out with its own efforts. Out of sheer compassion, someone else will have to remove the load and then pull the donkey out of the mud. We are also loaded with heaps of impressions of the previous numerous births, and in addition, are further trapped in the dragnet of sensual pleasures. Therefore, hardly any difference (exists) between us as we are and the loaded donkey. We too, therefore, need a compassioned soul, who himself is absolutely free, to unburden us and to pull us out of our misery; only then will we be able to see the Reality. The greatness of such a Master soul is beyond any description indeed. Such a competent Master enables us to visualize the Truth after freeing us from the effect of past impressions and by bringing our attention above bodily consciousness.[95]

To derive full benefit from the company of a Saint, you must be pure yourself.[96] Those conditions considered to be the result of the Negative Power will never touch us if we lead a pure life. The Negative Power is a great judge and is very just in his punishment. His pen writes according to our karmas. So what constitutes purity and goodness? A mind which is given up wholly to God. All trouble and strife will thereby finish. When the mind withdraws from the Lord and attaches itself to something else, then whatever the person does takes him further away from God. And the further he goes, the greater the sin. This is really the true definition of sin. The Negative Power says, "I will never punish anyone if people become pure." So, in the courts of Saints, this is the greatest teaching, the secret of all secrets: that God is won by him who will give his mind.[97]

Faith

A S A MATTER of fact, no one can know or find a true Master unless and until the Master is pleased to reveal his own identity himself to the innermost satisfaction of one desiring to confirm his faith in the Master. This is done according to the extent of one's receptivity, and to the degree that his capacity to understand and his love entitle him. It depends wholly on the kindness and sweet mercy of God through a Master. Some are given clues according to their desires. The faith of some in their Master is confirmed when a disciple is saved miraculously from some danger. A favorable response to the prayers made to the Master confirms faith in others. There are others who have book-knowledge and are satisfied by the examples of others, so they get confirmation that way. Masters have the knowledge of measuring the capacity and range of everyone's intellect and bestow faith accordingly. Sants know the merits and evils of everyone but they never disclose them.[98]

How fortunate is a child who will repose fully and surrender completely in the strong and protective arms and loving care of the Father! He then becomes carefree, leaving all the work to the Merciful and benign Father, of working out things as He deems best. Such a life becomes supremely sweet and all his problems become easier and his way becomes clear and smooth. The Master Power is constantly extending all feasible help and blessings. Let us fully repose our trust in him. The fortunate ones do as the Master says, and receive all the necessary material help, which goes a long way to assuage the severity of the karmic debts. The difficulties and troubles may come, but they pass off without leaving an ugly mark behind. Please do not lose heart.[99] He never fails His children.[100]

If you will put yourself completely in the hands of God, surely He will take care of you. One man went to the jungle for twelve years and hung himself upside down in a well by iron chains. A farmer came by and asked, "What are you doing?" "Waiting for God." The farmer said, "Oh, this is what one must do to find God," and he quickly ran to make a rope out of grass. Although the rope was so weak he hung himself in a nearby well. In ten minutes the farmer asked of the other, "Has your God come yet?" "No." "Oh," said the farmer, "Mine has." "What," said the other, "How can this be after only ten minutes? I have been here twelve years." The farmer had no iron chains but he put his faith completely in God once he knew the way to God, not caring for his life.[101]

Prayer and Gratitude

PRAYER IS THE KEY that unlocks the Kingdom of Heaven. It pulls up the sluice gates and releases from within immense power and resourcefulness.[102] Prayer and gratitude are akin. A gratuitous heart becomes the abode of all virtues.[103] Always seek His Divine guidance by invoking His mercy in humble supplication and inner intense longing for His darshan.[104]

A disciplined life is an asset; make it a principle to be always happy, cheerful and grateful.[105] Man's only duty is to be ever grateful to God for His innumerable gifts and blessings.[106]

Humility

ALL THE MASTERS of the past and present say that, "The Kingdom of God is for the humble of heart." So many of us, alas, are proud, vain, in ego lost; and blind to the wisdom, we do but wander from darkness to darkness.

The God that rules millions is the ego; enthrone on your heart the God of Love, and cease to wander—and what should be done to do so? Become as humble as ashes and dust.

The world is full of the proud of purse or power or learning. Whereas, we should be humble and simple and empty ourselves of all "self" that the Lord might do with us what He would.[107]

The truly humble are the truly happy. For want of humility, men and women are leading an unbearable, miserable life. All this misery is from within. It is not a change in our circumstances, but deliverance from the thraldom of the self, the petty "ego" that sits a tyrant, robbing us of the bliss that is our heritage as children of God. We are, as it were, in a cage of self-centeredness, and until this prison is opened by the key of humility, the swan bird of the Soul is not free and cannot swim to the regions of radiance and joy.[108]

When the light of humility dawns on the soul, the darkness of selfishness disappears and the soul no longer lives for itself, but for God. The soul loses itself in God, lives in God, and is transformed into Him. This is the alchemy of humility. It transforms the lowest into the Highest.[109]

St. Augustine said the way to God is, "First humility, second humility and third humility." He who is proud of possessions or of learning or of authority will not go to any Saint unless he is humble. Even if he goes to the Saint, but considers himself superior to Him, he will not listen to Him. A glass which is kept above a tumbler of water will remain empty—until it is put below the tumbler. You know what you know; just listen to what the other says. Perhaps we can learn something from him.

Yes, the branches of a fruit-laden tree bend of their

own accord. Even so, the man who, losing himself, finds God—finds Him everywhere and in everyone—bends before all, offers homage of his heart to all. This is true humility. It is not a forced sense of lowliness.[110] Such a one lives in unity with all. He is in others and others are in him.

It is the fake ego-self that gives rise to the sense of discord and separation. When the illusion of ego is broken, one feels, "I am not apart from others, but others are parts of the One—God—The Master—and all of us are engaged in the same service of God."

Each one of us is unique in his own way. There is a divine purpose behind the life of everyone who comes into the world; no one has been created for nothing. We have something to learn from everyone. This is the mystery of humility.

The truly humble person does not compare himself with others. He knows that none of us, however evolved, is perfect; none of us is complete in himself. The humble person does not regard one as better than the other; he believes in the divinity of each. If one says and asserts that he is better than others, then he is not perfect as yet.

It is only when one realizes his nothingness that God comes and fills him with Himself. Where man is, God is not; where man is not, God is! God cannot enter the heart of the self-seeking person. He who is full of himself considers himself as above others and so puts a limit on himself. God is without limit. How can the limitless enter the limited?[111]

True humility is freedom from all consciousness of self, which includes freedom from the consciousness of humility. The truly humble man never knows that he is humble.[112]

The humble man makes no fuss. He is at harmony with himself and others. He is gifted with a wondrous feeling of peace. He feels safe and secure, like a ship in harbor, unaffected by howling storms and lashing waves. He has found refuge at the Lotus Feet of the Lord and the storms of changing circumstances have no power over him. He feels light as air. The burdens which we carry all our life—the burden of the self and its desires—he has laid aside, and he is ever calm and serene. Having given up everything, he has nothing to lose, and yet everything belongs to him, for he is of God, and God is in him. Having broken the bondage of desire, he is as happy with a piece of dry bread as with a sumptuous meal. In every situation and circumstance of life, he blesses the Names of God.

He who would be humble regards himself as a student. He learns many new things, but what is more difficult, he unlearns many things he has learned. A scholar came to a Saint and said, "O Seer of the Secret, tell me what I may do to live the life divine." And the Saint said to him, "Go, unlearn what thou hast learnt and then return and sit before me."[113]

He who would walk the way of humility must renounce his earlier ways of living. He must give up the opinions he has formed, the standards to which he is accustomed. He must have a new outlook on life. The things the world would worship are to him of no value. His values are so different from those of other men. Rich food, fine houses, costly dresses, positions of power and authority, the applause of men, honors and titles, no longer attract him. He feels drawn to a life of simplicity. He is happy in living a hidden life in the Hidden Lord.

He is dead to the world; he is alive in God. At times he actually behaves like one dead.

Yes, the truly humble man is, in that sense, the "dead" man. He has "died." God alone lives in him. His self has been annihilated. His self has vanished into God, and only God remains. God works in him and through him, and God emits in his eyes. God speaks in his words. On his feet, God walks the earth, and through his hands gives His benedictions to all.

Such men are the real strength of the world—its illumination and inspiration. To see them is to commune with God, for God dwells in them. They are the living, moving Temples of the Lord. They are the ones who keep the world intact, though they do not know it themselves. The whole earth depends on them without anyone being aware of it. Their hearts and minds are in tune with the Great Heart and Mind of humanity. They are in complete accord with all that lives. They give their love to all living beings, as though they were the sons of the one sweet Mother. They have broken all fetters and entered into the freedom of the children of God. God does their will, because they have merged their wills in His. God fulfills their least desire, for it is He Who desires all their desires. They are the little saviors of humanity.

I wish each one of you to follow the lesson of humility, born of love and simplicity.[114]

Devotion

SO IF YOU WANT your devotion, your love of God, to bear forth fruit, then be wholly and solely devoted to One. Think of Him, see Him, hear about Him and know Him. Those who help us on the Way, we are thankful to them. Bhakti or devotion will bear forth fruit only when you are wholly and solely devoted to Him, so much that you forget yourself.[115]

God is One and He wants everyone to go to Him all alone. One should not think even of the body in which he is sitting, that he or the very Isht (object of devotion) is there.[116]

. . . Be wholly and solely devoted for a while, do one thing at a time. If you have such devotion, even if only for a few minutes, it will bear forth fruit. If you sit for hours and your attention is diverted, divided in so many things, such devotion will not bear forth fruit. Now see where you stand.[117]

The prayer which comes from the heart and is expressed through the brain and mouth will be heard. When you pray, you should go into your closet and pray all alone. If you are fully confident about your prayer and about the existence of the One to whom you pray and His competency, and that prayer goes out of your heart, naturally it will be answered. For example, there

is a story about four different types of devotion that wives
have for their husbands. The first type is attached to
other men, though outwardly she appears to be fully devoted to her husband. Truly speaking, wives and husbands should be as one soul working in two bodies. We
are like the woman who was outwardly devoted to her
husband but was always thinking of others. We have no
conviction, we are not devoted wholly and solely to God
or the Master. Some wives are devoted, but they want
something in return. That kind of devotion is second
class. If she is not given what she wants, she resents it.
The third kind of wife will pray to her husband if she
wants something, but whether he gives it or not, she remains devoted to him. But the forth and highest type of
devoted wife will think, "Well, my husband knows my
condition, he sees me daily and will look after my needs.
If I am acceptable to him in these ragged clothes, then
what more can I want!" This is the highest form of the
devoted soul. Whether we are rich or poor, happy or in
distress, He sees our fate. We are all His children after
all, is it not? So this type is the highest form of devotion.[118]

Kabir says, "What is the criterion of a man who is
devoted wholly and solely to God? If in a deep sleep state,
the word of God or the Master comes out of his mouth,
then such a man is wholly and solely devoted to Him.
What would I offer to such a man? I would offer my
flesh, my skin to make shoes for his feet." You follow,
which form of devotion bears forth full fruit? It is that
which is wholly and solely devoted to One. Our mind is

devoted to so many things. Such devotion will not bear
forth fruit. If we want our devotion to bear forth fruit
from day to day and that we should see this fruit in our
lifetime, then our whole attention should be riveted to
the Feet of the Lord, or the Lord manifested in the God-
in-man. The result will be that if you love all the World
for His sake, you will not be attached to the world.[119]

So try to live in the living present, forgetting the past
and the future—and fill every moment of your life with
simple trust in Him in all loving devotion. He will manifest in you when you choose and turn your face to Him.[120]

The disciple reaches his final Goal in proportion to his
own integrity, loyalty and devotion to Master.[121]

The more one gives weight to the Master's words, the
more he grows in grace. True devotion to the Master
consists in acceptance of, and doing, what he commands.
Guru Ramdas exhorts us that the thought of the Master
should ever be a companion, no matter what we may be
doing. The Master is hidden in his words, and his words
are in fact the real Master.[122]

We should give our obedience and devotion, and leave
the rest of the work to him.[123]

Impediments to Devotion

FIRST OF ALL, the ladies and men should not always be
thinking of the opposite sex or read such novels,
lovelorn novels I would say, which give lusty thoughts.
When you do not always think of the Master, He is left

aside and the other person of whom you are thinking intervenes, whether it is a man or a woman. What is the result? Your inner progress is stopped, because you are devoted somewhere else. So the ladies and men should not read those books where lovelorn tales are given. The ladies should not think about the men nor the men think about the ladies. This is the first impediment on the way. It does not mean that we should not love anybody. For the sake of the Master or God, we should love all who go to Him.[124]

For the purpose of devotion you may love, but it should be for the sake of the Master. Otherwise, this is one of the most effective impediments by which men are driven away and their attention diverted from a higher place to a lower one. This is one thing. The other thing is that if you are always reading about money and thinking that such and such a person has become a millionaire, or listen to talks about such things, you will develop greed within you. Third, a man is known by the society that he keeps. Don't have the society of someone who has given up to these two things, because by society, you become that. Those thoughts will always be reverberating in your mind. The fourth impediment is that sometimes you think of your enemy or that such a man is against you. This always comes into your mind, again and again you think of him, and this creates hatred within you. Sometimes for the sake of name and fame, we think that such and such a man is rising in the world, that he is becoming known in the world, and you wonder why you are not. A man like this may have been devoted at first.

One by one, these things that I have mentioned stand in the way, and our devotion does not bear fruit.[125]

Another impediment is when somebody is devoted to you. There is one example that I will give you. Suppose that you have got Rs. 100.00 or $100.00 in your bank. Whoever thinks or looks to you with all devotion sends in a debit bill against you. The one who is devoted will want a return for that devotion, whether you have got the money in your bank or not. You will become bankrupt, mind that! Those who can give something expect something in return. Nobody can give even a glass of water to you without any purpose. If anybody gives you sweets or something (leave aside the question of the Master—He is a Selfless Worker), he will expect something in return. Whether you want to give it or not, that is debited against you. You follow me now? That is why all Masters say, "Earn your own money, live on your own earnings and share with others." There should be give and take. Selfless work for the good of the cause is another thing. For that you should not want anything in return. Only then will it become selfless, not otherwise. If you want something done, you give something.[126]

Sometimes we act and pose and we become that. Really you are not that, you are deceiving your own self, the God in you first, then you deceive others. For how long can this continue? The cat must be out of the bag eventually. So you should not think of the opposite sex, whether you are a man or a woman. If you always think of the body, naturally you will think of the opposite sex. Christ said that husbands should love their wives as

Christ loved the church. Even husband and wife should not think of each other as a man and a woman. They may have one duty of begetting children but that is not everything. It is mainly to have a companion in life for the purpose that both of them should reach God.

So first, the men should not always think about the ladies and the ladies should not become too attached to the men. If you have to love one another, love for the sake of the Master, forgetting your sex. Second, if you have the society of someone who is very wealthy and you are always in that society, then you will want that very thing for yourself. Greed will develop within you. Third thing is that a man is known by the society that he keeps. Society develops its own quality quicker in us, no matter what sort of society it is. The fourth thing is acting and posing and doing things for the sake of name and fame and competition. These are the things which stand in the way of your devotion.[127]

If you have got a good companion, all the better, otherwise remain all alone with your own self, with the Master or the God within you. If you live in this way, your devotion or bhakti, even if done for a short time, will give you more, a hundred times more results than the other way. In the other way, devotion is lost. Another impediment is that those who are not believers in God will naturally develop some doubts too within you. So avoid all these things. If you can get good company, where you can develop love for your Master or God, well and good, otherwise live with your own self.

There is another thing that stands in our way that affects all, whether they are representatives, group leaders or anybody. That is when they say, "I am bigger than the next fellow." They act and pose, they want to be the boss and naturally this causes hatred and results in no progress. This attitude in due course becomes like a church and an imposition. But Sant Mat, the Teachings of the Masters, is colored through and through with humility, simplicity and love.[128]

So yesterday, I talked about the things, that if you follow them, will bring more results in your devotion. Today, I have talked about what are the things that are impediments on the way to devotion. These are things explained and you have to follow them. The more you follow them, the more progress you will have. Sometimes you progress and then all at once you feel barren. Why? It is because something else has intervened, interfered in the way. So we have to be very cautious. Think of God, or the God-in-man, in all your affairs. Let the needle of your compass be pointed always to the north, then you are safe. Love one another for the sake of the Master. If you love one another for the sake of the man concerned, this will stand in the way of our love for the Master. If you love the Master, then keep His commandments.[129]

The Words of The Master

WHEN A PERSON comes to a Master, he must come with an open-minded outlook. Since he knows that all his actions hitherto, individual as well as social, have not so far secured him salvation, he should bid goodbye to them and ask the Master for his instructions in the matter of spiritual practices.

Having obtained his instructions, he must then follow them scrupulously, and that alone should constitute his sole devotion. Whatever the Master ordains, that must be taken as Gospel truth, no matter whether it stands the test of mere human reason or not. Our intellect and our reason, after all, are limited and cannot reach the depths to which the Master penetrates. He knows the why and wherefore of his instructions, and like a fully responsible Field Marshall issues his commands. We must therefore learn to obey him implicitly like a true soldier, and do what he bids.[130]

We should try to carefully understand the Master's teachings and what lies behind them—not waste time in intellectual wrangling and reasoning. When an officer gives the orders to fire, the soldier must fire, and the responsibility of the decision rests upon the officer. So our duty is to obey, and die if necessary! As long as the condition of our mind does not develop to this kind of obedience, we will not get the full benefit that the Naam has to offer us. The Guru is not ignorant of the pathways to spirituality.[131]

Mere lip loyalty to the Master never pays. The Master wants full devotion to what he says, for therein lies the ultimate good of the disciple.[132]

Persons who time and again meet the Master come to love him more and more; and those who regard his words as Truth become beloved of the Lord. Whatever

the command of the Master may be, it must be followed
with unswerving zeal, so that you will be able to take
hold of the Shabd, which will lead you back to your native home.[133] Love of God means implicit obedience to
Him.[134]

The words of the Master cannot be detached from the
Master. It is from the abundance of heart that the tongue
speaks. The Master is embedded in the Word and his
words are expressions of what is in him; that is, Word,
Life-impulse, and Power. How then can the two be
separated from each other? His words undoubtably
pierce through the hearts of the aspirants and none other
can know the sweet pangs from which they suffer.[135]

It is absolutely necessary to serve the will of the Master, for in doing so lies the good of the disciple. Many
people indeed meet the Satguru, but that is not enough.
For salvation, one has to obey him in thought, word and
deed.[136] He who obeys the Guru's every word will realize
the Lord. But we choose to modify his commandments
to our own way of thinking.[137]

Some people hear in one ear and it goes out through
the other. Other people hear and give out through their
mouth, that they know so much. Both of these things do
not give you any real benefit, unless that very thing forms
a part and parcel of your life. The food that is digested
gives you strength; otherwise, it will result in diseases,
such as vanity and other things.[138] We simply make an
outer show of obeying the Master's orders but do not
live up to them. Even in His absence, orders are orders.
The very order is the Guru, is the Master. Those who

pay obeisance to the words of the Master are sure to be emancipated.[139] Even if you obey the Master's words blindly, you will benefit.[140]

He who obeys the Guru's wishes knows what God is. But do we obey? If only we would obey implicitly for six months, we would see the magical change in our condition. You can get salvation in this very life![141]

Darshan or having a look at the Master, may give you temporary peace and quietness of mind, but the moment you go away the mind begins to run riot again, and reigns supreme over body and soul. Thus, nothing but doing and performance count on the Path of the Masters. The Master's words sink deep into the heart; one can hardly think of not following him.[142]

The Negative Power comes in when we do not truly love, we do not obey, or we obey only so far as our mind agrees. This is what is called the power of negativeness.[143]

It may be possible that He says something that does not appeal to your intellect, but what is your duty? When the officer in the field orders, "Fire," what will the soldier do? He must fire. The Master will never say anything which is not becoming. It may be that you do not understand what He says at the time, but He has some noble purpose behind it for your betterment.[144] . . . Implicit obedience and reverential humility are two of the most helpful factors in spiritual progress.[145]

If there is a mound of filth, over which a silken cloth is spread, do you mean to say that there will be no odor from it? So we can deceive the world, but not the God within us. Take to your heart what is being said. See how far you have changed, or if you are the same man with the same low nature. Outwardly you are making obeisance and paying homage, but the heart is not changed. What did Christ say? He said, "Change your hearts, for the Kingdom of God is at hand." Change your hearts, this is what all Masters say. We don't listen to their words. We simply go on with the outward things or do not seek further than the worldly things that we require. How many are there here who have come only for God's sake? If they have come for God's sake they will have Him, sure and certain. If they have come for some other thing, then . . . ? They will have only that thing, not God.[146]

So it is said that those eyes that do not see the Master should be taken out. Those ears that do not hear the voice of the Beloved, it would be better if they were deaf. That head is blessed that bows down to the feet of the Beloved. Guru Nanak and Shamas Tabrez said that those arms should be broken that do not embrace the Master. So these are the feats of love. What does a lover want? Naturally to be near to the Master, the God in Him of course. He wants to listen to every word that the Master utters. He will follow it at any cost. "If ye love me, keep my commandments." These things follow as a matter of course, I would say. He who loves, will follow what the Master says, whether he is in the Master's presence or away. The Master is Word personified. Whether the disciple is thousands of miles away, he is still being watched, because the Master is the Word made manifest. Sometimes the Master also manifests physically. So just meet with the wishes of the Beloved. This is what love does. And what does it cost? It costs nothing. It asks only that you should have your whole attention riveted on the Beloved. All other things will follow naturally.[147]

The conduct of a disciplined initiate should reflect the greatness of his virtuous Master.[148] To go to a great soul and not to follow his teaching is to demean him.[149]

If you act on what you are told, only one Satsang is sufficient for your salvation.[150]

The Physical Presence of The Master

NOW THE QUESTION arises, how can we increase this desire for God, or give birth to it, if it is not yet awakened? By keeping the company with him who has what you want. If you wish to be a wrestler, keep the company of a wrestler, or if you are interested in learning, then keep the company of a learned person. The radiation absorbed whilst in the company of a Saint will bring untold benefit.[151] The company of a person who is self-centered will give you the radiation of His life. Maulana Rumi says, "If you have the company of a Saint (Saints referred to in the scriptures are meant here, not the so-called masters with whom the world is flooded today), and if you sit by Him for an hour, you will have His radiation. You will have more advancement and progress this way than by putting in hundreds of years of devotion.[152]

You can have His radiation where He is already manifest. Sitting close to the human body where God is manifest, even for a short time, will give you quicker results. That is why Satsang, or the company of a Saint, is talked of very highly in all scriptures. The process is quickened by radiation. The same God Power is within you but is not awakened. It will be awakened at the time of Initiation and further, it will be given a boost by the radiation of the Master. That is why it is said that one lyrical glance from a Saint that is radiated to your soul from outside can bring you up into your own self and you will see the Light of God within you. So one grace-pouring glance from a Master is sufficient for us. That will give a boost. That is what is meant by, "Have the company of a Saint; the more you get the better." The more receptive you get by sitting near him, the more benefit you derive. Simply to come and go won't do. It is receptivity that gives you substantial benefit. The more time that you can spend in the company of a Saint, the better.[153]

The Guru's tongue is drenched with the Lord's nectar, and when it speaks a charged intoxication radiates forth; so wherever the Guru goes, he intoxicates others. No matter how sweet may be the words of a lecture, if the person delivering it is not imbued with the love of God, there will be no spiritual effect. When the Guru's words are heard and put into practice, all hunger leaves, and that charging gives a tranquil and perfect peace.[154]

Every word, every look, every move, every touch, even the aura of a Saint is endowed with mercy, love and the grace of God. The atmosphere about Him is charged.[155] Indeed the personal aura of the Master has its unrivaled and unique effect. No words can probably discuss or describe its grandeur.[156] You are just to look at Him, intently, minutely, penetratingly, forgetting everything else, receive impressions, close your eyes and let those impressions be imbedded in your heart.[157]

Receptivity

BREATH FOR BREATH, he remembers you. Without the Master's remembrance, love for him cannot be born in the disciple. He sends out rays of love, and the disciple experiences a strong pull toward his Master. This is also a gift.[158] Even if the disciple does not set his attention on the Master, the radiation goes on emitting, and the effect of this is the making of him. If he becomes receptive, then the Master appears before him.[159]

Receptivity is developed when all foreign thoughts are driven out. You remain and He remains. You are working at the back of the eyes and the God-in-man is also working there. The eyes are the windows of the soul and He teaches others without any language through the eyes.[160]

The life of one who is receptive will become the abode of all good qualities.[161]

The gracious Master Power is the constant and nearest companion of the initiate. He is fully aware of your inner prayers and adoration.[162] Master always holds the hands He takes. There is never a thought of loosening that tight hold. Master Power will never leave nor forsake the initiate until the end of the world. He is a fathomless ocean of love incarnate. Love knows only giving. So He gives and gives. He continually sends His grace to them. When the initiate sees the Master's inner glory and charm and listens to the strains of Music, he or she must respond, no matter what those who are ignorant may say. This is a gift of the Master.[163]

Moreover, when Master initiates someone, He resides with him; He watches all of his actions, guides him further where it is needed; especially those who turn their faces to Him. If you forget, He does not forget.[164] See Him present in every experience and remember He is always with you, ready to assist whenever you turn your thoughts to Him.[165]

I should also like to say a few words about the numerous personal problems which the dear ones refer to me for a solution to their difficulties. While I am happy to give the right guidance, it should also be remembered that those initiated by me are looked after by the gracious Master Power working overhead, Who is ever with His children and can solve all of their problems if they but put themselves in a receptive mood. In this regard, an application of sound common sense together with a calm consideration of the facts can work wonders in developing receptivity to the Master Power. Receptivity is the key which can not only solve your material difficulties but can also unlock the Kingdom of Heaven within you.[166]

His words were like soothing balm on their raw wounds. The truth is that there is great power in the attention, and when one is helpless and feels that there is no hope, one will get full protection and assistance by turning one's face toward the Master. Whenever you feel lonely or lost, remember sweetly the Master and invoke His help and if it is a time that you can sit in meditation, do so with love and devotion. The true way to God starts when you rise above body-consciousness. There is no other way.[167]

I did find a Friend for you—a friend who is even now waiting patiently for you to turn to Him. He is constantly by your side loving you, wanting to share your life, wanting your love, your thoughts and faith. It is you who have drawn a thick screen of various thoughts in between you and your Friend. Try to remove this screen, then you will see a Friend waiting with outstretched arms, to embrace you with Love, to stand by you all through this life and thereafter. Do not despair, you are much loved. If only you would shed your negative attitude and be receptive, everything would be yours. He is with you always, extending all feasible help. If we turn our face to Him, He will be constantly with us, perceptibly and imperceptibly.[168]

Help and protection is always extended by the Master to His followers. He looks after their comforts in every way, both outer and inner. Even the effects of the reactions of the past—from the gallows to an ordinary pin prick—so much concession is given. As the mother sacrifices everything for the sake of her child, even so does the Master sacrifice everything for the sake of His children. The follower in fact does not dream of what the Master does for him. He fills his followers with His own thought, with His own life impulses. When we remember Him, He remembers us with all His heart and soul. He is not the body. He is the Word personified, the Word made flesh. To get the full benefit of the Master Power, the disciple must develop receptivity. It is impossible to develop receptivity until implicit obedience is given to the commandments of the Master. When you pay heed to the Master's commandments, then that is a sign that you are growing in love for Him, and the more you grow in love for Him, the more receptivity you will develop.

When you begin to develop this receptivity, all discomfort will vanish and you will truly begin to tread the Path in the firm assurance that you are on the right way, together with the loving companionship of one who will demonstrate more and more His greatness and His power on each step of the way until you find that it is the very God Himself who is your Guide and Mentor, who will never leave you until he has safely escorted you back to the true home of the Father.[169]

The more time you have in direct contact, so much the better. If not, because it is not possible to have it 24 hours of the day, then develop receptivity by sitting in your rooms. If that is developed, then you can go anywhere and still have it. So the Word is pervading everywhere. It vibrates throughout the universe and is especially concentrated in the Word made flesh. One vibration from Him also vibrates throughout the universe. It is only a question of becoming receptive to it, that's all. In that way it makes no difference whether a man is sitting here or afar. It is a matter of becoming attentive, receptive to the Word or Shabda, which pervades everywhere. Where it is manifest, that vibrates and that vibration goes on throughout the world. You know who the Master truly is now? Such like Masters are spoken of in all the scriptures.[170]

When you come to a place where a Master is sitting, you should forget everything. Forget the environment around you and who is sitting by you. Just be fully attentive to the eyes of the Master, which is where His soul has its play. You must become receptive to derive the full benefit of the company of a Saint. Those who come near the Master, and their mind is, what you say, tossing about from one place to another, and ripples are constantly arising in the pond of their mind, cannot develop receptivity. They cannot receive the full benefit of radiation that comes from the Master, through His whole body and especially through the eyes. This benefit you can derive even when sitting thousands of miles away. Through a radio, you hear what a man is saying from a long distance. Through a television, you also see who is speaking. The Word is everywhere. Word or Naam or Shabda are all one and the same. So the vibration of the man in whom the Word is manifest permeates through the whole world. Those who become receptive by stilling their mind and intellect, derive full benefit. Kabir says, "If the Master resides thousands of miles across the seas and the disciple resides this side, he should just direct his attention to the Master." The Word is everywhere, you have just to become receptive. When you become receptive, you will derive the full benefit of Satsang.[171]

What I am telling you is a very delicate point of course. You may be living for years with the Master and yet not develop Life. As you think so you become. That Life becomes infused in your life if you become receptive. You will become One, no more two. That is why Saint Paul said, "It is I, not now I, but Christ lives in me." This very thing has been given out by almost all Masters, whether they came in India or abroad. Maulana Rumi says, "I am so much filled up with my Master that I have forgotten what is my name, whether He is in me or I am in Him. I cannot differentiate." So this is something which comes to the fate of those who become receptive. He is all wisdom, grace, mercy and love. These qualities can be developed in you by becoming receptive, not by word of mouth. By word of mouth, you will understand at the level of the intellect, but Life cannot be radiated, infused in you, unless you become receptive. You follow my point?[172]

Master Power is always with you, working overhead, extending all feasible love and protection. A loving father would not like to see his child remain in the cradle forever, but would be happy to see the child stand up and walk and will surely offer his hand to the child in his efforts to stand up and walk.[173] The road is very long, but he gives his time to each individual; after all he has great love for each and every one—what can he do?[174]

To expand our capacities for receiving progressively upraising illumination may not always be easy; but the Master is patient in His Wisdom, and from out of His vast spirituality His assistance remains for ever at hand until we join Him in Sach Khand, the final ever-blissful Home of our true Spiritual Being.[175]

Man has not to exert himself, except in moulding himself ethically and morally to that climax of love, sincerity and humility, which will produce the necessary state of receptivity in him. Everything else is in the hands of the Master.[176]

Please do not grieve over your inability to be more receptive to the divine grace. Slow but steady wins the race. Fragrant flowers are fashioned into fairness delicately under Divine Will . . .[177]

When the Sound Current is strong, it reminds you that He is always with you, working overhead extending His grace. Turn your face to Him and benefit therefrom.[178]

You will agree that it is the loving devotion, and the anguished cry of the soul, when the mercy is invoked and one gets attuned.[179]

Who can teach you "The Art of Loving" except Him who is Love Personified and is overflowing with the intoxicating Love of God and all creation. There is no greater Love in all the world, than the Love of God and the Word made flesh. Whoever thinks of Him, reads of Him, talks of Him and meditates on Him, will become like unto Him. Know that nothing should stand between you and your Master. The more you give yourself in complete self surrender, the more you shall receive.[180] How wonderful it is to surrender completely to one who is Competent and Loving and to feel His loving presence and grace working in every sphere of life. The more one is able to develop receptivity by keeping His Commandments, the more he or she is able to feel, retain and enjoy His grace. The Master's grace is boundless.[181]

When the Word becomes manifested somewhere and you become receptive to it, your mind will be stilled. You can reflect your own self in it and can also reflect God within you. The only thing that stands in the way between God and you is the mind. You are not to put in anything from outside. It is already there. When the turbulent waves of the mind are stilled you can see your true face in it.[182]

You can only become receptive through love. The man who has love, even while sitting with thousands of people, he still remains all alone, because his whole attention is riveted on the Master, with whom he is concerned. This is the way how you can develop receptivity.[183]

The disciple's attention should be directed toward his Master. The speed of attention is very fast. One can judge from the force of electricity; the pranas or life currents have faster speed than electric current, and the attention is faster than pranas.[184]

Telepathy has now conclusively proved how heartstrings between individuals play in unison, irrespective of distance between the two. There is a tremendous power in thought vibrations and their range is unlimited. Thus the sympathetic chords between the Master and the disciples carry silent messages of love to and fro between them with a force that is unimaginable. This wonderful relationship one can establish with God. By being in tune with the Infinite one can by force of thought do a lot of good to others, as at bottom all are embedded in the same soil, the Divine ground.[185]

When a disciple remembers the Master, he experiences within him a soothing influence and a sort of Divine intoxication. This is known as telepathy or sympathetic communication from heart to heart from a distance. In the same way we can, by tuning our attention with the Infinite, draw upon the great good of others. For this purpose one has to unite his self in the Divine ground wherein all are embedded and from there pass on the heavenly influence to the individual or society desired to be benefited. In this attitude one has not to place the desires of others before the Creator, but has simply to invoke His loving pleasure and await His Grace to work out the desired result.[186]

We should always look up to the Master to guide us within, as nobody else can. It is, therefore, of great importance that we should constantly be aligned with the Master and owe lasting allegiance to Him and not allow anybody to come in between Him and ourselves. All the brothers and sisters in faith should lovingly cooperate for this highest purpose of life and in no way allow themselves to be distracted by anybody, howsoever apparently one may look to be highly evolved or developed. It is an undivided affectionate obedience which stirs the ocean of compassion and mercy within, and the gracious Master extends His kindly protection and timely help to the child disciple, whether one knows it or not.[187]

There are Satsangis and near Satsangis. By near Satsangis I mean one who has come in closer touch with the Guru. This teaching is the same for all children, but those who become receptive come closer to the Master; they get a special protection. Though his protection is extended to everyone—all are fed and eat the same bread —yet the child who is more hungry will receive more food.[188]

So, receptivity is important for success in all phases of life, both mundane and spiritual, and it can be achieved by following this right understanding. First, one must lead a God-like life; second, the spiritual diaries must be maintained in the accurate way; and third, one must learn to develop receptivity. If you succeed in the first two, the third will follow of itself.[189]

Spirituality cannot be taught, it must be caught like an infection which is passed on to the others, who are receptive.[190]

When a disciple comes near a Master, the latter's atmospheric influence is felt according to the degree of receptivity developed. When he or she has grasped the theory of the teachings of the Saints and has taken up the Way, it may be as an experimental measure at first, and full conviction comes only when he or she sees within. The evidence of others can only give inducement to take up the way, but first-hand experience is convincing, however small it may be.[191]

The Immaculate Naam is the constant companion of each initiate. The more a child grows in awareness, the more he or she will appreciate the sweet loving help extended by the Master Power, the Immaculate Naam.[192]

Those who are put on the Way, each thing comes up to them to awaken a higher outlook whereby the disciple may see the God Power working through all. To such ones there are books in rivulets and sermons in stones.[193]

The Master always holds His disciples in the innermost heart center. After all they all are His children. He does not look at their unworthiness. He is there to make them worthy. He cannot leave them—His love is so great.[134]

Please learn to be receptive to His grace and feel His kindly presence, riding with you on the buses, chatting with you in the street, sitting with you in the park, by your office desk, and accompanying you every morning to the office, slowing down by the lily pond to check new flowers and walking with you in the evening all the way back by the new moon. Master is always with the disciple and never leaves him or her until the end of the world. The Father will never disown His children.[195]

Live in God's Will: Become a Conscious Co-worker of the Divine Plan

*None can describe the condition of one who has
  made God's Will his own;*

Whoever tries to do so, must realize his folly.

*No supply of paper, pen or scribe can ever de-
  scribe the state of such a one.*

O, great is the Power of the Word;

But few there be that know it.[196]

JAP JI

The Master sets before us the goal, which is to attain complete oneness with the Lord— the One Being. We can reunite with the Source from which we once emanated, and regain our permanent abode in the Home of our Father, where joy and peace reign supreme beyond the reach of annihilation and ignorance, beyond all miseries of the troubled ocean of life.[197]

There are three things required of a Sikh or the disciple in relation to his Master to enable him to create receptivity of the Master's favor. He must sacrifice his body, his mind and his possessions—nay, even his very life should be consecrated at the feet of the Master. It is not because the Master is covetous of any reward from His disciple, but that the disciple should sacrifice all he holds dear in this life. The Master does not accept a speck of it, but gives them back, all intact, as a sacrificial offering. He instructs the disciple not to defile himself by misuse of his possessions, but to make the best use of them to the benefit of his brethren, the poor and the needy, the sick and the infirm, so as to help in the harmonious development of all around him. Let the disciple stand before his Master with his all at His feet, but the Master would accept naught out of it. He would thus stand in full resignation, ready to receive the Grace of the Master and the beginning of his realization. He has to make himself a vehicle for the Master, like a rebeck or a lyre to be played upon, creating sweet symphonies of the Holy Naam. All social connections, all attachments to worldly possessions, all clinging to name and fame, all the physical comforts, all the evil thoughts surging in

the mind, are to be placed before the Master, to let Him
work His Will through them.[198]

A disciple who follows the will of the Master gets the
Elixir of Life in his own right, and wins the Kingdom of
God as his birthright.[199]

Please, my Lord, listen to my appeal:
I wish only to be at thy Feet.

To be at His Feet means to obey him—to surrender unto
Him. He would like to dye you in the same color as his
own soul. In deep humility he has said I want to be at
Your Feet. He is wearily acknowledging his defeat in the
world; it is not a matter of force. It has also been said
that by force you cannot get, and by force you cannot
give. You can neither gain the inner knowledge by force,
nor can you learn to leave the body at will by force. Whoever feels that he can achieve anything through force is
welcome to try and see. All is in the Lord's hands; if He
wants to give anything, then you will receive. He most
definitely will give to one who will surrender to His Feet.
Dwell only on the understanding that the Guru has giv-
en; imbibe the virtues therein, and as you think, so you
will become. In this way you will absorb the radiation.[200]

He who becomes conscious of the Divine Plan
is the True Man.

In the true sense, the Lord's man is one who becomes a
conscious co-worker of the Divine Plan. How does he
recognize the Lord's commands? *By the Guru's blessing,*
he unravels himself. Also, *through the Guru's blessing he*
recognizes His commands by dying while living. At the

time of death the soul withdraws from outer environments and leaves the body. If this can be done while living, when the soul rises up she sees that Power at work, and retains the knowledge consciously. Unless that happens, one cannot truly know the Lord's commands. When he knows His commands in truth, he becomes a man in the true sense of the word.[201]

When you become the conscious co-worker of the Divine Plan, who is there to bring you back to the world? You may have been away from God for thousands of years, but once you meet a God-in-man, He gives you a contact with God. If you develop it, then naturally your coming and going is ended and you will go back to your Home.[202]

God wants, love demands, every sacrifice from us. Who is the lover of God? It is He who can sacrifice everything in the Name of God. Can we? Can we say that we have love for God? For trifling things we say that we have no time to remember God. So love demands sacrifice of everything, even of your life, what to speak of outer things.[203]

Discipleship truly consists in unswerving devotion and resignation to the Will and Pleasure of the Master. By complete resignation, all mental chattering is thrown overboard and then there are no more cravings or desires. The tumultuous hubbub of the life of the senses is replaced by calm and collected serenity born of resignation and true renunciation. It is in these silent hours that the spiritual consciousness begins to dawn.[204]

This body, this wealth, this mind, I have given to the

Master. It does not mean to give the body literally—that belongs to those with whom you are connected, as a re-action of the past. The Master guides your soul, so your soul should be surrendered to him, not the body. By giv-ing the mind, you should think as he wants you to think, and your wealth used for good cause—not for misuse, or to harm the lives of others. Share with others, and then eat. Think of everything as being the Guru's property given in your safekeeping, and use it in a like manner. If you do all this, what happens? You receive Par Brahm (God beyond Brahmand).[205]

Self-surrender was the natural corollary of such faith and love, and Baba Ji's letters return insistently to this theme:

Be not lost in yourself. Let this thought be firmly and unshakably fixed in your mind: "Body, mind and wealth, nirat and surat, eyes, ears, nose, mouth, hands, feet—yea all that is in the world is the Sat-guru's. I myself am nothing. Whatever you are do-ing, do it as Satguru's and always seek to do what is the best. Do not forget this even for a moment, but take it as a *hidayat,* a commandment.

(24th May, 1901)

Never let the idea of "mine-ness" find a place in your heart. Even if you get the lordship of Brahm-and, do not regard that you have any share in it: "I am only an agent." Everything is the Satguru's. Let the Master's injunction be ever in your mind: "I am nothing, I am nothing, I am nothing," and let the remembrance of the Lord be your constant thought and the form of the Satguru imaged in your heart always.[206]

(7th September, 1900)

What the Lord considers best He is doing. Do not bring yourself into the picture. Live by the words of the Master and continue performing your earthly duties. When the fruit is ripe, it will fall of its own accord, without injury to itself or the bearing branch, and the ripe fruit is held in great value. But if we pluck the unripe fruit forcibly from off the tree, the branch is injured and raw fruit shrivels and is of little use. Meeting a competent Master is the fulfillment of human birth: this is the fruit of life. To live by his commandments ensures its proper nurture. Daily Simran and Bhajan to the maximum possible are its best food and nourishment and mergence with Shabd is its ripening and falling off.

(3rd March, 1899)

Such was the progress of the soul. Its ripening was a matter of steady growth. Supported by the words of the Master, nourished by Bhajan, and borne on the Shabd Dhun, it transcended realm after realm until it left all coverings of mind and matter behind and reached Sach Khand. This was its True Abode, the realm of pure spirit. From there merging into the Divine it receded progressively into the Formless, until, passing through the Alakh and Agam, it reached the Anami, the Nameless and Formless source of all that moves and has its being.[207]

I quite appreciate your adoration for the Master and your anguish for mergence into His Divinity. Please relax so that the gracious Master Power engulfs you in Its splendor and glory. Let the ego be completely annihilated and you emerge out of and above the plane of duality, forgetting all about your "I-hood." Self-denial and abnegation is another stepping stone to the climax of Spirituality. Be completely immersed in the sweet glory of His remembrance, altogether oblivious of the past or future. Just resign and surrender in favor of His Divine Will. The Nectar of Life needs a most transparent receptacle, to be poured into, for distributing to the thirsty children.[208]

The elimination of the ego is the only remedy for liberation from the unending cycle of births and deaths. It is a clear test of those who have realized at-one-ment with the Everlasting Divinity, the spiritual current diffused in the world. All labor undergone for total self-effacement is an effort in the right direction. The secret lies in depersonalizing the soul of all that is personal. The many recipes for losing the "I" consciousness that flood the world today fail to gain for us the Goal of Liberation. For with such methods, the ego feeds itself and grows from strength to strength and is not effaced. Unless we become conscious co-workers with the Divine Plan, we cannot become selfless.[209]

God is within you, He is not to come from outside. It is your I-hood or ego that stands in the way. This ego comes up when you are conscious of the body, whether physical, astral or causal. When you rise above the physical body, the physical I-hood is eliminated. When you rise above the causal body, then you will completely understand who you are. Your will is the will of the Lord. The Lord's will is within you.[210]

Ego is the self-assertive principle in man that makes him feel that "I do this, or I do that." When one rises above body consciousness and knows himself and becomes a conscious co-worker of the Divine Plan, and sees that he is not the "doer" but is a mere puppet in the hands of God, he will cease to be responsible for his actions and will become *Jivan Mukta,* or a free soul. The ego in man is part of the grand delusion that he is laboring under. It will cease to act or will be nullified only when a great degree of purity has been attained by the disciple, in which all of his actions will reflect the Master in him. Like Christ, he will proclaim: "I and my Father are One."[211]

There is no place without God, and it is the height of illusion to consider that His creation is separate from Him. The whole world is His image, if Man could only see it.[212]

The devotion of oneself to the practical side of the teachings will prove the efficacy of the means devised by Nanak. A calm and Supreme Joy begin to reign over the mind at the very outset. With the progress of time and practice, sweet symphonies are set afloat in the living temple of the human frame, and a world of Heavenly Light is made effulgent. Ultimately, man is brought to face the "Effulgent Spirit" in its full swing. It is only then that the universe appears full of the Lord and that there is nothing of the world that is not the Word.[213]

The blessings of Hari Naam are too numerous to be recounted. One who becomes dyed in the color of the Word always chants the glories of God. All his works automatically take the right shape at the right moment. What he wishes must happen, for Nature herself is at his beck and call. He is freed from all ills and all evils. He loses all thoughts of I-ness and my-ness and never becomes vainglorious. He rises above the pairs of opposites: riches and poverty, comforts and discomforts, pleasure and pain, fame and obscurity, for he remains in a state serene and with equipoise. The poison of mind and matter can have no effect on him. While in the world, he is no longer of the world, but is unattached and carefree; he moves about wherever he likes. The illusions and delusions of the world do not affect him. He escapes the sway of Kal (Time) for time has no bondage for him, nor has space any limitations nor causation any spell. He gains life everlasting and once again wins back the Kingdom of God, the Garden of Eden from which he was driven because of his first disobedience to God. He not only saves his own soul but through the power of the Word saves the souls of many others who come in contact with him; yes, the souls of his ancestors and descendants as well.

Blessed indeed is a person who has the good fortune to come into the fold of a Sant Satguru and thus gains the summum bonum of life.[214]

When once this contact with Naam is established, the Sadhak always feels the presence of the Higher Power and

the Power remains forever with him wherever he may be
—on the snowy mountain tops or in the burning desert
sands. Reveling in the greatness of that Power, he leaves
all his cares to Him and becomes indifferent to everything around him. He cheerfully accepts whatever comes
his way as coming from Him for his benefit alone. He
consciously sees the Divine Will at work and smilingly
surrenders himself to it with words of genuine gratitude
on his lips. He has no longer any wishes of his own except what may be of God. Now he works as a mere instrument moving like an automaton under the influence
of that Power. He sees all creatures, high and low, just
as tiny specks set in an orderly harmony in the immense
Universe surrounding him. He now divines a procession
which is orderly, an order which is harmonious, obeying
a Will infinitely above him and yet infinitesimally careful of him. In this way is established a complete harmony
between the soul of man and the soul of the Universe.
At every step he cries forth, Let thy Will be done.[215]

Self-Surrender

THE ESSENTIAL advantage in the field of spirituality
is to be found not without but within. It lies not in
the absence of outer opposition but in one's inner capacity for complete self-surrender and love; and outward
obstacles may in fact act as tests and stimuli for the development of this capacity. This ability to conquer the
ego and to submit oneself to the Higher Will is as rare in

the East as in the West, and wherever it can be found, there you shall observe the true grandmark of spirituality.

It is this capacity that you must cultivate and develop if you really wish to make substantial progress in the spiritual field. I repeat that the path is not easy. You must crucify your ego and lay your selfhood at the altar of love for your Master. Rome was not built in a day and the True Abode of the Lord is not to be attained with a few weeks labor. Most seekers want quick results. They want miracles and sudden transformations. But the seed germinates rapidly only in thin soil and then withers away. The seed that must grow into the life-giving tree must grow more slowly. The science of spirituality as it has been taught by all Masters and as it has been given to you, is a perfect science. Its truth has been demonstrated by some initial experience. The rest depends on your effort. The Divine Grace is ever ready to pour itself into the vessel, but the vessel must first be ready.[216]

A loving faith in, and a complete surrender to, the Will of God or to that of His elect, the God-man, constitute the basic principles for the life of the seeker after Truth.

The sages and the scriptures alike all tell us that while living in the world, we should not conduct ourselves as if we are of the world, but maintain an attitude of self-abnegation or total detachment from the world and all that is of the world. We should, therefore, live like a lotus leaf which has its roots in the mire below but raises its head far above in the light of the glorious sun shining over the murky water, or like a royal swan that sails majestically on the surface of the water which is its native habitat, and yet can fly high and dry if and when it chooses or feels the necessity to do so.

This kind of disinterested isolation or separation from one's surroundings and above all from his lower self, the body, the mind, and the mental world, comes only when one dissolves his ego or the individual will into the will of God of the Will of his Guru, the God-man, for then he acts like a mere pantomime in a dumb show which dances and plays at the will of the wirepuller behind the screen. This is called complete self-surrender which silently craves for "Not my will but Thy Will, O Lord." Such an attitude easily helps a person become *Nehkarma*. While apparently doing one thing or another, he is now not doing anything on his own but is carrying out the Will of his Father—God or his Divine Preceptor for he verily sees within Him the Divine Plan as it is and he is just drifting along the Great Current of Life and finds himself a conscious instrument in the invisible hands directing all his movements.

Self-surrender then, means surrendering one's everything to God or his Elect, the Preceptor (God-in-man), including one's body, riches and his very self (the thinking mind). It does not mean a state of total bankruptcy for an individual, as some might be prone to think. The great God and His Elect are the giver of all these things and do not stand in need of those very gifts which they have already given freely and in abundance to their children for their best and legitimate use. We in ignorance think of these as our own and adopt an attitude of aggressive possessiveness and try to grab them by all means fair or foul and then guard them jealously with all our might and main. Attached to these gifts and clutching them fast, we forget the Great Giver Himself and herein creeps imperceptibly the great delusion, the root cause of all our sufferings. No doubt these things, having come to us, are ours, but they have been given to us temporarily as a sacred trust to be utilized according to the Will of the Donor which, of course, is all perfect and immaculately clean with no flaw in it. But as we live in the realm of matter, we, with all our worldly wits about us, cannot escape attaching to us the gross impressions and allowing them to accumulate freely from day to day until they form a granite wall around us and we, losing clarity of perception, become blind to the reality and come to identify the self in us with the *pinda* and *pindi-manas* (the body and the bodily mind).[217]

Truly sincere disciples of the Masters and the Masters themselves always consider that they have no individual existence of their own apart from that of the God-in-man or of God. Such people read the past, the present and the future as an open book and do things in conformity with the Divine Plan. This leads one to the irresistable conclusion that God helps those souls who do His Will. But this is only for men of firm faith and is not to be taken as a means of escape for ordinary individuals living always on the plane of the senses, for they are governed by the law that God helps those who help themselves. The quality of self-surrender, with whatever degree of faith, does bear its own fruit, and quickly, according to the level at which it is practiced. By gradual experience one learns of its full value as he advances on the Path until he reaches a stage when he altogether loses his own ego in the Divine Will and thus himself becomes *Neh-karma*, the crown and glory of all human existence. A loving faith in the inherent goodness of God and complete self-surrender to the Divine Will lead one on the high-road to spirituality without any great continuing effort on the part of the aspirant. These two things constitute the secret "sesame" and the magic key that flings wide open the portals of the Kingdom of God that lies within the temple of the human body which we all are.[218]

If once we rise above body-consciousness, then we know what we are, and how best to utilize our gifts in the service of God and God's plan and not in sinful activities born of carnal appetites, self-aggrandizement, or as a means for acquiring temporal power for personal benefit and gain. This was the great lesson which the sage Ashtavakra gave to Raja Janak after giving him a practical experience of the Reality. We have in fact to part with nothing but egoistic attachment to the treasure-house of the heart, and this makes us none the poorer for it but attracts more of the love-laden gifts from the Supreme Father when He sees the wisdom of His child, a prodigal son before but now grown wiser. This is called surrendering the little self with all its adjuncts of body, mind and riches, for the sake of the higher self (soul) according to the Divine Will, and becoming *Neh-karma*, the very goal of life.[219]

Surrender to the feet of the Master means to merge

one's individual will in the will of the Master, and to completely place oneself at his mercy. It is the surest and easiest way to escape from all cares and anxieties. It comes only when a disciple has complete faith and confidence in the competence of the Master.

This type of self-surrender is like that of a completely helpless patient who, trusting in the skill of a competent surgeon, places his life in his hands and quietly submits himself to his knife and lancet.[220]

In exactly the same way, the work of the Master does not consist in merely teaching the theory of Para Vidya (Science of the Beyond), but it includes the practical demonstration of results of spiritual experiments, and help and guidance through all the disciples' difficulties. A true friend does not only give theoretical lessons in how to escape from mind and matter; he helps in effecting the escape itself.

Suppose, for instance, that a person has to go abroad. He will begin by making inquiries as to the various means of transportation available: land, sea or air, as he may choose. After he makes his choice he enters the plane, ship or train, and relying on the skill of the operator, takes his seat comfortably without the least anxiety. Should the ship flounder, or the plane be caught in a storm, it is the duty of the captain or pilot to take every possible care to save the conveyance along with the passengers for whom he is responsible.

In exactly the same way, an aspirant for spirituality has, after careful investigation, to decide first about the spiritual worthiness of a Master, and then to submit himself wholly and solely to his authority and direction without any mental reservations whatever; for he alone knows the turns and twists of the spiritual path and is in a position to act as an unerring guide.

The term surrender therefore means that a disciple should have full confidence in the skill and competence of the Master, and scrupulously follow and act on his instructions whatever they may be, whether in conformity with his own reason or not—for his reason being limited may be faulty or fall far short of the depth or prove uncertain.

It is not for him to question the propriety of the Master's commandments. He must learn, like a soldier, to obey his command without knowing the why and wherefore of things; for the Master knows what is best and most suitable in each case. One must therefore obey the Master literally, and straightway engage himself in the sadhan or spiritual practice and discipline as it may be laid down for him. This is the only way to spiritual success; there is no other.[221]

When a disciple entrusts his all to the Master, he becomes carefree and the Master has of necessity to take over the entire responsibility; just as a mother does for her child who does not know what is good for him.

As the disciple develops in his sadhan, he fits himself to receive more grace from the Master. Under his kind and benign influence, the disciple begins to thrive from day to day, and all his wishes are fulfilled without the least trouble on his part.[222]

Self-surrender is not an easy task. To accomplish it,

one has to recede back to the position of an innocent child. It means an entire involution, a complete meta-morphosis, supplanting one's own individuality.

It is the path of self-abnegation, which not everyone can take.

On the other hand, the path of spiritual discipline is comparatively easy. Self-effort can be tried by anyone in order to achieve spiritual advancement.

It is, no doubt, a long and tortuous path, as compared with the way of self-surrender, but one can, with confidence in the Master, tread it firmly step by step. If, however, a person is fortunate enough to take to self-surrender, he can have all the blessings of the Master quickly; for he goes directly into his lap and has nothing to do by himself for himself.

He is then the Master's Elect, his beloved son, the son of God Himself. But very rarely even a really blessed soul may be able to acquire this attitude.[223]

With surrender to a Satguru, the Lord takes a jiva under His own protection and grants unto him the blessings of *Sahaj* (i.e., eternal happiness). All doubts and fears now disappear and he comes to his own real Self.[224]

> *Endless are His praises, endless the words of commendation;*
> *Endless His works and endless His gifts;*
> *Endless His vision, and endless His inspiration;*
> *Endless and beyond understanding is His purpose;*
> *Endless His creation and endless the ends thereof.*

Endless men's search in anguish for His limits,
but His limits cannot be found.
Endless He is and none can know His end;
The more we say, the more He is.
Exalted is the Lord, and exalted His abode;
More exalted still His Holy Word.
He who reaches His height,
He alone may glimpse Him.
O Nanak, He alone knows His greatness;
And it is only His glance of Grace, can lift us
to His height.[225]

JAP JI

From Master's Messages

ARISE, AWAKE, and stop not till the Goal is reached is the time honored message coming down, as it does from eternity, and I repeat it today with all the emphasis at my command. Make hay while the sun shines. The Kingdom of God verily is at hand and the Power of God unmistakably beckons you to it. Avail yourself of the golden opportunity that God has given you, for human birth is a rare privilege and thrice blessed is man. Make the most of it, while there is yet time. Let not dissensions creep into your thoughts and corrode your progress in any way. You are one of the fortunate children of Invincible Light. Live up to that sacred Truth. Master Power is always with you and will be extending you all the love and grace.[226]

There is need to take stock today where we stand, how far we have traveled. Let us do so calmly but seriously. The Journey may be long but has to be completed. Life is running out, let not vain pursuits deflect us from our Noble Path. The grace of the Master is overwhelming and is extending far and wide. Through His grace the long and tedious journey back to our Eternal Home is cut short and rendered full of melodious charm. His Gracious Love is overflowing, and He is waiting for you at the back door of your eyes to receive you. Ours is to invert and sit at the door. Let our steadfast devotion and whole-hearted faith in Him stand in our good stead.[227]

Love is the "Light of Life." This love is developed the more you pray from your heart and not lips, the more you are in contact with the Light and Sound Principle of God-in-Action Power, the holy Naam or Word with which you have been given a contact.

This course of life will develop true humility of the heart, which is the secret of growth in God, for the lack of which you are easily offended, become suspicious, upset when others speak ill of you, have secret desire to be popular, become dictatorial in your talk and conduct, irritable, artificial, ostentatious, complicated in your life and unkind to all those around you and below you.

The true "superman" is the great man, who serves God with humble heart. He is humble, simple, straightforward, gentle, kind and reverent to all. When we forget this, we have quarrels, controversies in the name of the Holy Cause we represent.

The great Sikh Gurus said, "Child-like simplicity and

unattachment bring one nearer to God." So did Christ say, *Except ye be as little children, ye cannot enter the Kingdom of Heaven.*[228]

Your duty is two-fold—corporeal and spiritual—as you have the body and the spirit. Both are intertwined and interlinked and need to be performed diligently and lovingly without dampening your enthusiasm in any way. For to shirk one's duty is timidity, to face it with determination is manly, to take the results with cheer is bravery and to adjust one's life according to one's environments is invigorating and peaceful.[229]

You have only to do your duty with love, faith and enthusiasm and rise into conscious awareness of the Great Power within you. Now or never should be the motto. There are no windfalls as a general rule. You have to work your way up. Every one reaching the top step has ascended the steps below.[230]

How can your life be sublime? Set up some ideal before you and work for that with heart and soul.[231]

If you want to be happy, make others happy. If you want to be blessed, bless others. Those who injure others, are injured. Such is the Great Law.[232]

Blessed indeed is the hour when the Timeless comes into Time. The Formless assumes a Form and the Wordless becomes the Word, and the Word puts on the mantle of flesh to dwell amongst us. Verily ye are, essentially and potentially, the Timeless, the Formless and the Wordless. The Word is in you and you live in and by the Word, though you may for the time being be living on the plane of senses and unaware of your real identity.[233]

There is suffering in the world, and men and women wander in darkness. In such a world let us go about giving love and compassion to all. Let us serve the poor and broken ones, serve our brothers and sisters, serve birds and beasts and all creation in whom is the breath of Life. Let us not waste energy in questions and controversies. Let us light a few candles at the altar of suffering humanity. This will be achieved by having right understanding, viz., all mankind is one. The soul in all is the essence of God. We are members of the same family of God. We are all brothers in God. When we learn that God resides in every heart we should have respect and love for all. This realization must dawn on mankind.[234]

In silence we test ourselves to find weaknesses to be weeded out. We have to wrestle with darkness and develop moral muscles and receive the message of the spirit. We must be, for some time at least, alone with God. When we enter more and more into silence, our desires will be eliminated, purity attained and the body and the mind sanctified, and we taste the Elixir of Naam Divine and know how sweet the Name is.

In silence the heart illumines; veil after veil is removed. In the heart shineth the Light, and the very silence becomes vocal giving vent to the Music of the Spheres reverberating in all creation. When the Light is seen shining within your heart and the Music of the Spheres becomes audible, you behold the Light in all that is outside, you see the one Light in all. This is the Universal Vision that the One is in all and all are in One. Blessed is he, the man of Illumination, for wherever he be, he dwelleth with the One Eternal.[235]

To attain this Goal purify your nature by living a good life. Manifest truth, purity, love, selflessness and righteousness in your life and activity. Give up all hatred, eradicate egoism and anger. Eschew violence, pledge yourself to love, sincerity, humility, forgiveness and non-violence. Abandon war. Abandon lust for power. Let the Law of Love prevail amongst you, which should be radiated to all nations and races. Let true religion of heart be the ruling factor of your lives. Love God, Love all, serve all and have respect for all as God is immanent in every form. Preach the Gospel of oneness. Spread the message of oneness and live a life of oneness. There will be peace on earth. This is the Mission of my life and I pray it may be fulfilled.[236]

God is love and the Master (God-man) is Love Personified. When our soul comes in contact with His overflowing love, we are saturated with His love through and through, which washes away all dirt of sins of the past and merges us into oneness with the Father.[237]

You are protected by the Master Power working overhead. Depend on Him. You will have all the necessary inner help. The Master is waiting for His dear children to come to Him within.[238]

I have great love for all of you. Indeed, if you knew how much I love you, you would dance for joy. You would become so intoxicated by His love that it would carry you straight into the arms of your Beloved within.[239]

The love of the Master for you is boundless.[240]

Let your inner self be overflowing with the Love of

the Master so much so that all thoughts of yourself be lost in Him.[241] God-Master sees all and showers grace on all who do the Will of His Father.[242] I am in India but my heart is with you all and I send my heartfelt love to each one of you.[243]

REFERENCES

References

The references to the books of Kirpal Singh can be found in the following editions:

The Jap Ji—second edition (1964)
The Crown of Life—third edition (1970)
Spiritual Elixir—first (one-volume) edition (1967)
Morning Talks—first edition (1970) or third edition (1974)
The Wheel of Life—first edition (1965)
Prayer—third edition (1970)
Baba Jaimal Singh—third edition (1971)
The Mystery of Death—first edition (1968)
Godman—second edition (1971)

BOOK ONE
NEW LIFE IN THE WORLD

1. *Wheel of Life,* pp. 61-62
2. *Spiritual Elixir,* pp. 1-2
3. *Ruhani Satsang,* pp. 21-22
4. *Excerpts from Letters to New York Satsangis,* p. 42
5. Letter to an Initiate
6. *Morning Talks,* p. 229
7. *Morning Talks,* p. 238
8. *Jap Ji,* p. 81

9. *Jap Ji,* p. 82
10. *Spiritual Elixir,* pp. 90-92
11. The Master on Marriage (Circular)
12. *Spiritual Elixir,* p. 293
13. *Spiritual Elixir,* p. 221
14. *Sat Sandesh,* December 1971, p. 10
15. *Spiritual Elixir,* p. 283
16. *Spiritual Elixir,* pp. 254-255
17. *Spiritual Elixir,* p. 254
18. *Spiritual Elixir,* p. 126
19. *Spiritual Elixir,* p. 283
20. *Baba Jaimal Singh,* p. 81
21. *Sat Sandesh,* September 1970, p. 12
22. *Sat Sandesh,* December 1971, p. 11
23. *Morning Talks,* pp. 154-155
24. *Baba Jaimal Singh,* p. 100
25. *Morning Talks,* p. 80
26. *Sat Sandesh,* March 1972, p. 6-7
27. *Sat Sandesh,* April 1971, p. 14
28. *Receptivity,* p. 12
29. *Spiritual Elixir,* p. 93
30. *Excerpts from Letters to New York Satsangis,* p. 78
31. *Spiritual Elixir,* p. 161
32. Message on birthday of Baba Sawan Singh, July '68
33. *Spiritual Elixir,* p. 237
34. *Spiritual Elixir,* p. 16
35. *Sat Sandesh,* March 1972, p. 31
36. *Sat Sandesh,* March 1972, pp. 2-3
37. The Way of Love (circular)
38. *Sat Sandesh,* June 1970, p. 26

39. Message on birthday of Baba Sawan Singh, July '68
40. Circular No. 2
41. Master's Birthday Message, February 1963
42. *Sat Sandesh*, December 1970, p. 2
43. *Sat Sandesh*, June 1970, p. 29
44. *Spiritual Elixir*, p. 288
45. *Spiritual Elixir*, pp. 133-134
46. *Excerpts from Letters to New York Satsangis*, p. 79
47. *Spiritual Elixir*, p. 105
48. Circular No. 17
49. *Morning Talks*, p. 18
50. *Excerpts from Letters to New York Satsangis*, p. 52
51. *Excerpts from Letters to New York Satsangis*, p. 52
52. *Spiritual Elixir*, p. 290
53. *Sat Sandesh*, June 1970, p. 30
54. *Spiritual Elixir*, p. 108
55. *Spiritual Elixir*, p. 95
56. *Spiritual Elixir*, p. 126
57. *Sat Sandesh*, February 1971, p. 9-10
58. *Spiritual Elixir*, p. 289
59. *Spiritual Elixir*, p. 235
60. *Excerpts from Letters to New York Satsangis*, p. 62
61. *Spiritual Elixir*, p. 239
62. *Spiritual Elixir*, p. 236
63. Circular No. 27 p. 9
64. Circular No. 27, p. 10
65. *Spiritual Elixir*, p. 290
66. *Spiritual Elixir*, pp. 7-8
67. *Spiritual Elixir*, p. 211
68. *Sat Sandesh*, December 1970, p. 10

69. *Sat Sandesh,* December 1970, p. 14
70. *Spiritual Elixir,* p. 214
71. *Sat Sandesh,* April 1971, p. 28
72. *Spiritual Elixir,* p. 254
73. *Spiritual Elixir,* p. 178
74. Letter to an initiate
75. Circular No. 68
76. *Spiritual Elixir,* p. 164
77. *Sat Sandesh,* December 1971, p. 6
78. *Sat Sandesh,* December 1971, p. 11
79. *Sat Sandesh,* December 1971, p. 9
80. Circular No. 27, p. 5
81. *Spiritual Elixir,* p. 102
82. *Excerpts from Letters to New York Satsangis,* p. 63
83. Letter to an initiate
84. *Spiritual Elixir,* pp. 53-54
85. *Morning Talks,* pp. 69-70
86. Letter to an initiate
87. The Master on Marriage (circular)
88. *Excerpts from Letters to New York Satsangis,* p. 20
89. The Master on Marriage (circular)
90. *Spiritual Elixir,* p. 79
91. *Excerpts from Letters to New York Satsangis,* p. 60
92. *Spiritual Elixir,* p. 240
93. The Master on Marriage (circular)
94. Letter to an initiate
95. Letter to an initiate
96. Letter to an initiate
97. *Spiritual Elixir,* p. 236
98. *Excerpts from Letters to New York Satsangis,* p. 62

99. *Spiritual Elixir,* p. 106
100. Letter to an initiate
101. *Sat Sandesh,* December 1971, p. 6
102. *Sat Sandesh,* April 1971, p. 26
103. *Excerpts from Letters to New York Satsangis,* p. 54
104. *Spiritual Elixir,* p. 213
105. *Excerpts from Letters to New York Satsangis,* p. 26
106. *Spiritual Elixir,* p. 46
107. *Sat Sandesh,* June 1970, p. 26
108. *Sat Sandesh,* June 1970, p. 27
109. *Sat Sandesh,* June 1970, p. 27
110. *Sat Sandesh,* June 1970, p. 29
111. *Spiritual Elixir,* p. 243
112. *Spiritual Elixir,* p. 84
113. *Sat Sandesh,* June 1970, pp. 26-27
114. *Sat Sandesh,* June 1970, p. 28
115. Letter to an initiate
116. *Morning Talks,* pp. 21-22
117. *Sat Sandesh,* June, 1970, p. 27
118. *Excerpts from Letters to New York Satsangis,* p. 17
119. *Baba Jaimal Singh,* pp. 85-86
120. *Wheel of Life,* pp. 31-32
121. *Sat Sandesh,* December 1971, p. 24
122. *Spiritual Elixir,* p. 178
123. *Excerpts from Letters to New York Satsangis,* pp. 55-56
124. *Morning Talks,* p. 127
125. *Spiritual Elixir,* p. 285
126. *Spiritual Elixir,* p. 278
127. *Spiritual Elixir,* p. 134

128. *Spiritual Elixir*, p. 262
129. *Excerpts from Letters to New York Satsangis*, p. 42
130. *Excerpts from Letters to New York Satsangis*, p. 16
131. *Spiritual Elixir*, p. 289
132. *Wheel of Life* p. 50
133. *Spiritual Elixir*, pp. 261-262
134. Message on birthday of Baba Sawan Singh, July '68
135. *Prayer*, p. 58
136. *Spiritual Elixir*, p. 252
137. *Excerpts from Letters to New York Satsangis*, p. 26
138. *Excerpts from Letters to New York Satsangis*, p. 80
139. *Excerpts from Letters to New York Satsangis*, p. 27
140. *Excerpts from Letters to New York Satsangis*, p. 24
141. *Prayer*, p. 47
142. *Prayer*, p. 50
143. *Prayer*, p. 57
144. *Prayer*, p. 43
145. *Excerpts from Letters to New York Satsangis*, p. 51
146. *Baba Jaimal Singh*, pp. 124-125
147. Circular No. 2
148. *Sat Sandesh*, September 1970, p. 11
149. *Spiritual Elixir*, p. 128
150. *Spiritual Elixir*, p. 94
151. *Spiritual Elixir*, p. 156
152. *Sat Sandesh*, August 1970, p. 14
153. *Morning Talks*, p. 233
154. *Morning Talks*, p. 206
155. *Spiritual Elixir*, p. 55
156. *Spiritual Elixir*, p. 148
157. Circular No. 2

158. *Excerpts from Letters to New York Satsangis*, p. 56
159. *Excerpts from Letters to New York Satsangis*, p. 72
160. Letter to an initiate
161. *Sat Sandesh*, April 1971, p. 31
162. *Morning Talks*, p. 140
163. *Spiritual Elixir*, p. 266
164. *Spiritual Elixir*, p. 253
165. *Morning Talks*, p. 141
166. *Morning Talks*, p. 142
167. *Wheel of Life*, p. 48
168. *Excerpts from Letters to New York Satsangis*, p. 81
169. *Spiritual Elixir*, p. 39
170. *Spiritual Elixir*, p. 282
171. *Sat Sandesh*, November 1970, p. 5
172. Circular No. 27, p. 15
173. *Sat Sandesh*, October 1970, p. 8
174. *Sat Sandesh*, July 1971, p. 31
175. *Spiritual Elixir*, pp. 219-220
176. *Spiritual Elixir*, pp. 251-252
177. *Sat Sandesh*, July 1971, p. 30
178. *Spiritual Elixir*, p. 83
179. Circular No. 2
180. *Morning Talks*, p. 43
181. Circular No. 2
182. *Man Know Thyself*, pp. 26-27
183. *Wheel of Life*, p. 31
184. Letter to an initiate
185. *Wheel of Life*, pp. 52-53
186. Letter to an initiate
187. From a tape from Sawan Ashram, February 1970

188. Letter to an initiate
189. *Baba Jaimal Singh*, p. 89
190. *Baba Jaimal Singh*, p. 90
191. *Baba Jaimal Singh*, p. 91
192. *Spiritual Elixir*, p. 135
193. *Sat Sandesh*, August 1970, p. 25
194. *Sat Sandesh*, August 1970, p. 26
195. *Sat Sandesh*, August 1970, p. 26
196. Circular "On Military Service"
197. Circular No. 69, August 18, 1969
198. *Spiritual Elixir*, p. 129
199. *Spiritual Elixir*, p. 262
200. *Sat Sandesh*, December 1971, p. 28
201. *Sat Sandesh*, December 1970, pp. 9-10
202. *Sat Sandesh*, December 1970, p. 14
203. *Excerpts from Letters to New York Satsangis*, p. 52
204. *Sat Sandesh*, January 1971, p. 10
205. *Spiritual Elixir*, p. 269
206. *Spiritual Elixir*, p. 54
207. *Excerpts from Letters to New York Satsangis*, p. 74
208. *Excerpts from Letters to New York Satsangis*, p. 14
209. *Excerpts from Letters to New York Satsangis*, p. 74
209a. *The Wheel of Life*, p. 36
210. *Sat Sandesh*, January 1971, p. 4
211. *Sat Sandesh*, January 1971, p. 5
212. *Sat Sandesh*, January 1971, p. 5
213. *Sat Sandesh* January 1971, p. 6
214. *Sat Sandesh*, January 1971, p. 9
215. *Sat Sandesh*, January 1971, p. 9
216. *Sat Sandesh*, January 1971, p. 10

217. *Sat Sandesh,* January 1971, p. 10
218. *Sat Sandesh,* January 1971, p. 10
219. *Sat Sandesh,* January 1971, p. 11
220. *Sat Sandesh,* January 1971, p. 11
221. *Sat Sandesh,* January 1971, p. 11
222. *Sat Sandesh,* January 1971, pp. 13-14
223. *Sat Sandesh,* January 1971, p. 14
224. *Sat Sandesh,* January 1971, p. 14
225. *Sat Sandesh,* January 1971, p. 14
226. *Sat Sandesh,* January 1971, pp. 14-15
227. *Sat Sandesh,* January 1971, p. 15
228. *Sat Sandesh,* January 1971, p. 15
229. *Sat Sandesh,* January 1971, p. 15

BOOK TWO
NEW LIFE IN GOD

1. Circular No. 17
2. *Morning Talks,* p. 36
3. *Morning Talks,* p. 228
4. *Morning Talks,* p. 57
5. *Sat Sandesh,* December 1971, p. 29
6. *Morning Talks,* p. 48
7. *Morning Talks,* p. 46
8. *Morning Talks,* p. 32
9. *Spiritual Elixir,* p. 108
10. *Morning Talks,* p. 49
11. *Morning Talks,* pp. 255-256
12. *Morning Talks,* p. 211

13. *Morning Talks,* p. 204
14. *Sat Sandesh,* February 1972, p. 12
15. *Morning Talks,* p. 205
16. *Baba Jaimal Singh,* p. 124
17. *Morning Talks,* p. 221
18. *Morning Talks,* p. 230
19. *Morning Talks,* p. 50
20. *Excerpts from Letters to New York Satsangis,* p. 26
21. *Sat Sandesh,* February 1970, p. 11
22. *Morning Talks,* p. 207
23. *Morning Talks,* p. 221
24. *Spiritual Elixir,* p. 126
25. *Morning Talks,* p. 40
26. *Spiritual Elixir,* p. 256
27. *Spiritual Elixir,* pp. 117-118
28. *Sat Sandesh,* February 1972, pp. 7-8
29. *Morning Talks,* p. 215
30. *Spiritual Elixir,* p. 132
31. *Morning Talks,* p. 205
32. *Morning Talks,* p. 103
33. *Morning Talks,* p. 206
34. *Morning Talks,* p. 223
35. *Morning Talks* pp. 203-204
36. *Morning Talks,* p. 204
37. *Morning Talks,* p. 204
38. *Morning Talks,* p. 46
39. *Morning Talks,* pp. 37-38
40. *Baba Jaimal Singh,* pp. 99-100
41. *Morning Talks,* p. 207
42. *Morning Talks,* p. 206

43. *Morning Talks,* p. 207
44. *Spiritual Elixir,* p. 250
45. *Spiritual Elixir,* p. 232
46. *Sat Sandesh,* January 1971, p. 12
47. *Morning Talks,* p. 247
48. *Sat Sandesh,* November 1971, pp. 28-31
49. *Sat Sandesh,* November 1971, p. 28
50. *Simran,* pp. 11-12
51. *Sat Sandesh,* June 1971, p. 3
52. *Spiritual Elixir,* p. 184
53. *Simran,* p. 15
54. *Simran,* p. 20
55. *Spiritual Elixir,* p. 184
56. *Spiritual Elixir,* pp. 135-136
57. *Simran,* p. 15
58. *Spiritual Elixir,* p. 173
59. *Spiritual Elixir,* p. 184
60. *Wheel of Life,* p. 37
61. *Simran,* p. 30
62. *Sat Sandesh,* April 1968, p. 12
63. *Simran,* p. 21
64. *Simran,* p. 24
65. *Spiritual Elixir,* p. 170
66. *Spiritual Elixir,* p. 302
67. *Simran,* p. 23
68. *Simran,* p. 24
69. Letter to an Initiate
70. *Excerpts from Letters to New York Satsangis,* p. 21
71. *Spiritual Elixir,* p. 175
72. *Excerpts from Letters to New York Satsangis,* p. 45

73. *Excerpts from Letters to New York Satsangis*, p. 54
74. *Sat Sandesh*, February 1972, pp. 12-13
75. *Excerpts from Letters to New York Satsangis*, p. 52
76. *Morning Talks*, p. 153
77. *Sat Sandesh*, February 1970, p. 10
78. *Godman*, pp. 156-157
79. *Morning Talks*, p. 143
80. *Godman*, pp. 156-157
81. *Godman*, p. 159
82. *Godman*, p. 161
83. *Godman*, p. 160
84. *Godman*, p. 140
85. *Godman*, p. 162
86. *Godman*, p. 161
87. *Godman*, p. 158
88. *Spiritual Elixir*, p. 258
89. *Sat Sandesh*, November 1970, p. 5
90. *Prayer*, pp. 55-56
91. *Prayer*, p. 56
92. Circular: "Sant, the Master"
93. *Sat Sandesh*, January 1968, p. 28
94. *Sat Sandesh*, April 1968, p. 11
95. *Sat Sandesh*, April 1968, pp. 6-7
96. *Morning Talks*, p. 185
97. *Sat Sandesh*, November 1970, p. 3
98. Circular: "Sant, the Master"
99. *Spiritual Elixir*, pp. 277-278
100. *Spiritual Elixir*, p. 226
101. *Excerpts from Letters to New York Satsangis*, p. 29
102. *Prayer*, p. 58

103. *Excerpts from Letters to New York Satsangis*, p. 78
104. *Spiritual Elixir*, p. 107
105. Circular: "The Way of Love"
106. *Prayer*, p. 57
107. Circular: "Humility"—p. 2
108. Circular: "Humility"—p. 2
109. Circular: "Humility"—p. 2
110. Circular: "Humility"—p. 2
111. Circular: "Humility"—p. 3
112. Circular: "Humility"—p. 4
113. Circular: "Humility"—p. 3
114. Circular: "Humility"—p. 4
115. *Morning Talks*, p. 95
116. *Morning Talks*, p. 94
117. *Morning Talks*, p. 97
118. *Morning Talks*, pp. 251-252
119. *Morning Talks*, p. 95
120. *Sat Sandesh*, December 1970, p. 2
121. *Spiritual Elixir*, p. 120
122. *Godman*, p. 187
123. *Sat Sandesh*, May 1971, p. 9
124. *Morning Talks*, p. 99
125. *Morning Talks*, p. 99
126. *Morning Talks*, p. 100
127. *Morning Talks*, p. 101
128. *Morning Talks*, p. 102
129. *Morning Talks*, p. 103
130. *Godman*, p. 184
131. *Sat Sandesh*, June 1971, p. 32
132. *Godman*, pp. 184-185

133. *Godman*, p. 188
134. *Morning Talks*, p. 224
135. *Godman*, pp. 186- 187
136. *Godman*, p. 189
137. *Sat Sandesh*, March 1971, pp. 14-15
138. *Morning Talks*, p. 255
139. *Morning Talks*, p 134
140. *Sat Sandesh*, March 1971, p. 15
141. *Sat Sandesh*, June 1971, p. 9
142. *Godman*, pp. 185-186
143. *Sat Sandesh*, June 1971, p. 32
144. *Morning Talks*, pp. 131-132
145. *Spiritual Elixir*, p. 106
146. *Morning Talks*, pp. 43-44
147. *Morning Talks*, pp. 47-48
148. *Sat Sandesh*, April 1968, p. 5
149. *Sat Sandesh*, April 1968, p. 5
150. *Sat Sandesh*, April 1968, p. 5
151. *Sat Sandesh*, August 1970, p. 12
152. *Morning Talks*, p. 68
153. *Morning Talks*, pp. 187-188
154. *Sat Sandesh*, February 1972, p. 32
155. *Spiritual Elixir*, p. 203
156. Letter to an Initiate
157. *Morning Talks*, pp. 110-111
158. *Sat Sandesh*, September 1970, p. 13
159. *Sat Sandesh*, September 1970, p. 14
160. *Morning Talks*, p. 164
161. *Morning Talks*, p. 164
162. *Spiritual Elixir*, pp. 212-213

163. *Spiritual Elixir*, p. 215
164. *Sat Sandesh*, October 1971, p. 18
165. *Spiritual Elixir*, p. 96
166. *Sat Sandesh*, September 1970, p. 10
167. *Spiritual Elixir*, p. 251
168. *Spiritual Elixir*, p. 207
169. *Excerpts from Letters to New York Satsangis*, p. 82
170. *Morning Talks*, p. 189
171. *Morning Talks*, pp. 185-186
172. *Morning Talks*, p. 164
173. *Spiritual Elixir*, p. 120
174. *Sat Sandesh*, September 1970, p. 11
175. *Spiritual Elixir*, p. 77
176. *Spiritual Elixir*, p. 114
177. *Excerpts from Letters to New York Satsangis*, p. 74
178. *Spiritual Elixir*, p. 261
179. *Spiritual Elixir*, p. 158
180. *Excerpts from Letters to New York Satsangis*, p. 52
181. *Spiritual Elixir*, p. 258
182. *Morning Talks*, p. 187
183. *Morning Talks*, p. 166
184. *Sat Sandesh*, September 1970, p. 11
185. *Prayer*, pp. 50-51
186. *Prayer*, pp. 52-53
187. Circular 27, p. 12
188. *Sat Sandesh*, September 1970, p. 12
189. *Receptivity*, p. 14
190. *Spiritual Elixir*, p. 110
191. *Spiritual Elixir*, p. 213
192. *Spiritual Elixir*, p. 179

193. *Spiritual Elixir*, p. 149
194. *Spiritual Elixir*, p. 218
195. *Spiritual Elixir*, p. 306
196. *Jap Ji*, p. 97
197. *Jap Ji*, p. 82
198. *Jap Ji*, pp. 66-67
199. *Godman*, p. 190
200. *Sat Sandesh*, September 1971, p. 31
201. *Sat Sandesh*, March 1972, p. 10
202. *Morning Talks*, p. 224
203. *Morning Talks*, p. 221
204. *Spiritual Elixir*, p. 270
205. *Sat Sandesh*, December 1971, p. 14
206. *Baba Jaimal Singh*, p. 99
207. *Baba Jaimal Singh*, pp. 109-110
208. *Spiritual Elixir*, p. 93
209. *Spiritual Elixir*, p. 225
210. *Morning Talks*, p. 61
211. *Excerpts from Letters to New York Satsangis*, pp. 81-82
212. *Sat Sandesh*, March 1972, p. 10
213. *Jap Ji*, p. 81
214. *Godman*, pp. 190-191
215. *Prayer*, pp. 76-77
216. Circular 17
217. *Wheel of Life*, pp. 76-77
218. *Wheel of Life*, pp. 80-81
219. *Wheel of Life*, pp. 78-79
220. *Godman*, p. 177
221. *Godman*, pp. 177-179

222. *Godman*, p. 179
223. *Godman*, pp. 180-181
224. *Godman*, p. 59
225. *Jap Ji*, pp. 107-108
226. *Spiritual Elixir*, pp. 338-339
227. *Spiritual Elixir*, p. 310
228. *Spiritual Elixir*, p. 359
229. *Spiritual Elixir*, p. 325
230. *Spiritual Elixir*, p. 326
231. *Spiritual Elixir*, p. 343
232. *Spiritual Elixir*, p. 344
233. *Spiritual Elixir*, p. 335
234. *Spiritual Elixir*, pp. 364-365
235. *Spiritual Elixir*, pp. 364-365
236. *Spiritual Elixir*, p. 326
237. *Spiritual Elixir*, p. 319
238. *Spiritual Elixir*, p. 330
239. Birthday Message, January 1970
240. *Spiritual Elixir*, p. 320
241. Christmas Message, December 1962
242. *Spiritual Elixir*, p. 324
243. *Spiritual Elixir*, p. 319

OTHER BOOKS

BY KIRPAL SINGH

Godman: Finding a Spiritual Master
The Crown of Life: A Study in Yoga
Morning Talks
Naam or Word
Prayer: Its Nature and Technique
A Great Saint—Baba Jaimal Singh: His Life and Teachings
Jap Ji: The Message of Guru Nanak
Spiritual Elixir, Vols. I and II
The Teachings of Kirpal Singh (compiled and edited by Ruth Seader)
    Vol. I: The Holy Path
    Vol. II: Self-Introspection/Meditation
    Vol. III: The New Life (complete in one book)
Heart to Heart Talks—Vols. I and II (edited by Malcolm Tillis)
The Night Is a Jungle and Other Discourses of Kirpal Singh
Man! Know Thyself
Spirituality: What It Is
The Mystery of Death
The Wheel of Life: The Law of Action and Reaction
A Brief Life Sketch of Hazur Baba Sawan Singh Ji Maharaj
God Power, Christ Power, Guru Power

BY DARSHAN SINGH

Spiritual Awakening
The Secret of Secrets: Spiritual Talks
The Cry of the Soul: Mystic Poetry
Inner Space
The Meaning of Christ

BY OTHER AUTHORS

Portrait of Perfection: A Pictorial Biography of Kirpal Singh
The Beloved Master, edited by Bhadra Sena
Classics & Creations: A World of Vegetarian Cooking
The Ocean of Grace Divine, edited by Bhadra Sena
Seeing Is Above All: Sant Darshan Singh's First Indian Tour,
    edited by H.C. Chadda
Kirpal Singh: The Story of a Saint
    compiled and adapted for children; with illustrations

ORDERING BOOKS

Books listed on the preceding page may be ordered through your bookseller or directly from Sawan Kirpal Publications, Route 1, Box 24, Bowling Green, VA 22427, or Sawan Kirpal Publications, 2 Canal Road, Vijay Nagar, Delhi-110009, India.

SAT SANDESH: THE MESSAGE OF THE MASTERS

This monthly magazine is filled with practical and inspiring articles on all aspects of the mystic experience. Discourses by the living Master, Sant Darshan Singh, provide the initiate and seeker with information and guidance on meditation and the spiritual life. Also included are articles by Sant Kirpal Singh and Baba Sawan Singh. Poetry, photos, and other features appear in each issue. For subscription information write: Sat Sandesh, Subscription Dept., Route 1, Box 24, Bowling Green, VA 22427.

FURTHER INFORMATION

Mr. T.S. Khanna, General Representative, 8807 Lea Lane, Alexandria, VA 22309.

Olga Donenberg, Midwest Representative, 6007 N. Sheridan Rd., #14-B, Chicago, IL 60660.

Sunnie Cowen, Southern Representative, 3976 Belle Vista Dr. E, St. Petersburg Beach, FL 33706.

Sant Darshan Singh resides at Kirpal Ashram, 2 Canal Road, Vijay Nagar, Delhi-110009, India.